Concepts in Film Theory

Concepts in Film Theory

Dudley Andrew

OXFORD UNIVERSITY PRESS
Oxford   New York   Toronto   Melbourne
1984

OXFORD UNIVERSITY PRESS
Oxford   London   Glasgow
New York   Toronto   Melbourne   Auckland
Delhi   Bombay   Calcutta   Madras   Karachi
Kuala Lumpur   Singapore   Hong Kong   Tokyo
Nairobi   Dar es Salaam   Cape Town

and associate companies in
Beirut   Berlin   Ibadan   Mexico City   Nicosia

First published by Oxford University Press, New York, 1984
First issued as an Oxford University Press paperback, 1984

Library of Congress Cataloging in Publication Data

Andrew, James Dudley, 1945–
  Concepts in film theory.

  Bibliography: p.
  Includes index.
  1. Moving-pictures—Philosophy.   I. Title.
PN1995.A49   1984   791.43'01   83-17365
ISBN 0-19-503394-9
ISBN 0-19-503428-7 (pbk.)

Versions of several chapters of this book received prior publication as
follows: Chapter 1 in *Research Opportunities in Film,* ed. Herbert
Bergman (East Lansing, Michigan: Film Research Center Publication,
1981); Chapter 5 in *The Horizons of Literature,* ed. Paul Hernadi
(Lincoln: University of Nebraska, 1982); Chapter 6 in *Narrative Strategies: Original Essays in Film and Prose Fiction,* ed. Syndy Conger
and Janice Welsh (Macomb, Illinois: Western Illinois University Press,
1981); Chapter 9 in *Iris* 1, no. 1 (Spring 1983); and Chapter 10 in the
MMLA Bulletin 15, no. 1 (Spring 1982).

Printing (last digit):   9 8 7 6 5 4 3 2 1

Printed in the United States of America

To
Brigid, Ellen, and James

Preface

Certainly in some sense this volume is a sequel to *The Major Film Theories,* for it begins in 1965, virtually where that earlier book left off. Just as Jean Mitry was seen there as the culminating figure of the classic era, so here he is situated at the outset of the modern era. Because film theory has grown so institutionalized, taken up as it has been in universities, promulgated in professional societies and at academic conferences, advanced in dissertations and in specialized journals, it seems proper to approach it through topics rather than through careers of individuals. Of course this limits my discussion to those issues that obsess our journals, conferences, and seminars. Maverick thinkers, some perhaps of lasting importance, are perforce left unheard in such a survey of recent trends. But I do not apologize for this, since more than mere convenience has urged this strategy. It is my belief, argued throughout this text in its method as well as in its propositions, that film theory exists as a discourse among theorists and with films. Hence I have gone straight to the noisiest corners of that discourse and have sought to make sense of the yelling and the whispers overheard there.

Are the topic headings sufficient to circumscribe this babble of modern theory? They are meant to be, and the reader is challenged to locate significant omissions along the way. Within the discussion of each topic, however, no pretense to completeness can be claimed. I present the arguments that most disturb or inspire me, and whenever useful, adduce enough background to situate a given film problem within its proper intellectual tradition.

All this is properly antecedent to the book's barely submerged and chief concern: to express, through a dialogue with the theories of the day, my own views on each particular concept and, more ambitious still, my own sense of the interdependence of these concepts. No doubt my predilections are readily discernable to the critical reader of *The Major Film Theories,* but there I struggled to let the figures I selected betray their insights and conundrums on their own. The present volume, for several reasons, is different. First, no names in today's theory are printed quite so luminously as to compel deference to their ideas, for this is genuinely an age of schools of thought more than of lone geniuses. Second, history has yet to sanctify or excuse the discourse of our era and everyone can feel freer with it than with the canonized systems of the past, no matter how far we may think to have outstripped them. Third, my own thoughts about film have matured exactly during the era this book chronicles. This is the theory generated in the institutions which have supported me, and I am happy as well as obligated to take a forthright stance within it. Nor is it treacherous to conclude, as I will, that the era of pure theory is over and that the task before us consists in confronting film concepts not with logic or with paradigms derived from other fields, but with exemplary films and sequences of films. To claim, as I also will, that theory must be led in some respects by criticism, history, and analysis, is an important *theoretical* claim. In a current volume I try to make good on that claim *(Film in the Aura of Art,* Princeton University Press, 1984).

Obviously the honesty as well as utility of this book is imperiled by a number of factors: an admittedly incomplete survey of the available positions, the tendentious way this survey conforms to my view, and the absence in this text of the kind of film analysis called for by the argument. Enter the Classified Bibliography. Great care has been taken to select enough citations relevant to each chapter to permit the responsible enthusiast to pursue the arguments initiated in this text far beyond the limited and parochial attention they receive in a book of this size.

While many items in the Bibliography may challenge my position, I look upon the Bibliography *in toto* as an ally. For I will be satisfied when any reader, stimulated by the arguments presented here, or by my personal assessment of those arguments, or even by the enticing titles in the Bibliography, recognizes that the concepts isolated in this book are anything but isolated, and can begin to see them as part of the history of ideas, as part of contemporary intellectual life, as part of an overarching view I am indirectly tracing, or, most important, as part of the questioning of the medium that goes on within the work of films themselves. I will be satisfied, I say, because the discourse initiated in such recognitions is one with the discourse of this book. It is in fact the very discourse we label "Film Theory."

Iowa City   D. A.
May 1983

Acknowledgments

Film theory, I begin by saying, is now an institutional endeavor. Let me then thank the University of Iowa for the time it has given me through its Faculty Scholar program and the National Endowment for the Humanities for its summer support. In fact, this series of essays took shape during the NEH Summer Seminar I offered in 1977. To its dozen clever and enthusiastic participants as well as to my assistant in that seminar Mary Ann Doane I owe the impulse to have my say in matters of contemporary film theory. Mary Ann contributed further with comments on particular chapters, as did Dennis Giles and Jacques Aumont. Ana Lopez with the aid of Dana Benelli, Andréa Staskowski, Robert Arnold, and Daryl Iogha, organized the Bibliography. To all these I am indebted but to none more than Pamela Falkenberg, the closest and most generous reader I have had. While subscribing to few of my ideas, she brought me to test and then to express them as forcefully as possible. In a way her sympathetic intelligence exemplifies the premise of my methodology, that film theory fulfills its mission not when transcendental logic or external system steps in to make sense of the flux of film life, but when the encounters we have with films and ideas urge us to adjust ourselves so that we can fully hear them, truly understand what they might have to say, and in understanding them, understand ourselves and what we might be.

In this spirit I am brimming to acknowledge the deepest debt Stephanie and I have to our children who must be bewildered to see themselves mentioned in the context of a book which interests them, if at all, only as a subject to ridicule at the dinner table. But insofar as I have learned the give and take of the hermeneutic enterprise I advocate in these pages, it is from them, or rather with them in their growing, in our growing together, that I have learned it.

Contents

Concepts in Film Theory

1

The State of Film Theory

FILM THEORY AND THE ACADEMY

In *The Major Film Theories* I gave attention to several powerful individual thinkers who constructed complete views of the cinema. In writing now about contemporary theory, I find it far more useful and honest to treat key concepts rather than key personalities and to build an overall view of film based on positions taken in relation to those concepts, specifically to perception, representation, signification, narrative structure, adaptation, evaluation, identification, figuration, and interpretation. Why have these issues come to dominate our era in film theory? More important, why has a method based on such reflective concepts dominated other, more direct approaches to film?

In this introduction I want to argue for the propriety of these concepts and, more generally, for the propriety of a kind of enterprise that ceaselessly discusses, modifies, and rewrites theory in relation to such concepts. Modern theory approaches nothing directly, neither the audience through questionnaires and neuro-physiological experiments, nor the films through minute formal analyses and experiments. Such audience studies and formal experiments which do go on in mainstream film theory are invariably guided by the current general discourse, that is, by reflective concepts. For this is the state of film theory as it has come to be, an accumulation of concepts, or, rather, of ideas and attitudes clustered around concepts. Film theory is, in short, a verbal representation of the film complex.

How have we gotten into this state of affairs where direct approaches to the field are unfeasible, where theory aims at explanation or "picturing" rather than at "prediction" and "verification" as it does in the sciences and social sciences? How is it that even within the current paradigm of theory as reflective explanation, we can no longer expect a single thinker to take full command of the field by reorienting our view of it as Aristotle did in drama centuries ago or Kenneth Burke did in rhetoric decades ago?

To clarify the state of film theory we ought first to interrogate the terms we use to describe the study of anything. Too much of our vocabulary relating to research derives from the "allegory of the quest." We say that we engage in the "pursuit" of learning, that we "conquer" a field or hope for the "domination" of the known by the knower. I would like to substitute for these heroic and aggressive terms others of my own: "discourse," "representation," "adequation," in which a theory sets us reasonably before a picture of our field so that we see it in a comprehensive and fruitful way.

Perhaps even the term "field" has duped our expectations. Fields of research do not lie open for parceling out, homesteading, or development in the way the metaphor wants to suggest. They are social constructions, the first act of research, not eternal caches of riches passively awaiting the scholar's pick and axe. We may think that the heavens comprise a clearly delineated field, marked off by the earth's horizons and the power of our telescopes; nevertheless, there exist at least two subjects, astrology and astronomy, which have been established by societies in relation to this "same" field of stars.

What kind of social construction is the field of film? What is the potential workplace film theorists have hoped to inhabit? This essentially sociological question can be addressed by a sociological index: What has academia done with film? When and where has film been admitted as a subject of serious and progressive study?

No doubt a detailed history of the field would trace a complicated root system for film; still I think we can posit with justness that film attained some respectability in the early 1960's in American universities and this was primarily due to the enthusiasm of members of humanities departments. Alternative locations for film study, options which were occasionally exercised, would include the social sciences (especially communication research and sociology) and the fine arts.

It was no doubt inevitable for film to land in the humanities during this epoch. The social sciences were growing so rapidly that they had little time or energy to do anything exceptional with regard to cinema. Certainly some data were collected and hypotheses advanced, but such study was normally carried out alongside the analysis of other expressions of mass culture. No systematic or consistently thorough examination of film could be initiated in a discipline which had much bigger game to stalk.

For their part, the fine arts in our era have been dominated by interests in the production of art. Consequently, those film departments lodged within the fine arts have emphasized production. Not only has this been at the expense of theory (though theory is almost always represented in such departments) but the literal expense of film production has stunted the potential spread of this conception of the field. Not many schools have been able to afford to place film within the fine arts.

The humanities, on the other hand, were primed to profit from the rising interest in the study of film. As the largest academic division within American universities, not only were there excesses of students eternally seeking new (and "relevant") courses, but excesses of faculty eager to teach them. Since the humanities were not experiencing anything like the growth pattern of the social sciences, their faculty were trying to achieve distinction in a crowded arena. The development of film as an extension of this arena gave many English, philosophy, theater, and language professors opportunities to find a new audience to teach, new journals to publish in, and renewed enthusiasm for their professions. When academic requirements in the humanities began to loosen up and even disappear in the late 1960's, film studies became a way to uphold enrollment for many departments, primarily language departments.

Of course the development of a field does not depend exclusively on the economics of higher education. It is also closely tied to the current movements of culture that interest the intelligentsia. Here again humanities professors were in a privileged position for they were connected to a native tradition of semi-academic writing on film and to a flow of ideas from Europe which began with ever greater frequency to take the cinema seriously. Actually these two lines of inheritance may serve to divide the types of humanities scholars who sought to involve themselves in film study. One group, a dominant and conservative one, readily formalized the prolific but haphazard cultural consideration of cinema which had always gone on outside academia (in the film re-

views of reputable journals and newspapers, in essays by cultural critics, at film festivals, and in the then few existing film magazines like
Sight and Sound and *Film Quarterly)*. The English teachers who took
their cues from this tradition generally developed courses in adaptation, in film as drama, or in the analysis of serious auteurs like Bergman and Fellini. Such courses undoubtedly added to the prestige of
film study and gave it a large undergraduate base, but they were not
otherwise terribly useful to the progress of film theory.

Humanities divisions, moreover, are also notorious hiding places for
radical cultural critics, some of whom saw in film study an opportunity
to help shift the ground of the whole realm of humanities. These were
the scholars who received their strength in part from European models
made available to them at conferences and in scholarly journals. Because of their training, humanities professors are equipped to learn from
foreign language texts. Popular essays by Lévi-Strauss, Barthes, and
Eco and the extension of their insights by continental cultural critics
had the effect of giving shape to a rebellious American sub-profession
and of turning that rebellion onto new objects of culture. Film was a
major recipient of this attention throughout Europe, a logical focus for
the energetic disciplines of semiotics, psychoanalysis, and ideological
analysis. Many American radical scholars eagerly turned to film as an
open set of texts where new theories appeared even newer, and where
there were as yet no traditional ways of dealing with the subject. Film
study became a regular offering in many comparative literature departments, for instance, and was an integral part of radical journals
such as *Diacritics* and *New Literary History* born at the end of the 1960's
and of *Enclitic* and *Sub-stance* coming out of the 1970's. This subversive induction of film into academia aroused great hostility among traditional humanities scholars and drew fire as well from both film buffs
and critics. All felt that cinema was being "used" for questionable
purposes by people who knew little about it. The jargon associated with
continental criticism was deemed most inappropriate for a fresh art like
the cinema. While such complaints were to a varying degree justified,
the discipline of film theory made great strides in this atmosphere.

Such advances would have been unthinkable were film a part of the
social sciences, for in this country professionals in communication study,
sociology, and so forth have exhibited comparatively little interest in
the scholarship coming from other countries. Nor have historians and
critics of the fine arts been particularly cordial to radical continental

developments in cultural criticism. Indeed, they have not been eager even to link themselves to the conservative tradition of American film criticism. After all, film criticism in this country has appeared mainly in middlebrow journals and has concerned itself with popular narrative genres. Few fine arts professors have had the inclination to descend into this discourse.

Only the humanities have been sufficiently eclectic and outward looking to benefit from the various strains of thought that have become important to the field of film. And so cinema seems to have been most logically and happily housed in departments of English, theater, speech, and foreign language. Still, this location has deprived film studies of the research strategies and goals routinely pursued in non-humanities disciplines. We can lament the plight of communication theory in relation to film study, for a start. During the 1950's and 1960's numerous empirical studies of audience response were conducted leading to some promising generalizations concerning the aesthetic and rhetorical effects of the medium; yet today this brand of work, when it appears, seems almost haphazard and without context even though the field of communication research has grown into a highly sophisticated discipline, completely bypassing its early flirtation with cinema.[1]

The same fate awaited rhetorical theory despite the close ties it has always kept to literary and cultural criticism (and hence the easy access to film study it has enjoyed in a way denied to the empirical methods of communication research). Unfortunately American rhetoricians have in the main neglected or ignored the expanded notion of rhetoric developed by structuralists such as Barthes, Todorov, and Genette and have thereby failed to rendezvous with the mainstream of modern film theory. Aside from occasional essays on isolated films and individual genres, rhetoric has made very little contribution to film theory. This will change. With the growing awareness of modern philosophical traditions in the field of rhetoric, and with the publication of books such as Berger and Luckman's *Social Construction of Reality* as well as the key translations of the work of Habermas, Schutz, and Barthes,[2] there is certain to be a a wave of interest by rhetorical theorists in the concerns of continental cultural criticism and hence in cinema. Nevertheless, because of their tardiness, any theories that may develop are nearly bound to retrace a familiar scenario: sweeping generalities will be advanced one after another until such a time when smaller, more careful theories may try to establish a progressive investigation of the problems of the field.[3] In other words, the heroic ethos will prevail. Unfortunately, the more focused studies are of greatest use now: the investigation of rhetorical figures in film, the speech act dimension of the film experience, the concepts of enunciation and interpretation, and so forth. It will be a long time before the "sociology of cinema" gets around to treating such questions.

The lack of input from the fine arts has had even more regrettable consequences. Not only has the avant-garde film received scant attention, but the theory of narrative cinema has until recently been deprived of key concepts in art theory. We would expect art and music theory to play a crucial role in the search for a modernist alternative to popular narrative film, yet Duchamp and Schoenberg are called upon far less than Bertolt Brecht and Robbe-Grillet, no doubt because even in this "alternative arena" it is the literary critics who control the discourse about film.

Equally damaging has been the retardation of a purely formal theory of film. Had film theory grown up in music or art departments, there might have been far more attention given to the properties of the medium, more experiments done in the classroom on editing rhythms, color, film syntax, and so on. Slavko Vorkapitch[4] emphasized precisely this sort of research and a number of East Europeans have contributed modestly as well,[5] but a film theory along the lines of music theory seems very far away. In sum, the direct, scientific impulse in film study, whether testing audiences or testing aspects of films, has not attracted much following. Such study dominates television research, on the other hand, no doubt because networks, advertisers, and government agencies hope to predict the effects of the medium. Even Hollywood, cinema's largest economic force, is no longer large enough to support such research, though it did so in the 1950's. Besides, Hollywood has access to its own empirical data, box office receipts, a type of evidence unavailable to the broadcasting industry.

Still, some research generated by sociologists of television has spilled over to film study, particularly the type of theory known as "visual literacy." The psycholinguist John Carroll has contributed to this field developing a transformational grammar of film, employing films of his own devising as test cases in his search for grammaticality in film.[6] Working less in the social science tradition and more in that of art history, Noel Burch, David Bordwell, and Kristen Thompson are heading an investigation of the "grammar" of constituted bodies of film, like the Hollywood system, the pre-Griffith system, the 1930's Japanese system.[7] Such work involves the close analysis of hundreds of films chosen, in Bordwell's and Thompson's case, by means of a random statistical algorithm. Both the psycholinguistic, Chomskyan approach, and this art historical approach proceed as though direct analysis of films and of their effects is possible, using empirical data. This work goes against the norm for it is symptomatic of the humanities that dominant film theory has not only neglected empirical studies of all sorts but has erected a rationale for this neglect. The psychoanalytic impulse in film theory, for instance, based on the founding concept of the unconscious, can allow for no alliance with communication research which depends on the tool of audience questionnaires, where conscious attitudes of subjects provide the data for generalization. This is but one example, although a privileged one. All in all, the film theory born in the world of the humanities has been one based on the efficacy and import of *metaphors* about the film phenomenon. Since metaphors are more readily generated than are computerized analyses of audience questionnaires or minute descriptions of hundreds of obscure films, the discourse of film theory is destined to remain in this literary world.

Empiricists are quick to point out that many of the metaphors devised by humanists are open to testing and verification, that a carefully constructed film sequence shown in controlled circumstances to various audiences might substantiate or disprove statements routinely advanced about the effects of editing for instance or the relation of sound to picture. Similarly, Bordwell and Thompson implicitly question current notions of the classical Hollywood film in their statistical sampling of thousands of such films. Those humanists who are willing to admit such "help" from empirical sources are likely to do so, however, only under the rule that speculative theory leads to empirical testing rather than the other way around. The humanities approach to film theory has, in other words, developed a tradition that is virtually self-sufficient.

THE DIRECTION OF MODERN FILM THEORY

While nearly all film theorists agree about the rules governing their discourse, arguments within that discourse abound. The first such argument, one which has already been cited, has been between traditional humanists and cultural critics. The name "humanities" connotes something of the immutable when it is pronounced. Those who study the humanities are connected to the Renaissance and through the Renaissance to classical antiquity. Some theorists have emphasized this relation, claiming that film ought to be studied as the modern evocation of the human spirit that in other days produced the _Oresteia_ trilogy, the miracle play, and the Elizabethan tragedy.[8] The philosophers in this group have felt that at the very least film should be open to traditional speculative inquiry. The most prestigious seat of such speculation has been the _Journal of Aesthetics and Art Criticism,_ that refined organ of philosophers of art and beauty, which in its very first year of publication (1941) eagerly incorporated cinema as a subject deserving its attention. Since that year no fewer than fifty-three articles on the cinema have appeared there by philosophers and art critics, with more than half published in the past six years.[9] Yet it is instructive to note how little impact this journal of aesthetics has had on the study of the aesthetics of film. True, certain philosophers coming from the tradition it represents, most notably Stanley Cavell and Arthur Danto, have begun to publish in film journals[10] and at least one film theorist, Noel Carroll, has lately called for the redirection of film theory along the lines of dominant strains in American aesthetics;[11] nevertheless, in the main, film theory, criticism, and critical theory have been untouched by these "timeless" speculations. Whether because of its novel subject (the cinema) or because of the epoch of suspicion to which we belong, serious and progressive film theory has taken root and flourished primarily as cultural criticism. Discussion about the medium and its properties (which is always "essential," or timeless discussion) has fallen to concern over the function, impact, and context of the cinema as a "practice." This is so much the case that the word "aesthetics" has nearly dropped from the vocabulary of film theory.

Some may proclaim this orientation to be anti-humanistic, yet few scholars, especially modern ones, have ever considered the humanities to be immutable. Not only has the extent of their domain constantly grown (for example, to include cinema) but their ruling approaches and methods, in short their ideology, have a history. In an important sense film theory came to life by burying a work that was representative of all earlier film theory: 1964 was the date both of the publication of Jean Mitry's _Esthétique et psychologie du cinéma_ and the appearance for the first time of the work of Christian Metz.[12] Mitry stood for the old tradition of film theory in a very literal way through his copious citation of nearly every important theorist before him. His efforts are representative in another sense as well, for their encyclopedic range is organized according to a logic which claims to ensure for the work its totalizing aspirations. Nearly all earlier theorists wrote under an explicit or implicit urge to totalize the field; in this sense most theorists up to 1960 were Aristotelian. They sought to divide the "film complex" into a series of hierarchically related questions and to conquer this complex with consistent propositions.

The modern era in film theory began in reaction against these aspirations in a way that is modest and haughty. The modesty arises from the refusal of the encyclopedic tone of much early theory. Metz and his followers are content to isolate particular theoretical issues and to shed light on these without recourse to lofty overall principles. In this way they see themselves more in the line of modern science than of Aristotelian science. Modern theorists lord it over their predecessors, however, by pointing to the range of sophisticated disciplines whose intersection in the cinema was never felt to be problematic before 1960. Whereas no one can hope to master the anthropological, psychoanalytic, linguistic, rhetorical, and ideological theories (to name only the most evident) now considered crucial to a full understanding of the field, all modern theorists can smirk at the naïveté of an era in which full understanding was considered attainable by means of direct reflection.

One of the obvious duties of modern theory is to place more clearly the propositions of traditional theory. If older theories suffer from a type of naïveté, modernists can reconstruct the intellectual context within which these thinkers so confidently wrote. More than being simply a history of film theory, such studies would help us save older theories by specifying, in a way they themselves were unable to do, the manner in which they must be read. Traditional theory would then no longer be something to be defended or discarded. It would be used with precision and with neither reverence nor apology.[13]

Recent theory is not exempt from the kind of historical context it sees as an inevitable limitation in traditional writing on the subject. Naturally it assumes that its more modest ambition, especially its refusal of a totalizing view, protects it from the excesses of idealism. In addition, self-consciousness is integral to its method. Modern theory, critical and self-critical, meditates upon and uses its own situation, whereas earlier theories believed they could transcend the moment of their writing and speak of cinema for all time.

Largely due to this cultivated self-awareness, modern theory has been closely tied to developments in the general intellectual community. Whereas in the past a theorist might ground his views in whatever philosophy or movement personally interested him (Neo-Kantianism for Münsterberg, Marxism and the behaviorism of Pavlov for Eisenstein, and so forth), the inevitably partial scope of current work necessitates a view of theorizing which is communal and in which theorists see their work as part of cultural thought in a given historical moment.

Opponents of the current trend readily label this impulse as fad-oriented, mocking its predictable itinerary from structuralism to semiotics to ideological analysis, psychoanalysis, deconstructivism, and the study of cinematic *"écriture."* No one, least of all the theorists themselves, would deny that film theory has hitched rides on popular developments in these other fields. The alternative is to strike out on one's own guided by some illusory glimmer of truth. But few of us believe truth is available in this way to even the heroic or Quixotic searcher. Meaning is seen in our era as something constructed, tested, deconstructed, and adjusted. The critical attitude prevails. Hence it is not only predictable but appropriate for film theorists to learn from the other master critiques of culture, from linguistics, psychoanalysis, ideological analysis, and critical philosophy.

In sum, film theory today consists primarily in thinking through, elaborating, and critiquing the key metaphors by which we seek to understand (and control) the cinema complex. This can be done only in public, discursive events, in classrooms, journals, and conferences. It can be done only collectively. When Charles F. Altman tried to explain the importance and impact of psychoanalytic thought in relation to cinema,[14] for example, he correctly noted that the old notions of spectatorial relations to the screen had been dominated by an interplay or synthesis of the metaphors available: frame and window. Bluntly put, Eisenstein and Arnheim conceived of the spectator as being before a framed image (as a painting); Bazin claimed he sat before a window; and Mitry intertwined the notions finding that cinema's specificity lay precisely in the oscillation between window and frame.

The impasse apparent in the Bazin versus Eisenstein arguments (arguments that filled countless film theory papers into the 1970's) was broken by the entry of psychoanalysis. It brought a new metaphor, that of the mirror, to complicate the notion of spectatorial position in front of the screen. This inspired metaphor gave rise to the elaboration of it in film theory (from studies concerned with ideology and technology in perspective views, to the analysis of the spectator's identification with the basic cinematic apparatus) and in film criticism (readings of films in relation to spectator position and to identification). But this metaphor too must be criticized. Altman explicitly attempted such a critique when he countered the myth of Narcissus (a central psychoanalytic scenario stemming from the mirror) with that of Echo, and thus turned his attention to the soundtrack, an aspect of the film complex scandalously neglected up to that time. Soon after, he was able to edit a full issue of *Yale French Studies* (No. 60) devoted to Cinema/Sounds, containing articles by modernist theorists prodded to rethink film theory on the basis of a newly privileged metaphor. Thus goes film theory and thus, in my mind, should it go: metaphor and critique, constantly modifying our representation of film in human history.

The genesis and development of the modern approach to film theory has not been so haphazard and bound to fad as its opponents often claim. First of all a consistency of attitude and goal binds the various approaches even when they seem to overthrow one another. Then, just as important, the state of film theory from 1964, from which all these "critical" projects launched themselves, has had a controlling effect by delimiting the terms of its own critique.

In 1964, a single representation of the film complex dominated the field—Jean Mitry's. Not only is his range encyclopedic, but his books form a compendium of quotations from the classic era of film theory. Mitry goes beyond those he quotes by demonstrating the dialectical interplay between realism and formalism. Where earlier theorists emphasized one aspect of cinema over the other, Mitry contends that a full theory of the medium must see these terms in dynamic interrelation, and this is what he provides. Mitry's position in the short history of film theory is like Hegel's in the history of philosophy. It is in its very effort a summation and reconciliation of all earlier views. It is a history of theory as well as a theory itself. It is grand, comprehensive, and idealist. It sees itself as an endpoint.

Mitry never enjoyed, even on a proportional scale, anything like Hegel's popularity or the general acceptance of his views. But, like Hegel, he quickly attracted critics bent on dismantling his edifice. Not only was Mitry's theory pompous in its scope, it allowed subsequent theorists little or no room within which to maneuver. Those coming after him would, by historical necessity, need to develop a critical theory. The fact that this moment, 1964, coincided with the fall of phenomenology (a synthetic approach to cultural experience to which Mitry's work owes great debts) and the rise of materialist (critical) approaches only made the break seem wider.[15]

While most modern theorists have tended to ignore Mitry as belonging to an earlier, cruder era, the topics modern theory addresses derive largely from him. Christian Metz, certainly aware of this, composed a review of Mitry's second volume which ran to forty pages.[16] Sadly, in English-speaking countries that review is far better known than its still untranslated subject.

Mitry's synthesis deals essentially with the twin experiences spectators are given in every film: that of recognizing something they can identify and that of constructing something worth identifying. Corresponding to realism and formalism, respectively, this tension between recognition and construction operates at every level and in every film, although according to varying ratios.

Though remaining staunchly neutral regarding the ultimate dominance of either "construction" or "recognition," Mitry nevertheless demands interaction between these two activities. This is where he locates the uniqueness, the specificity of the cinema, and this is what gives him the criteria for the evaluation of given films. The sheer recording of an event (for ethnographic reasons, for instance, or in the case of certain static adaptations of plays and ballets) fails to attain the level of *cinema* just as do, from the opposite direction, avant-garde films which, in their concern with abstract rhythm and shape, refuse to offer a recognizable signified.

This criterion applies not only to determining a canon of legitimate films, but can be used to evaluate specific cinematic strategies within any film as well. Here we encounter head on Mitry's conception of levels or thresholds. The spectator must move from the perception of objects presented in a certain way to an understanding of a state of affairs (story, argument) and finally to a comprehension of its poetic and rhetorical significance. This trajectory is controlled and guaranteed by the poetic movement of the well-made film. For Mitry this movement is always from the ground up, photographed images congealing into a shaped story whose values are inscribed via formal devices (repetitions, allusions, figures of all sorts) which come out of and extend the world developing on the screen. At each of these levels (image, narrative, poetic) the tension between the real and the abstract must be operative; in great films it is creatively operative.

Now Mitry's essential conservatism in taste, indeed his very audacity in making value judgments, has been enough to convict him in the eyes of his more critical and "scientific" successors. Nevertheless the categories of formalism, realism, image construction, narrative, and figuration have proved to be the key areas for contemporary theory as well. More important, Mitry's intuition that a theory of film would have to deal with both its language and its psychology could not have been more precocious, even if what he meant by cinematic language and the psychology of the film experience were quite different from more current attitudes about these concepts.

Modern theory, then, may be seen as an interrogation of Mitry's key concepts, driven by a desire to get beyond them so that they no longer exercise their infatuation over us and no longer lock together in a way that makes both the theory and the cinema it supports seem so unalterable.

This operation of criticizing the concepts of traditional theory begins with a rewriting of the names of those concepts. For instance, instead of a study of cinematic realism we now have a critique of realism via a study of "representation" and "verisimilitude," [17] terms much less value-laden and much more open to the investigator. Similarly, the formerly pristine notion of the "objectivity" of the image is broken apart in a study of the work of film technology, the cultural effort to create machines whose operations will return to that culture an image constructed in such and such a way. [18] The study of representation, resemblance, verisimilitude, and the mechanics of technology has given modern theorists space to play in a field that for too long has belonged to the loaded terms "realism" and "objectivity." Yet these newer terms are loaded in their own way and point to the unquestioned master notion of *work*. In the arena of modern film theory, meaning, significance, and value are never thought to be discovered, intuited, or otherwise attained naturally. Everything results from a mechanics of work: the work of ideology, the work of the psyche, the work of a certain language designed to bring psyche and society into coincidence, and the work of technology enabling that language to so operate.

At Mitry's first level, then, the theory of the image is studied under the rubric of semiotics. The formalism and realism of the first stage of the cinematic experience are joined in analysis by a general science of signs. Their more abstract patternings correspond to Mitry's formalism; their particular analogical arrangements (creating representations and illusions of things) correspond to his realism. Currently the semiotic aspects of film technology are becoming more and more the locus for a theory of the image, including the "sound image" which is receiving special attention.[19]

Although it may appear that all theorists working at this level are in harmony against their idealist precursors, there actually has developed a strong debate over the status of the semiotic laws which have been formulated. This debate involves the question of history as it affects, or even controls, semiotics and technology. For all their concern to document the ideological underpinnings of the lens and its perspectival image, for example, the *Cahiers du cinéma* theorists, and Jean-Louis Comolli in particular, can be indicted for their own brand of idealism, since they have essentially reified technology for all time. Recent work in America has tried to show the complex interplay of historical context in the invention and use of new technology.[20] Obviously there is a danger here in allowing history to usurp all the explanatory power which formerly was in the hands of theory, but clearly in the next several years we may expect a struggle between the claims of history and those of structural theory.

At the second level, that of narrative, the great advances in structuralism have allowed the modern theorist to build the rules for the "natural" sequence of events. Once again verisimilitude is shown to be a complex construction of signs, not a privileged mode of knowledge connected to the nature of things. If anything is natural, it is the psychic lure of narrative, the drive to hold events in sequence, to traverse them, to come to an end. Here a structural psychoanalysis has been instrumental in laying bare the workings of identification, teleology, spectator positioning, especially in sexual difference, and point of view. These are the new names for concepts struggling with narrative in cinema. Here cinema's relation to the other narrative arts, to painting, theater, and the novel is provoking speculation; yet once again this speculation is riddled with debate over the historical dimension of the question. In the theory of adaptation, for instance, I mark a turn away from the comparisons of media essences and toward a kind of sociology of adaptation which will explore the types and functions of borrowing.[21] Adaptation is a historically determined phenomenon operating differently in different epochs. Surely the culture's idea of "What is Cinema?" is at stake in every adaptation, and so the question of the essence of the medium and of the legitimacy of transference from one art form to another is perpetually with us, but it is with us now as a perpetually historical question which cannot be answered once and for all. The same is true of studies of point of view. Bordwell and Thompson's essays on Ozu, Branigan's work on point of view, and Burch's discussion of alternate cinemas suggest that Metz's early optimism about a semiotics of the cinema has been replaced by the sober realization that there is no semiotics of the cinema but only a semiotics of this or that cinema during this or that epoch.[22]

Mitry's highest level is that of the "poetic," a term obviously straining to patch up a problem. Modern theory, especially in its most recent turnings, has interested itself in this level, not to find some non-mechanical ultimate realm in film, but precisely to detail the mechanics of cinematic expression. The concepts of enunciation and filmic *écriture* (the work of writing) are here examined with special focus on the study of figures, those physical constructions of meaning which become the locus of special value and, later, the vocabulary of the medium. Most important to note here is the dependence of modern theory on the detailed analysis of well chosen films or segments.[23] Unquestionably film criticism and film theory have become more interdependent than ever before. The relation between the events of history (actual films) and generalizations about our experience (theory) could not be closer than in this interdependence.

At all levels, then, from the technology of the medium to the basic units (images) and their concatenation in moments of discourse where signification is forced upon a set of conventions, the film complex is seen as a set of multiple, interlocking systems inflected by work. This is its analytic base, and this its materialism. I hope to show, however, that despite its very different attitude toward the medium and toward research itself, modern theory (as critical theory) has taken off from the elaborate constructions of the past. The break, which I locate in 1964, is not so much a break as a turning of theory around upon itself. The questions named by the terms perception, representation, signification, narration, adaptation, valuation, identification, figuration, and interpretation have always been with film theory. Yet these new names are not merely the product of pretension and fad. They are a response to the social reconstruction of the terrain of the humanities. Film theory has not only profited from that reconstruction, but has actively contributed to it by recognizing itself as a social practice in picturing and repicturing our understanding of film, of society, and of art. This is the basis of its growth and of its pride.

2

Perception

THE CURRENT DEBATE

Although perception has been an explicit starting point for most film theories and must implicitly sit at the base of them all, it has seldom seemed problematic enough to merit extensive treatment. In effect only two positions have been available throughout the era of classical film theory: the realist and the Gestaltist. Bazin and Kracauer represent the realist camp finding little essential difference between perception in the cinema and in the world at large.[1] While Bazin's notions of standard perception derive from Bergson and Sartre and are substantially more complicated than Kracauer's naïve realism, both men think of cinema as extending, rather than altering, perception.

Mitry, who always tries to give every issue and every side its full due, believes that cinema's quasi-natural perceptual base distinguishes it from all other art forms.[2] This is why his is at once an aesthetics and a psychology of cinema. Psychologically, cinema does indeed affect us as a natural phenomenon. Viewers employ their eyes and ears to apprehend visual and aural forms corresponding to things, beings, and situations in the world. The full machinery of cinema, the cinema as an invention of popular science, ensures that we can see anew, see more, but also see *in the same way*. Most important, this naturalness suggests an attitude for spectators that involves curiosity and alertness within a ''horizon'' of familiarity. In no other art form are these natural attitudes toward the art material so present.

But Mitry's psychology is by no means realist. The mind, he feels, interacts with visual phenomena in ways that take him several chapters to explain.[3] His view is ultimately Gestaltist, insisting on the constructive rather than receptive function of the eye. This forces him to attend to the crucial differences between cinematic and standard perception. Like Arnheim before him, Mitry finds in the distance between these modes of perception space for the artistry of film. Without such differences cinema would truly be a re-presentation of visual experience, whereas perceptual deviation in cinema makes possible the conferring of value on this or that aspect of perception, the filtering here and enlarging there which makes a representation significant.

Mitry has deftly threaded his way between the two classic positions of film theory, the realist and the formalist. He has used realist arguments to help differentiate cinema from the other, purely conventional artistic systems like painting and literature; and he has used formalist arguments to redeem cinema from the servile task of mere reproduction (to separate it from tape recording, for instance). Thus he has nodded at the evident importance of questions of perception in film theory only to quickly dismiss them; perception is a necessary process which becomes interesting only insofar as it is made significant through artistic re-working. Mitry's film theory is centered on that re-working, not on perception.

Since the publication of Mitry's formulations in the mid-1960's, perception itself has become far more an issue, and it is the artificiality of cinematic perception, not its alliance with normal vision, which has been stressed and studied. Theorists were uniformly impressed with the labor required to produce Mitry's "natural" threshold of perceiving the filmic image.[4]

As early as 1967, Umberto Eco challenged Mitry's complacent theory with his notion of the multi-articulation of the cinematic code.[5] Eco reasoned that all systems designed to mediate experience for us (and he was happy to call these "languages") depend on the interrelation of their elements, not on the relation of the medium to its referent. The medium represents the referent only by a certain articulation of those elements, while the elements themselves need not be connected in any way to the referent being represented.

Where Mitry, following Bazin, thought of the basic film unit as the represented object or action (as an index, actually connected to its referent before being welded into a new "filmic" structure), Eco goes deeper to the pre-objective blotches of light, dark, and color which are the atoms of every image. Like the elementary particles of other semiotic systems (spoken language and music) these blotches are articulated via position and opposition to form fragments of recognizable semantic forms (triangles, vectors, and so forth) which are themselves articulated into iconic forms such as arms, legs, and trees. Thus only after two transformations can we speak of the represented objects as being "given" on the screen. Just as a newspaper photo is an array of dots of varying degrees of light and dark, none of which by itself stems from reality, so at its base cinema is a flow of grain organized into codes of iconic representation. The non-representational films of Paul Sharits and Peter Gidal support Eco's views by manipulating film grain in non-objective patterns.

Eco's argument seeks to win cinema over to the master discipline of semiotics, depriving it of any privileged status in relation to reality. Cinema is a seductive, but ultimately conventional language like painting, poetry, stained glass, or Morse code. It can be used to communicate known truths or it can serve the aesthetic function of questioning and expanding itself as a code; but in no case can it ever engage us directly with the world. Its ability to construct untruths, to lie, seals this point as far as Eco is concerned,[6] because the world itself never lies; it is only lied about by humans who represent it. Cinema is just such a human means of representation, despite the adage that "the camera never lies."

Here as elsewhere semiotics has hungrily consumed an entire human activity, diminishing perception in the cinema to nothing while raising signification to 100 percent. Although it is evidently possible to redescribe all behavior semiotically (to understand sight, for instance, as neurological communication, or to think of genetics as functioning by means of the semiotic codes of the DNA molecule), Eco's insistence on the category of "truth and lying" ought to limit semiotics strictly to intentional behavior. We may mistake the implication of some natural symptom (taking a mirage for water), but in such cases nature is not deceiving us in the way a person may when lying with signs.

No one would deny that cinema mediates reality for us. The disagreement hinges on the degree of intentionality behind such mediation. Eco and his fellow semioticians insist on the fully intentional character of all cinema. Bazin together with those we might classify in the phenomenological camp (Cavell, Morin, Merleau-Ponty, and

V. F. Perkins) contends that beneath the semiotic language of film lies a perceptual "manifold" which is never fully exhausted by the film's message. The cinematic signifier differs from all other artistic signifiers in its quasi-natural existence. We are permitted to look at it not only for what it explicitly says but for what our scrutiny can discover in it.

Morin finds this split between reading and scrutinizing the film sign to be peculiar to cinema from its inception.[7] He has shown, eloquently, that cinema began as an instrument of popular science, as a perceptual machine he calls the "*cinématographe*," whose function was to provide views of things formerly unseen or unseeable. Hence the fascination with slow and fast motion, with extreme close-ups and unlimited repetitions giving our eyes access to the world of nature. The importance of the "cinématographe" to biologists and physiologists is a matter of record.

At nearly the same instant, this very machine also began to function within an entertainment industry catering to a voracious public appetite for "curiosities." Through the cinema, magic shows, actualities, and spectacles were fed to audiences enamored of postcards, dioramas, and wax museums. Here cinema disseminated what were already highly organized cultural rituals. At first this function might seem to be equivalent to the scientific function in that the *cinématographe* extended perception, bringing to light things formerly unavailable or difficult of access. Soon, however (and perhaps immediately, if we recall the case of Georges Méliès), this machine started behaving like a language, reorganizing what it presented, abstracting and operating on the world through its images. Thus the *cinématographe* quickly became that phantasmagoric language we know as the *cinema*. But for Morin, Bazin, and many others the phenomenon of the movies is incompletely described unless this tension between perception and signification, between the *cinématographe* and the cinema is maintained. The cinema may be a language, but as Bazin said, "it is *also* a language,"[8] that is, not entirely language. Its other dimension, which he lodged in the psychology rather than the semiotics of the image, separates it from all other arts and gives to it the fascination which has engendered so many claims about its connection to the world.

Eco would surely debate this distinction between the cinematographic device and the language of cinema, between perception and signification in motion pictures. And he would be aided by a contingent of French theorists who in this same period (1968–71) took as their object of analysis not the language of cinema as Eco was doing but what they saw as the language of the device.[9] They were put on their guard by the complex technology required for this seemingly simple and natural augmenting of vision. A certain culture with specific needs went to great trouble to invent it. The complicated history of the development of this machinery must dampen the sunny idealism of Morin, Bazin, and all others who are tempted to speak of film images as quasi-natural products springing from the earth "like a flower or a snowflake."[10] Part of the discourse of culture, the cinema intervened in and altered that discourse in specific ways.

The lens which permits the formation of a representational image, for instance, stems from the camera obscura and Renaissance optics. The cinema thus inherits the desire of Renaissance culture for the centered representation of any visual field. The mechanisms satisfying this desire are hardly innocent. Indeed Marxist theorists see them as the products of a nascent capitalism that needed to replace the representations of cosmic and religious space (the feudal era) with a space of cultivated landscapes ruled over by proprietors who, in other pictures, are figured in rooms cluttered with objects of wealth.[11] Each individual spectator is in this way encouraged to desire and possess a consumable space from his or her own perspective, a space in fact requiring the presence of an "an individual" for its lines (perspectival) to be justified.

Bazin often spoke about perspective as a "Fall" from sacred to secular space, an original sin which necessitated a later cinematic redemption. But for the Marxist, cinema did not so much redeem the world by bringing art down into the flesh of the earth; instead it reified and naturalized these framed and centered images as though the world itself were thought to exist as so many rectangular cut-outs presented for our knowledge and delectation. The spectator is master of the universe when it is presented this way. The supposed scientific base of cinema guarantees the permanent rights of individuals to rule the world with their eyes just as science itself rules it with knowledge and a bourgeois class rules it with capital.

The tendentiousness at the base of the filmic system also directs the kinds of subjects that system has repeatedly treated: stories of objects lost and found, suspense tales in which the viewer in the end "possesses" the key, visions of expanses or of material opulence stretched out before a spectator who, for a small admission fee, can call them his own for a while.

Even if we question this hypothetical relation between the machine of cinema and its products (as many do, including dissenting Marxists),[12] we cannot deny the central thesis that the technology making possible the perception of images in cinema is a product of labor and of history. Where labor and history command, "nature" and "natural activity" become terms designed to mystify. The *cinématographe* as a machine is a willed transformation of nature for purpose and profit.

This analysis of the cinematic apparatus supports Eco in that it strives to explain how the conventions underlying cinematic perception go unnoticed and function ideologically. As a master concept "ideology" always implies the hiddenness of its operation. A vast outlay in capital and genius produced this machine to perform a central function, that of supporting a belief in the mastery of the eye over a scene (tantamount to the mastery of capital over labor and of the individual over larger social orders). For Eco, too, a perpetual labor quietly and surreptitiously adjusts human "subjects" to the machine of cinema and, through this machine, to a cinematized version of reality. While advertising itself as fully open to the visible world, cinema is a highly delimited, conventional emitter of messages about how things look and how they should be treated.

Labor is the notion that directly joins Eco's work to that of the theorists of the machine of cinema, for labor is at work in this tool of perception just as it is in the operation of communication. This is an important discovery, going beyond Mitry for whom film theory proper begins with "given images." Nothing is "given" we have come to learn. Far from overwhelming further investigation, this realization must push our analysis of the functioning of cinema toward a kind of subtlety that has been sorely lacking from Marxist critiques. Even if we do not perceive with an innocent eye through the cinema, it is crucial to find out just how we do perceive through it. The question remains even if the stakes of the response have changed.

THEORIES OF PERCEPTUAL PSYCHOLOGY

No matter what seductive metaphors we may cavalierly spin about cinema being the language of reality (Pasolini) or the entry door to nature

(Morin), it is clearer today than ever before that cinema is a fully cultural instrument created for various cultural activities. Each member of the culture organizes his or her experience through this mechanism; thus cinema works on the subjects of culture. But there is a prior work required first, that by which subjects learn to use the mechanism; here the question of perception presents itself unmistakably. Succinctly put: What sort of labor is required to learn to watch cinema? How does this learning differ from that required for the other media? How does it differ from that which enabled us to perceive in our daily life, if we can speak of this as labor at all?

When Metz declared that we must "go beyond analogy"[13] he meant that we must not let the striking quality of the film image overwhelm us or keep us from analyzing it. We must examine not just the codes that add themselves to the image, cultural codes seeking to naturalize their messages through realistic presentation; we must examine first and foremost those codes which permit an image to appear at all, the codes of resemblance.

The discovery that resemblance is coded and therefore learned was a tremendous and hard-won victory for semiotics over those upholding a notion of naïve perception in cinema. Every moment of cinema is now at the mercy of the analyst. We must theorize the very perception of images. But saying that they function by learned codes of resemblance is only a beginning; for how does natural perception work? We need a tentative theory of perception to undergird any useful theory of film perception. We can no longer afford to treat natural perception as a zero degree.

The labor involved in bringing film stimuli into recognizable images is not a unique or special labor. Something like it must happen in every perceptual case. So too, the corollary that we must *learn* to perceive film images is a corollary that must apply in some way to all visual life. This at least has been the opinion of most scholars since "nativist" arguments fell to the growing empiricism of the seventeenth and eighteenth centuries. Nativists had claimed that brightness, size, and (most critical) form were qualities immediately seized by every viewer.[14] But after John Locke, the perception of form came to be considered a product of long experience which stimuli evoke. Connections built up over the years and supplemented by the refining power of our other senses and by our bodily movement in the world help constitute, on the bases of the brightness and size of stimuli, the distribution, volume, and interdependence of elements in a visual field. In this way retinal stimulation leads to fully formed images. One of the classic formulations of this process goes:

> Perception is a complex act involving presentative and representative elements. After discriminating and identifying a sense impression, the mind supplements it by an escort of revived sensations producing an integrated percept, an apparently immediate apprehension of an object in a particular locality.[15]

This highly positivist view held sway over the nativist school into our century only to succumb to less atomic and additive modes of explanation. Foremost among these, and foremost in the history of film theory, was the Gestalt theory.

Originating modestly as a way to explain certain specific visual phenomena unaccounted for by the empiricists,[16] Gestaltism quickly developed into a full-fledged psychology, nearly a metaphysics. Essentially the Gestalt view downplays the individual element (or atomic unit) in favor of the field of configuration of which it is a part. Certain forms (at the base, these are invariably geometrical) are innate, structured into the physiology of the eye and the neural arrangement of the brain. We cannot help but see certain patterns in the world when stimuli bring these patterns into play.

The Gestalt theory is of the nativist variety for it denigrates the importance of both experience and learning. Indeed, its experimental method is close to a phenomenology in employing naïve subjects or ridding experienced subjects of their preconceptions. Thus Gestaltists hope to arrive at the basic structures of perception operative in all cases, though these are often hidden from us by clouds of habit and learning.

The fact that this theory became popular just as the first film theories were born helped seal a bond between film theory and Gestalt psychology which has never really been severed. Hugo Münsterberg and Rudolf Arnheim explicitly invoke it while many other theorists are tacitly under its sway.The Gestalt position has been especially attractive to aestheticians in all the arts for reasons that are easy to understand. First of all, art plays an important role in the theory as a diagram of the perceptual patterns at work in ordinary perception. Art is an activity that directly pictures the formal predispositions that we bring to experience. Even when the Gestalt view began to lose its hold on the field in the 1950's, its antagonists frequently recognized its fertility for aesthetics.[17]

In fact the Gestalt view has not so much been abandoned as re-worked by such recent theories as connectionism and functionalism that refute the myth of immutable structures or Gestalts but that retain the notions of "field" and "figure/ground." Even if there exist certain perceptual predispositions based on the neuro-physical makeup of the ocular system, as the Gestaltists contend, it now is deemed foolish to assume that these always work in the same way or produce the same results. The functionalists invoke the phrase "act of seeing" as an in-tentional act that differs according to the life situation of the organism at any given moment.[18] To search the heavens as an astronomer does involves quite a different process from reading a book or looking dreamily into the eyes of one's lover. Functionalism would describe the contexts of vision and the operations of the ocular system within those contexts. Obviously for the functionalists seeing is very defi-nitely an acquired skill; indeed it is a series of skills based on the need for action or orientation. Functionalism effectively blends the nativist and empiricist impulses in the psychology of perception by altering the definition of seeing, refining it into many subclasses of acts (search-ing, recognizing, gazing, and so forth). Such acts are both natural (na-tive) and acquired in experience.

In broadening their concern to the contexts of perception, recent psychologists have tried to bypass a strictly neurological study of seeing. No doubt the brain operates by means of geometric and digital patterns of stimuli and response, but "perception," it should now be clear, in-cludes many aspects, only one of which is, strictly speaking, neuro-logical.

The breakthrough made by functionalism in dissolving the cluster of questions that have been lumped together under "perception" has been much advanced by certain philosophers of language eager to ana-lyze the precise meanings of "perception names." Importantly, three of these philosophers, Nelson Goodman, Max Black, and Arthur Danto, have been particularly concerned with artistic perception and represen-tation, with Danto even having written an essay on the cinema.[19]

Scouring their work, one finds that even the simple notion of the visual image (in film, painting, or other media) is ruled by a plethora of terms that name the types of relation between image and our expe-rience of reality. Some of these are: designation, denotation, resem-blance, expression, exemplification, depiction, representation, signifi-cation, imitation, and reproduction.[20] Though these terms overlap to some extent, they can by no means be considered coextensive, and the choice of one term (or function) over another has many consequences. If we accept the image as a "denotation" or "signification," for instance, we treat it as something to be deciphered and we attend far more to its motivation than to its detail, or rather, as in a caricature, we look at detail only for its motivation (for the black tooth in Richard Nixon's smile). If we treat the image as a depiction or representation of reality, on the other hand, we may be encouraged to study its details for themselves and for what they may reveal (as when an image sent back from Mars is scrutinized by scientists). Thus the depictive powers of the transmitted television image share a relation to perceptual reality closer than that maintained by caricature, for we search the television image as we search fields of vision, whereas we look at a caricature only to recognize its subject and message. The relation between cognition and re-cognition differs in these cases.

Even this brief inquiry proceeds on the assumption that we know what "ordinary visual perception" consists of. Yet the most cursory linguistic analysis of the issue brings into relief the differences we sense not just between cognition and recognition but between perception and cognition, sensation and perception.

Let us begin with sensation. Is it coded and must it be learned? When certain semioticians insist that all vision is coded and that there is no direct access to things as they are, what does this imply? Surely sensations come to us naturally. We have sensations in the normal course of events when vibrations stimulate our nerve endings. If in its first encounters it takes some time (as it seems to) for our organism to learn to organize sensations so that they can be distinguished by shapes, colors, sizes and brightness, once this rudimentary skill is learned, it applies universally and unprogressively. An infant may at first have been unable to distinguish triangles from squares, but by two years old it can do this as well as a sixty-year old. Similarly, all optically endowed animals receive sensations, so that to speak of sensations as having to be learned defeats the cultural thrust of the notion of learning and of codes. If animals also must learn to see, then we must talk about a supplementary learning for humans; otherwise the term has lost all power to discrimate.

Now if we equate the perception of a situation with an ability to distinguish (and thus potentially name) objects and events making up the situation, then learning pertains to perception just insofar as it pertains to the elaboration of a specific cultural world. Perception, as distinct from sensation, is coded. Indeed it may very well be semantically coded in that Eskimos have some seventeen terms for snow, presumably because they are able to sensorially discriminate this many gradations. Belonging to a different cultural world, these gradations are invisible to the rest of us.

Doubtless, perception, no matter how defined, is in league with cognition and even with language. Why else would feminists lay such stress on altering the dictionary, unless they believed that with a new vocabulary our culture would *perceive* women differently and thereby would form a different reality altogether. But surely some of the transformations by which sensation becomes perception stem from human physiology (the configuration of rods and cones) and from universal features of earthly existence (day and night, the horizon line, and so on). Not all perception is culturally specific and alterable. To speak of learning to see is to speak of attaining (very early) a threshold after which vision becomes a source of orientation and action. Even if we point to the distance of vision from reality (optical illusions, the "constancy" principle, and other effects proving that what we see is a projection made from limited cues), it is clear that vision is in no sense arbitrary. Subjects who were fitted with glasses inverting everything they saw had difficulty negotiating their visual worlds for only several hours, after which they perceived everything in a normal manner.[21] They had adjusted their sensations in a regular way, with the regularity giving them confidence in using their sensations as legitimate indications of the environment.

Vision, then, is a skill involving our experience, language, other senses, and perceptual apparatus. If it is not in any strict sense the world internally given, but instead is the transformation of stimuli, the regularity of this transformation permits a consistent world to be constituted, one generally in harmony with our other senses and with the experience of other people. So much is this the case that vision is our main source of new information about our environment. We use it to search perceptual fields when recognition breaks down or when other people report or predict a discrepancy in "their" constituted worlds. Arguments about unidentified flying objects are excellent exemplifications of this.

Without involving ourselves further in the issues of veridical perception, we can now make some comparisons between it and the perception of images in the arts and in cinema. E. H. Gombrich has most forcefully and continually insisted on the conventional nature of artistic illusion as opposed to the more or less automatic aspect of natural perception.[22] Every man-made representation derives its power not from its relation to real perception but from its deployment of a system of marks which, through use, has become "readable as" an image of the real. The artist works to make the marks of the system equivalent to the distinguishing marks of the perceptual field he or she hopes to represent. The viewer works to decipher the marks, using his experience with the system and interpreting the strategy of the artist to interpolate a complete scene.

The tasks of constructing such images and of deciphering them require sophisticated training, far beyond the basic threshold of perceptual learning that we noted for natural vision. Whole schemas must be internalized, together with a sense of their use in history. It makes sense in this case to talk of "learning" a visual language for only the sustained reinforcement of a particular capability by a particular environmental need or pressure could produce the skill of transforming marks on a flat surface into the legible representations of three-dimensional objects and scenes. Even if we insist that all human perceptual *activity* (in distinction from *passive* functions such as sensation or emotion) requires learning, we would do well to reserve a special category for those perceptual practices which are fostered by particular types of needs and are thereby cultural rather than universal activities. Everyone physically fit will necessarily learn to see, but not everyone will learn the codes of representation operating in Japanese *ukiyo-e* prints. Natural languages are those which necessarily emerge in any environment; this would include a spoken language. But cultural learning develops only in the context of a specific pressure and reinforcement. This would include written language, ancient languages, and the languages of visual representation. The process of learning may be structurally similar in every case (for acquiring spoken language as for acquiring a driver's license), but cultural learning occurs only in a restricted milieu whereas natural learning occurs anywhere on the globe and at every time in human history. To cite our subject at hand, viewing a representational painting seems natural to us because we live within a milieu of painting. It seems less natural to a baby, a backwoods child, or an adult aborigine, all of whom nevertheless have learned to perceive the world around them just as readily as have we, and to equal effect.

Evidently the terms cultural and natural are inadequate in distinguishing human activities and learning; nevertheless, the overall thrust of our inquiry demands that we strive to discriminate amongst types of learning, no matter how we label these types. In the case at hand, we can say that the kind of learning required to decipher artistic paintings is of a different order still from both natural vision and picture viewing. Artistic vision demands continual attention through a lifetime of refinement, but object recognition in pictures is a skill once learned, never forgotten. Like the use of a simple tool (reading a scale, for instance) object recognition depends on the invariable application of an automatic process. The production of representational pictures, unlike that of artistic paintings, often depends on an apparatus to ensure this automatism. The camera obscura by which painters from as early as the fifteenth century facilitated the reproduction of likenesses is only the most obvious of such apparatuses. The geometrical schema on which perspective rests is equally an apparatus, a by-product in fact of the geometrical tools developed for projective mapmaking, some argue, to aid the booming maritime exploration industry of the pre-Renaissance.[23]

This geometrical scheme, built into our photographic lenses, is doubtless a conventional system, requiring that we submit to reading marks in just such a way and from just such an imagined position in order for perspective to "work." Yet this system, conventional as it is, is not arbitrary.[24] Its exact mathematical base is related to the task it fulfills, so that, once "seen," perspective is something we can hardly not see when it is employed. This is why, despite its cultural development (a product of Western Europe at the birth of capitalism), perspective was quickly and easily taken over by other cultures such as the Japanese, to coexist with native forms of representation. This intrusion of the West into other cultures was not like the adoption of English or French by those with time and money to learn it; it was more like the introduction of a new machine or tool, the rifle or the telescope. Minimal instruction was necessary for its proper use, but once used properly it immediately produced its promised effects.

Far from struggling to learn a complicated language, we traverse mechanical representations so smoothly that we must rather learn the halting of them. In Gombrich's terms it is "the limits of likeness" which must be recognized if we are to keep from misapplying or overapplying this tool. We must learn when the laws of representation are in effect and where they run up against their boundaries. In our viewing of newspaper photos, we do not need to educate ourselves to turn black and white dots into images of objects; rather we must learn to recognize two-dimensionality and the border of the frame outside of which a different kind of vision prevails. *Trompe l'oeil* paintings and illusions of all sorts trade precisely on the ease with which recognition works. We apply the tool in a milieu where it is uncalled for; or we apply the wrong tool.

Actually mistakes made in viewing images are not unlike mistakes we are prone to make in so-called normal viewing situations when we try or need to adjust perception to extended domains. If we put on sunglasses, for instance, our perception is "like" normal viewing but "limited" in respect to hue and brightness. If we peer through a key-hole, we must adjust our sense of object arrangement to the unaccustomed angle we have adopted and to the limited field provided by the frame. Learning has to do not just with the transforming of sensations into percepts but with adjusting those percepts to achieve a continuity of visual life. Otherwise each moment would have a hallucinatory quality, whereas "hallucination" is a word we reserve for those percepts to which we are unable to adjust.

Today even the most empirical psychologists hold that learning to see should mean the acquisition of *connections* among perceptual elements rather than the reception of those elements themselves. "Sensorial organization is not a product of learning so much as a primordial fact of existence."[25] In cinema too we must learn the limits, applications, and adjustments required of the sensations which come to us in a virtually primordial state.

CINEMA AND PERCEPTION

While there no doubt exists something like a cinematic language, the bare apparatus that produces recognizable images for spectators has much more to do with tools for expanded visual possibilities, tools like telescopes, periscopes, and so on, than with decipherable codes. Although the mechanism of the tool is complex (including photochemical, optical, and mechanical aspects), its operation is relatively simple, requiring minimal instruction. This is particularly so for the viewer. Learning to watch a film image is like learning to use a periscope. Disoriented at first, we soon transform the visual sensations into floating percepts which we learn to place in our world. Similarly, while the cinema transforms an open, three-dimensional, colored field into a framed, flat, often colorless image, it does so with an automatism so regular that we can adjust to it and then use it as an extension of veridical perception. The security policeman scanning fifteen closed-circuit television monitors is actually viewing the full perimeter of the bank it is his job to protect. He can respond correctly to information coming from any screen once he has learned the appropriate adjustments called for by this tool of his trade.

In this way cinematic reproduction is first of all a fact, not a code, of visual life. If we insist on considering the constant adjustment we make to it as reading a code, then we must extend the domain of the coded to cover most of visual life. Whenever we see something as something else (a portrait as a representation of someone, an actor as a character, a flower as a sign of spring, a piece of paper as a dollar's worth of labor or goods, a woman as a sex symbol) we would then be employing a code. Many theorists contend just this, that we see nothing except through the cultural codes which continually regulate our perception and present us with just this certain world. Such an extension of the term to all our visual life makes it ineffective, however, when applied to a particular form of perception like the cinematic. Yet such an extension makes an important point beyond even its political thrust: that there is little we can call "pure perception," and that most vision is only the unconscious application and interrelating of various skills of vision. Cinema is one of these. It must be distrusted like all such skills for it fails to present us with reality itself; yet it can be trusted as much as other skills for it stands in some definite relation to the real. Cinema thereby takes its place in our visual life, a place of perception not of language. Admittedly, of course, language is intimately involved in perception,[26] especially in such modeling perceptual activities as the cinema.

Current perceptual theory validates this place in many ways, by demoting stimuli in favor of organization. Whereas empiricism held that stimuli become percepts on the basis of earlier, recollected stimuli, theorists today in the main describe the formation of percepts as involving not the mechanical replay of past experience or of timeless Gestalt patterns, but other categories of visual and non-visual information which we put into play in given contexts. In consequence of this, seeing would be the master skill of organization in which subskills like binocularity, memory, eye-hand coordination, language, and the whole of nervous-mental life take their proper place. The world is elaborated within each perceptual act or moment.

Merleau-Ponty described this process in terms which, while troublesome for many perceptual psychologists, nevertheless remain true to this modern post-Gestalt view and play neatly into the hands of film theory as well.[27] Perception, he says, is not an exchange between solid stimuli emanating from solid objects and a coherent consciousness; it is instead a process by which my body entertains shifting yet organized relations to that which is outside it.

Because every perception occurs within a given horizon or project, there can be no single master law providing the key to organizing percepts. Instead we find an exchange between the body (together with its projects) and a material world which is pregnant with form. Hence it is impertinent to decompose perception into elements of sensation or to analyze an image into atomic parts of a code (the dots of a photo, for instance). For perception is an experience of totality even when, as always happens, it incorporates lacunae (the back side of the lamp I am focusing on). Nor do we accord the status of "the real" only to present stimuli. "When I share a landscape with a friend standing near me, I don't share my private sensation with his via a code; nor do we share some abstract knowledge of the scene which our words express. Instead I project myself into another myself and stand before a scene as socially given, not as known or deciphered."[28]

It is precisely this aspect of perception "as given" which so enthused the film theorists of Merleau-Ponty's era: Bazin, Morin, and Mitry. "Given" here ambiguously reminds us that the image comes from the attention of "another myself," while at the same time what we see has not been digested, abstracted, or communicated but is prior to all such operations. We view a scene which has been socially pointed out. This is certainly not a matter of simply viewing reality, as Kracauer seems naïvely to have thought; on the other hand, neither does it consist in the deciphering of a code.

How can we describe more clearly cinema's peculiar relation to perception? The term "image" can help us here, for cinema is a procession of images, and images are basic units of veridical perception too. No image, not even the normal, veridical image can be considered fully real, for perception as we have seen is a construction, not the end point of neural stimulation.

Since our constructions are so easily tricked (by illusions) and since images can be produced electrically without recourse to direct ocular stimulation, it is clear that there is no perfect rapport between eye, mind, and world. But there is surely some rapport, for the images we live with achieve a kind of trustworthiness, if not solidity, when verified by further encounters, by the other senses, and by reports from other observers.

The distance between stimulation and image requires a transformation that we can think of in terms of psychic work. Whatever the mechanism (and neurophysiologists have theories and evidence of all sorts) there would seem to exist three levels, tiers, or stages of visual organization to describe this distance and this work: (1) stimuli which perpetually bombard the eye; (2) focused fields which the active eye helps construct out of these stimuli and which may be called percepts; and (3) significant images which attain a stability we can refer to. The space separating each level from the others allows for errors, misjudgments, and values to enter; and the work that permits passage from stage to stage may be related thereby to a mechanism of ideology. Nevertheless, such workings are in an important sense "natural," automatic, and consistent.

Cinema replicates this process of vision. It depends on bridging the gap between a steady stream of optical stimuli and the organized fields and forms we call film images. Further, it routinely insists on the importance and stability of certain images. Thus cinema is above all things a representation of visual life itself. It mimics the continual work of seeing by means of its own work (technological, psychological, and sociological, respectively). As a representation of this process it can also pose questions about seeing, permitting us to reflect on the process as we undergo it. It can play with the relation of stimuli to visual fields (as in the experimental films of J. J. Murphy and Paul Sharits); it can play with the relation of perceptual fields to solidified images (as in Michael Snow's work); and it can insist upon or interrogate the cultural form of stable images (Bruce Conner and Kenneth Anger come to mind here).

All of this allows the simple generalization that in both cinematic and veridical perception, an image is any visual unit that sustains itself as a unit. Static images are already endowed with "significance" for us, frozen as they are in the flux of changing fields and amidst the stimuli which race perpetually behind and beyond these fields. These are the readable images that doubtless deserve a cultural reading of their inevitably rhetorical presentation. The publicity still, the artful snap-shot, the composed longshot—these photographic forms have their counterparts in those key percepts of our daily perception which Pasolini termed "im-signs,"[29] percepts which permit us to feel at home in a fluctuating visual world.

But images may have a temporal component too as they present an entire gesture, action, or scene. Here we can feel a perceptual flow working toward a significance which is conferred only when the wholeness of the fragment is sensed. Images are holding places in visual life: whether static or temporal they permit us "to go on from this point."

Most films trade only in solid images, easing us from one visual block of significance to the next; but films can suggest, show, or fore-ground the work of image production, that is, the work of perception itself. In these cases we understand more then ever that making visual sense is a labor and a risk in cinema. At the same time, we sense it as a labor and a risk in life generally. Hence, in spite of all recent attacks, cinema remains tied in a special way to the perception of reality. In an important sense, it is a *real mode* of perception.

3

Representation

THE WORLDS WE REPRESENT

In the second chapter we saw that the seemingly simple substratum of the cinema, visual perception, is an immensely complicated and disputed concept. In contrast, the issue of representation which stands before us now as the next level to be treated has never been thought of as simple by anyone and has been an explicit battleground for competing theories of the cinema. It will be even less possible here to present a satisfactory summary of views and arguments surrounding this issue, so vast is it, touching even upon the nature of thinking itself. But we can highlight and isolate the special conditions of representation which govern the cinema and the peculiar questions which the cinema raises as questions of representation.

Amidst all the varying types of experiments with perception, barely outlined in Chapter 2, there dominates a nearly univocal belief in the importance of ''attention'' in visual life. Only acts of cognitive expectation permit our eyes to move and focus in such a way that we see images. D. W. Hamlyn, berating all mechanistic discussions of perception, including even Gestalt psychology, demands that we study not just eye, the stimuli, and the neural patterns of the brain, but the general conditions at play in any moment of perception.[1] Our eyes work differently in different circumstances, literally forming different images depending on the expectations which guide their use.

Given this framework, we would have to say that the general circumstances of perception for the cinema spectator seem quite limited and specific in the first instance. We enter a theater and stare in front of us at a two dimensional screen for two hours. Yet within this strait jacket our eyes expect to coagulate film grain into shapes, objects, actions, and scenes; more important they expect to do so in ways which mimic the nearly unlimited viewing circumstances of life in the world. Cinema perception is a mode of "seeing as" wherein we see an array of light and shadow as a particular object and we see several hundred fragments of a full film as a particular world. Far from being a rare occurrence in perception, or a particularly devious one, cinema here joins myriad other instances of "seeing as," instances in which we notice an oscillation between what our senses deliver to us and how we identify this. Certainly the most startling cases of this involve illusions, but as E. H. Gombrich, Nelson Goodman, and others have stressed, this structure of experience is ubiquitous.[2] In daily life we are prone to identify geometric patterns of stimuli (an oblong, for example) as objects named by a different geometrical figure (a round table, set obliquely to our eyes). If this is the case for veridical perception, how much more pervasive is "seeing as" for explicitly judgmental visual acts which organize percepts into coherent wholes. We identify a set of varied stimuli not only as human beings, but as a group we call "the class" and oppose it to another blend of stimuli which we name "the teacher." Our experience, in short, does not merely add to our perception, it makes perception possible, for we perceive inferentially.

Goodman has pursued the consequences of these observations to the end, arriving at a pluralistic and nominalist philosophy which makes explicit use of art. There is no primary real world which we subsequently subject to various types of representation, he contends.[3] Rather it makes far more sense to speak of multiple worlds which individuals and groups construct and live within. Worlds are comprehensive systems which comprise all elements that fit together within the same horizon, including elements that are before our eyes in the foreground of experience, and those which sit vaguely on the horizon forming a background. These elements consist of objects, feelings, associations, and ideas in a grand mix so rich that only the term "world" seems large enough to encompass it.

Goodman is fond of using art as an explanatory model for his notion of "world." We step into a Dickens novel and quickly learn the types of elements that belong there. The plot may surprise us with its happenings, but every happening must seem possible in that world because all the actions, characters, thoughts, and feelings represented come from the same overall source. That source, the world of Dickens, is obviously larger than the particular rendition of it which we call *Oliver Twist*. It includes versions we call *David Copperfield* and *The Pickwick Papers* too. In fact, it is larger than the sum of novels Dickens wrote, existing as a set of paradigms, a global source from which he could draw. Cut out from this source are anachronistic elements like telephones or space ships, and elements belonging to other types of fiction (blank verse, mythological characters, and even accounts of the life of royalty).

It should be clear that even such a covering term as "The World of Dickens" has no final solidity or authority. A young reader of *David Copperfield* and *Oliver Twist* might consider these texts to be versions of a world of education and family relations which concern him outside of literature. The Dickens scholar naturally would consider these texts to be part of the complete writings of Dickens. What they represented for Dickens himself, who lived within them during the years of their composition, no one can say. One goal of interpretation has always been to make coincide the world of the reader with that of the writer. Although not a futile enterprise, the difficulties of accomplishing it, or of knowing that it has been achieved, are obvious.

Artworks are indeed suitable examples of worlds and worldmaking, for they are cut off in time and space from our everyday life. Not only is "The Woman Weighing Gold" a world within a frame which can hold a viewer's entire attention, so also is the Vermeer room in a museum featuring his work. The museum itself is a kind of world that we enter and leave bringing with us expectations, memories, particular codes of behavior, and a very special type of perception.

But out on the bustling street we likewise live in a world divided by comprehensive types of interest. For most of us the world of politics exists as a separate sphere to which we occasionally attend. This is an immense world frequently represented for us on the news or in papers. The New York *Times* editorial on "detente" is a version of part of this world as is the rebuttal of this version printed the next day in *Pravda*. Whatever encompasses our attention is a world we have constructed to live within. Whatever organizes our sense of that world or of some portion of it is a version; and versions we call representations.

THE WORLD OF AND IN FILM

Goodman's formulation makes it possible to speak of standard sense perception as "representational" in that each percept consists not only of its own quality but also of an indication pointing to the world to which it belongs. "This is a chair in the dining room" or "this is a swarm of molecules" is an equally true statement pertaining to a single ocular impression which the physicist had as he came down to breakfast. The first statement fits into his domestic world and the second into his professional world. Nor can we say that one statement is truer than the other, if both are in fact true to the worlds in which they belong.

The philosophical issues here go back centuries and can hardly be solved in this chapter. Does the Eskimo actually live in a world of multiple cold, white substances that we identify grossly and simply as snow? Goodman refuses to accord priority to the world of the chemist for whom such substances are particular definable states of the H_2O molecule.[4] Whether we agree with him or not, it is enough that recent philosophy has provided us with the room and the terms to permit a subtle description of the processes and effects of art in general and of the cinema in particular. Fortuitously, the relevant issues that crystallize around the notion of "world" derive not just from Anglo-American language philosophers like Goodman but from continental phenomenology. Sartre's writings on the imagination, Alfred Schutz's sociology of "life-worlds," and Mikel Dufrenne's "Phenomenology of the Aesthetic Experience" give weight to the common parlance of film critics who have always been comfortable with phrases like "Chaplin's world" or "The World of *Citizen Kane*."[5]

Instinctively we have cut off from our other experiences the special sensibility, gestures, and objects that belong to Chaplin's films or that fit into the kind of sepulchral space exemplifed by *Citizen Kane*. More generally theorists and the average spectator have cut off from ordinary life the world that exists within the movie theatre. "The World of Film" suggests the mechanism by which anything reaches the screen and, on reaching it, affects us. Instead of being a catalogue of things appearing on the screen (as in the Chaplin and *Kane* examples) "the world of film" is a mode of experience, rather like "the world of imagination." How does the cinema represent anything for us? In trying to answer this question Goodman advises us not to measure the adequacy of our representations against some supposed "reality" existing beyond representation but to isolate and analyze the peculiarities that make up the representational system of the cinema and that make its effects distinctive.

Now the first elements of cinematic representation are perceptual. Earlier we discussed the tension of belief and unbelief in cinema as equivalent to the oscillation between looking and seeing or seeing and recognizing which is the integral structure of perception in general. It is this equivalence that permits the casual, though philosophically naïve, claim that "reality" is rendered in cinematic perception. More accurately we should say that the structure of cinematic perception is readily translated into that of natural perception, so much so that we can rely on information we construct in viewing films to supplement our common perceptual knowledge (which is also, as we have often noted, constructed knowledge). This explains the confidence that jurors place in cinematic records submitted by a lawyer, or that astronomers have in video images sent back from Mars, or that ethnologists have in footage brought back by explorers to distant lands. In all these instances cinematic information supplements what we know about one or another of the worlds we inhabit.

To some degree the tension between belief and doubt operates in every iconic sign system: the cinema, still photography, drawing, painting, and so on. In each of these an image strives to produce the *effects* of natural perception through a *process* quite different from natural perception. We *effectively* recognize our friend in an image *processed* by Kodak.

If cinema heads our hierarchy of such sign systems, so that the jury accepts a filmed record of the murder but rejects a drawing by an eyewitness and even a still photograph, it is due to cinema's mechanical and temporal aspects. The automatic registration of light on celluloid involves us in squinting at the image to "make out" the object in the glare and the grain (whereas a drawing could be much more clear). And the temporal flow which throws us from one image to the next demands that we adjust our recognition of what we see to the overall image which organizes itself gradually before us. But it is just this work that makes us assent to the film image, for ordinary perception involves precisely the same types of work even if the actual visual cues (the stimuli) are somewhat different. So at its basis cinema may be said to represent the numerous objects signified in light and shadow over the course of an hour or two. But cinematic representation is more than a sequence of photographs, for the thousands of *photogrammes* meld into pictures of scenes enduring over time. Instinctively we strive to put disparate scenes together so that the entire projection coheres. Thus, from the automatic operation of the phi phenomenon which produces movement out of static and separated *photogrammes* to the classification of an entire film, the mind actively constructs images from the light that stimulates it. At the first level the percepts we identify in the flowing grain depend in a major way on our expectation that they will contribute to the larger representation which is at stake in the film.

These still images then become animated and begin to pull us through the film along what Béla Balázs called a current of induction[6] toward a final representation. It is this ultimate sense of a developing representation that makes the individual *photogrammes* readable and that likewise assures their smooth linkage in montage. Yet what is this final representation other than a construct built up of the individual fragments it supposedly makes comprehensible? Just as the basic percept of cinema is a unit constructed out of light and shadow on film grain, so the entire cinematic representation is a major unit our mind puts together. More important, the structure of cinematic representation from beginning to end is one of process, where fragments are ruled by the wholes they add up to, and where belief and unbelief keep our eyes on the screen while our mind glides into the world of the representation.

Quite simply the oscillation at the heart of all instances of "seeing as" becomes in the cinema a vacillation between belief and doubt. The cinema fascinates because we alternately take it as real and unreal, that is, as participating in the familiar world of our ordinary experience yet then slipping into its own quite different screen world. Only an unusually strong act of attention enables us to focus on the light, shadow, and color without perceiving these as the objects they image. And, on the other side, only an equally strong hallucinating mode of attention can maintain from beginning to end the interchangeability of what we perceive and the ordinary world, negating all difference of image and referent. Cinema would seem to exist between these two extremes as an interplay between "the real and the image." The film experience in general and every instance of viewing a film can be analyzed in terms of a ratio between realistic perceptual cues and cues which mark an effort and type of abstraction.

Contributing to the sense of reality (of immediate apperception and non-mediation) are at least four elements, some of which Christian Metz outlined in his earliest writing.

1. Experimental preconditions, such as the darkened auditorium.
2. Analogical indices such that the image of an object shares actual visible properties with its referent.
3. The psychological imitation which cinematic flow provides of the actual flow of reality. Importantly, movement in the cinema is actual movement, not represented movement, and our mind is brought alive by it.
4. Finally, the lure of sound, which establishes a second sense to verify the first and which analogically is more exact than image representation.[7]

All of these characteristics tend to put us in front of a filmed image as if we were in front of a real scene in life. What keeps us from accepting the image as life is a fissure which we sometimes leap, sometimes refuse to leap, and most often straddle. Consisting of such experiential counters as bodily immobility, of nonanalogic aspects such as foreshortening, and of the more basic fact that the scene has been put before us by another, these anti-illusionistic elements lead us to treat the film not as life but as an image in the Sartrian sense, as a presence of an absence.[8]

All films present themselves to us as real/image according to various ratios. To move across the bar is to shift intentionality in a manner not unlike what happens in figure/ground experiments. Reality is here taken to be a type of consciousness characterized by certain indices of appearances and a certain mental activity. To shift to the imaginary is to move, as in daydream, to another "realm" while still adhering to many of the phenomena associated with our reality state.

The crucial marker of this particular experience of oscillation is the frame itself. The frame is the physical embodiment of the bar between image/reality and it marks as well the case that this experience is presented to me by another. I must attend "there" to the frame and not elsewhere. Classically stated, the screen as "window" is a place of perception; as "frame" or border it delimits and organizes perception for signification. Jean Mitry saw this long ago.[9]

The frame keeps us off our guard. We search the screen as we search any perceptual field, yet we feel the force of "this particular" disposition of objects and shapes. The superfluity of the facts of the visible world imprints itself on every image, but the frame demands selectivity and motivation. We are given over to the world, yet we are given over to signification. Nor is this the end of it, for the image changes before our eyes; both the film and the world move on. The fact of movement introduces the category of narrative or, at least, its possibility. For while the framed image dissolves before us and the vibrant life of perception is reaffirmed, this flow engages a narrative intentionality marked by reframing and shot changes. Although we perceive the dissolution of every scene, we group scenes into events that are not allowed to fall away but are held together as on a chain.

From the angle of phenomenology, narrative refers to a type of consciousness into which audiences lock themselves when attending to the chain of movement in a film. It involves a particular form of image processing wherein sensations are read as significant in their temporal and causal interrelation. The study of narrative in cinema ought therefore to begin with a determination of our relationship to the images and to the current of induction which runs through them, pulling us after it. Such determinations would amount to genre studies if we formalized their results, since they would name and describe the customary relation into which spectators lapse (or against which they struggle) with regard to the filmed material and its organization.

If every film is a presence of an absence, we are still obliged to differentiate the types of imaginary experience possible within various ratios of this relationship. A filmed image may be considered the presence of a referent which is absent in space (live TV coverage) or in time (home movies). It may also be taken to be an image which is non-existent or whose existence is not in question one way or the other.

Consciousness immediately makes decisions about the status of the image and from these decisions it processes the filmic flow in different ways. If the absent referent is deemed nonexistent we attend to the peculiarities of the image, necessarily striving to give existence to an unknown. If, on the other hand, the absent referent has solidity for us (as a friend or a public figure in whose existence we believe), we may utilize our recognition of the image to launch our consciousness into a state which calls up a *mise-en-scène* of the imaginary, producing nostalgia, desire, and the like.[10]

In this way we can consider our relation to the flow of various types of movies. In the home movie situation each point interests us not as an accumulation of a past (retention) throwing us into a necessary future (protention), but only as a potential triggering device allowing a shift of consciousness. We wish to transcend the home movie by means of one or two of its images and attain a more private state. In other words, the intention of "conjuring up the past" lords it over the basic intentionality of "movement," using the life of movement to restore the dead past. Our frequent recourse to still-frame and creep-speed projection techniques certifies this hierarchy.

Documentaries achieve a variety of ratios of presence/absence or image/referent. Since in most cases we know and believe something about the referent and its world, the documentary can sometimes serve the imaginary function already described in relation to home movies. We use and discard a hundred minutes of the Rolling Stones in order to recognize those five minutes that are sufficient to launch us into a reverie. The sound track in such a film already guarantees this sort of response. But if the film is about an obscure woodcutter of the Northwest, we must attend to the specifics of the image and try to build a sense of a world about which we know little even though we may have "faith" in it. Every documentary relies on our faith in its subject and, more important, utilizes our knowledge of it. Barbet Schroeder's portrait of Idi Amin[11] summarizes a good deal of data through voice-over narration in its first five minutes, but otherwise forces us to process the images of Idi within a field of consciousness already full of the Idi story. Indeed like many documentaries, Schroeder's film was under little compunction to achieve formal closure since his subject would continue to survive and his spectators would in fact have a greater understanding of the denouement of his film than he possibly could have had in 1973, not knowing Idi's final atrocities.

Every fictional film likewise relies on some substratum of spectator understanding of the type of world that becomes the subject of the film. We bring our own sense of boxing to Rocky and of the strictures of bourgeois life to any Douglas Sirk film. But the fictional film, at least in most of its genres, quickly transfers our interest to the world of the image, calling on, but not playing to, our knowledge of its referent.

In the fiction film all moments become significant as we construct a referent whose absence is determinant, not merely accidental or logistical. Movement in fiction film is coterminous with the film itself. The viewer is asked to swim in a time stream, and he cannot look away without the fiction threatening to disappear. As Hugo Münsterberg noted fifty years ago,[12] our mental flow coincides with the filmic flow in those fictions that produce the strongest mental events. Whereas the techniques and codes that construct the illusion of the continuity of movement in the fiction film may be the product of history and labor (may change from era to era), the mode of consciousness by which spectators have always participated in the construction of a fiction is ahistorical and transcendental to the degree that it stems from certain conditions of perception and cognition operating in the everyday life world (conditions such as retention, protention, filling in, and so forth). It is for this reason that those filmmakers who break the cinematic flow (Godard, for instance) need to labor to do so, for they thwart the mind in its act of seizing something that seems to disappear for it when stopped.

Among fiction films themselves we can categorize different ratios of perception to signification and begin to list genres and styles as we do so. *Nashville* and *Paisa* affirm an overbrimming perceptual flux out of which certain stories have eddied. *The Third Man* and *Rosemary's Baby,* on the other hand, construct tight networks of signification which wither all but certain perceptual possibilities. In all fictional cases we appropriate the situation of the narrator by succumbing to the film flow in the proper way. Propriety varies from genre to genre, from *Paisa* to *The Third Man,* but the demands of narrative consciousness remain— demands that include its drive toward totalization, identification, explanation—even while these demands operate in different ways for each genre.

Some of the differences amongst genres and films can be catalogued as functions of the imagination. The supplying of background information is negligible in the standard Western for our minds instantly fill the horizon of these films with the appropriate atmosphere, landscape, and props. But in a film like *Wind Across the Everglades* or *Dersu Uzala,* both of which depend crucially on the relation of atmosphere and landscape to character and both of which are set in landscapes unfamiliar to most filmviewers, the filmmakers must continually offer background shots, through composition in depth, pans away from action, and descriptive exposition.

The film noir, to take another genre and another aspect of film construction, frequently employs both voice-over narration and returns to past action. The viewer is asked to gauge the action represented on the screen in relation to an overall judgment which is, so to speak, simultaneously present with the action. In standard gangster films, on the other hand, the straightforward, third person approach to the action asks us to project the end of the film (the death of the gangster) in the actions he sequentially institutes. The film noir hero, on the contrary, not only appeals to us through first person address, but speaks from a point where the action has reached its end.

More modernist narratives like *8½* or *Last Year at Marienbad* befuddle those viewers unable or unwilling to supply interconnections, background data, multiple categories of image status (dream, wish, memory, reality). By taking our powers and aspirations for explanation, totality, and identification to the limit, such films bring out into the open the value, the labor, and the fragility of representation in the cinema.

THE IDEOLOGY OF REALIST REPRESENTATION

In laboring to thwart the normal "way of the cinema," the radically avant-garde film draws attention to the strength and ubiquity of that "way." No matter what appears on the screen, audiences will instinctively shape it into a representation of something familiar to them. The film that gratifies this attempt, the most satisfyingly representational film, we call realist. Such a film will cut up the world of appearances into perceptual images organized into patterns that make sense to us because these images and patterns exist in our culture. Without effort we can identify in the film something we have identified already in our culture as important. Thus the film reinforces the world we have constructed.

Recent critics of realist cinema have shown all too clearly that this mapping of cinema on life is hardly natural at all but is the product of enormous technical resources and traditional knowledge. The cinema reproduces identifiable parts of our world by framing, focusing, and juxtaposing aspects of the visible in "acceptable" ways.[13] Furthermore it does so teleologically; it shows the dramatic or rhetorical significance of a certain arrangement of these parts from an integral and integrating perspective.

The history of the cinema is usually measured as the progressive adequation of the rules of cinematic organization to the habitual ways by which we organize life in our culture. The movement from long shot to mid-shot to close-up, for instance, termed in the industry the "accordian sequence,'' imitates our usual method of surveying the context of a situation and only then attending to human speech.

This and other codes of representation are meant to disappear as we grasp (identify) and assent to the representation itself. In other words, realism in the cinema is driven by a desire to make the audience ignore the process of signification and to grasp directly the film's plot or intrigue; for most filmviewers, the plot is precisely and fully what a film represents. In this way realism stabilizes the temporal dimension of film, turning the flow of pictures into a single large picture whose process of coming into being has been hidden behind the effect of its plot. While the semiotic work of such theorists as Metz and Barthes [14] has disclosed the cleverness of the realist system, it has simultaneously provided an impetus for both the critic and the filmmaker to go beyond realism.

This modernist ideal is in harmony with Gombrich's celebrated *Art and Illusion*. [15] Just as Gombrich sought to trace the invention of strategies in drawing and painting that produced the illusion of reality for each succeeding generation, so Barthes suggests a method whereby narrative can be treated as a practice, conventional and even rhetorical, in which fragments are joined in a way to promote an illusionistic experience. Plot in narrative is analogous to design in graphic art: we think of it as the first thing seized, as that which structures the whole, as meaningful in itself, as referential. The other elements in narrative, we believe, flesh out the plot, just as texture, color, and ornament operate on design. Like designs, plots can be more or less intricate; they can be produced by continuous line, broken line, or successive approximations. In the classic (or as Barthes has called it, ''readerly'') narrative, action has been organized for a reader-viewer which places him or her just as definitely as perspectival painting situates its viewer in relation to a vanishing point. The scene is intelligible only through the complicity of the spectator, a task we take on every time we read a classic story or see a classically built film. We exhaust such realist works once we have successfully identified what they are about, once we have, for example, arrived at the final clue which makes the entire detective plot clear to us.

The solidity of such plotted films puts us at ease before the fictional world, but it greatly restricts the possibilities of art. First of all, it assumes that every work wants to express precisely what it represents. While this may be true in science or ordinary discourse, artistic expression frequently is at odds with what it represents. This is why we find so many "still lifes" in painting, all of which may represent a bowl of fruit but each of which expressing a different mode of vision or feeling, a different way of painting. The narrative or the design in art ought really to be thought of as one element in a mobile system. Roland Barthes is the prophet of this view of artistic texts urging us to escape the trap of narrative, a trap that naturalizes conventions by relating the "view" of the story to views we have of the world at large in our non-literary experience.

In *S/Z* Barthes systematized the aspects of any narrative text which command our interest and attention. He calls these aspects codes and he lobbies for a free interchange between codes instead of the dominance of one of them, narrative. Barthes here gives definition to insights which Bazin and Eisenstein arrived at years ago. After discussing the movement from aggregate impressions to the "whole image" of Forty-fifth Street Eisenstein makes an important distinction (familiar to students of Russian Formalism) between the function of representations in life and in art.

> We have seen that in the process of remembering there are two very essential stages: the first is the *assembling* of the image, while the second consists in the *result* of this assembly and its significance for the memory. In this latter stage it is important that the memory should pay as little attention as possible to the first stage, and reach the result after passing through the stage of assembling as swift as possible. Such is practice in life in contrast to practice in art. For when we proceed into the sphere of art, we discover a marked displacement of emphasis. Actually, to achieve its result, a work of art directs all the refinement of its methods to the *process*.
>
> A work of art understood dynamically is just this process of arranging images in the feelings and mind of the spectator. It is this that constitutes the peculiarity of a truly vital work of art and distinguishes it from a lifeless one, in which the spectator receives the represented result of a given consummated process of creation, instead of being drawn into the process as it occurs. . . .
>
> Hence the image of a scene, a sequence, of a whole creation, exists not as something fixed and ready made. It has to arise, to unfold before the senses of the spectator.[16]

Eisenstein here has gone beyond the rather Pavlovian view which supported his earlier notion of montage of attractions.[17] He has also gone beyond much current semiotics which has been reluctant or unable to describe the path by which perceptions in the cinema become absorbed in the overall narrative representation. Semioticians assume the simultaneity of signifier and signified. It makes no sense, in the science instituted by Saussure, to speak of the sensory base of a sign preceding the mental image it brings up. Yet it is precisely in the space between seeing and recognizing that, in the second chapter, we lodged the specificity of cinema and it is in just an indeterminant space the Eisenstein here finds the specificity of art in general.

It is instructive to note that while Bazin too looks for cinematic value in perceptual labor leading up to signification, he grounds this value not in the tradition of the arts, as did Eisenstein, but in the phenomenology of everyday perception. This indeed is the heart of his realism, a realism obviously at odds with that nineteenth-century narrative realism and with the realistic illusions of classic Hollywood cinema. On more than one occasion Bazin explicitly ridiculed standard cinema because it had inherited the codes of style and content made obligatory by Balzac and Zola. Against this he affirmed a realism of perceptual experience wherein the daily life habit of apperception, recognition, and mental elaboration is structurally reproduced in the cinema.[18]

This insistence on active intentionality in the bringing into existence of cinematic representations of events, places, states of affairs, characters and the like, leads to the classification of types of representations as genres. Whereas "realism" appears to be a zero degree of cinematic representation (one involving no marked labor), we have seen how dependent it is on conventions and habit. Other genres such as neorealism, expressionism, even science fiction, clearly depend on extraordinary operations before their content will body itself forth with the proper effect.

Yet even though our consideration of representation once again has dispelled the hegemony of realism, it has not thereby removed the notion of representation from that of reality. Representation is obviously dependent on textual cues and is in an important sense a textual effect, but this does not of its own throw us into a realm of artistic anarchy. First of all a given textual arrangement produces a limited number of representations in its audience. We are not free to construct whatever we like from these cues, for our minds fill in, filter, delete, and emphasize according to laws or habits. More important, since in every case representation establishes a relation between a text and something outside the text, our sense of that which is outside is constitutive of the representation. As a relation, rather than a pure construction, representation is governed by issues of adequacy, novelty, usefulness, and even rightness. To return to Nelson Goodman's terminology, a representation is always a version of some world or other. Though it is not for us to decide about the priority of one world over another, and certainly not to insist on a real world against which all representations are pale copies, nevertheless we are entitled to demand of a version that it be better, more instructive, richer, more useful than an earlier version. Representation insists that we examine not only the text but the text in relation to the world it produces through our imagination.

REPRESENTATION AS PLOT AND PROCESS

Because it maintains a relation to the world it calls up, cinematic representation has been a concept under siege in our era. Both modernists and traditionalists have attacked it for its purported rootedness in things. Traditionalists from Erich Auerbach on have accorded to the representation of reality the highest cultural function, yet they have sequestered cinema somewhere in a cave beneath true representation, believing that it has condemned itself to pornographic spectacle. Modernists like Barthes and Gombrich hold little regard for representation deeming it to be an overvalued, purely psychological lure which distracts our attention from the possibilities of art. Ever since the age of realism our culture has been obsessed by plot in literature and design in painting. Cinema, seeming to combine both these representational traits, is the heir to this retrograde tradition and has therefore made fewest strides in escaping its servile and puerile function of merely duplicating a sense of the world for a mass populace.

The traditionalist position has been most forcefully advanced by Roger Scrutton who pushes the Bazinian position to the limit, claiming that cinema enjoys a relation to the physical world that is so tight and unmediated that neither human intentions nor values can enter in. For Scrutton, as for Auerbach before him, representation is always an act of will, a shaping of materials to produce a significant picture of the world.[19] Cinema for them is too easy, too like everday perception. Scrutton gives an example. Suppose we frame a street scene through our viewfinder in the middle of a city. Would we say, as we got ready to shoot, that we were looking at a fine representation of that street? "The very idea is absurd," says Scrutton, for we are looking at the street itself. Similarly, when that button is pushed and the film developed and projected, it is outrageous to him to claim we are watching a representation of the street, for what we see is effectively what was there.

Earlier, on the basis of Nelson Goodman's remarks, we suggested that our ordinary perceptions involve intentions and might be called representations, since they signal the world to which they belong. Scrutton need not deny this to maintain his point, for all he declares is that cinematic perception operate at the same level and in the same implicatory way as natural perception. True representation drives a second intentional wedge between what we see and what it means, as when Giacometti's small, stick forms in bronze represent a man, or man himself. Cinema is basically pornographic to Scrutton since it keeps our attention on the texture and quality of that which it depicts. It is a simple substitution for experience. This is why its inventions bring it ever closer to the original (sound, scope, depth). For we go to the cinema to sense life, not to encounter a view of life. Our bodies more than our minds assent to what we behold.

Scrutton's moralism, his undisguised elitism, is not the only thing that needs refuting. Even if we grant that at the purely perceptual level cinema does indeed enjoy (or is condemned to) an affinity with standard perception, the construction of an entire film out of such percepts would seem to be an act of the highest intentionality. In the first place we can point to those cases where two or more cinematic versions depict the same man, story, or state of affairs, recalling that in Goodman's vocabulary a version is precisely a representation. Think of the Frank Borzage version of *A Farewell to Arms,* so different from the David Selznick version of 1957. Scrutton would claim that the cinema in both cases merely reproduces dramatic representations and that the differences we sense in these films derive from differences in dramatic construction. The speciousness of this retort is answered by another example: What about two versions of New York City as proposed by the 1920 *Manhattan* and the Willard Van Dyke 1938 *The City?* Through camera angle, editing, lighting, and organization we are here given two quite different versions (representations) of the same city.

Where Scrutton discusses cinematic representation as a special or enlarged case of perception, modernists of the semiotic and post-structural camps treat it as a special and limited case of signification.[20] To them cinematic discourse, like any discourse, proceeds by the articulations of codes producing a myriad of meaning effects. One of these effects is representation, which, far from being deprived of intention, is a fully ideological effect whereby a picture of reality arises out of the interplay of differential signs. For the health of society as well as for the satisfactory working of the cinema, the solidity of such pictures must be dissolved back into the mechanism of signification which gave it life. Only in this way, they argue, can communication free itself from the automatic reproduction of ideology (or false pictures of reality) and open up the more logical or anarchic possibilities of signs.

Semioticians tend to stress the instantaneous and invariable movement from signifier to signified in the articulation of cinematic meaning. This automatic operation implies a spectator whose role is that of a relay in an impersonal movement of cinematic and cultural language. Post-structuralists, given over more and more to the free play of the signifier, revel in constructing an indefinite variety of provisional significations out of the materials (codes) of film. Whereas the spectator would appear to have a more crucial role here, that role is limited to teasing out the possibilities embedded in the codes themselves. Once again the material codes of the system rule the spectator, taking him willy-nilly in the endless flight of texts. Anti-humanists applaud this.

Representation is doubtless a humanizing term, for it suggests that texts exist in part by means of the relation they establish between readers (spectators) and a world of some interest. Although representation should not be thought of as the terminus of a film (as should no single aspect of what is always an interacting system), its peculiarly intermediate status tells us a great deal about the experience of watching a film. When leaving *North by Northwest* we will feel correct, though inadequate, if we characterize it as a thriller (genre) or as a film about a man pursued by unknown enemies (premise). Yet these descriptions are surely more apt than one which would label it ''a film about a man in a taxi'' or ''about a man on Mt. Rushmore,'' for neither of these fragments gets at the overall picture the film renders. If pressed to elaborate that picture (as the scriptwriter must have been when he proposed the film to the producer, or as we are when our friends are deciding whether to see it), we generally recount the plot, that is, we indicate the characters, the intrigue, and the values that are at stake.

In this way we identify what can be expected and suggest how the film ought to be perceived.

Although the plot is clearly no substitute for the film, it does relate the primary aspects of perception with the ultimate experience of meaning and value. The perceptual level of cinema is nearly intangible, while meaning and value surround the film like a horizon, out of reach almost by definition. Plot, on the other hand, is accessible for it is a sum of perceptual fragments (though not the aggregate of these) and it is an example of the world to which it belongs and which it delivers to us in specific form.

Considered this way as plot or argument, representation acts as a special kind of label allowing us to identify the whole picture before or after we fully immerse ourselves in it. Like any label it is a convenience and a fully conventional one. We identify a representation as whatever large unit holds and directs our attention. Eisenstein spoke always of a grand theme producing a controlling image capable of infusing and organizing the particular fragments of a film.[21] We make and watch films according to levels of intentional blocks or units, any of which we can term a representation. Even if such units are technically dissoluble into the elements which constitute them, they play a determining role in our experience of the film. The situation here is analogous to that which we found in perception where the raw stimuli could never fully account for the percepts they constitute. Attention and intention, guiding perception, operate even more apparently at the level of narrative organization. We identify an array of light and shadow as "a marching army," or "a man harranguing a crowd," and we label an array of such percepts as a representation of the life of Lawrence of Arabia, or as a version of Tolstoy's *War and Peace*. Viewers may differ in the labels they feel compelled to supply for what they see, but the compulsion to see films as representations is universal and universally functional in the overall film experience.

Representation's intermediate position between the fragments of a film and its overall possibilities of significance should surprise no one familiar with Freud's use of the term, for representation appears as the indispensable form under which fantasies and dreams may exist.[22] Although listed as one of the four operations of the dreamwork, representation is clearly the first and necessary condition permitting condensation, displacement, and secondary elaboration to operate. Doubtless because of Freud, representation retains its connotation of an unconscious drive in which figures arise and present themselves forcefully to us. Closer to the common notion of symbol than to that of code, psychic representations demand a work of interpretation in which we must adjust ourselves to the meaning that seems proposed but not completed by the representation. This is exactly like the work of filling in, filtering, and underlining the cues provided by the images and the soundtrack of a film.

The modernists are right to insist on the limited range of representation. As in the Freudian case, it operates as a threshold permitting the real work (dream or artistic) to create value and significance. Representations are often used in texts which turn against them. A filmmaker may signify something quite ambiguous or even negative about the representation his film develops as Werner Herzog does with *Aguirre* or as Tony Richardson does with the Crimean War in his *Charge of the Light Brigade*. Irony is only one of the figures of discourse that work with and on representations to form signification. But as this chapter has sought to point out, representation (at least in the conventional cinema) is a necessary precondition for discourse. One can maintain that Piero de Cosimi's ''Visitation'' turns on the brilliance of its color with the excessive use of red signifying perhaps a hostility to earlier paintings or a revolt against the patrons who commissioned the piece, or that it expressess Piero's massively unresolved psychological tensions. Nevertheless his painting *represents* Mary encountering her sister Elizabeth as reported in the first chapter of St. Luke's Gospel.

Representation marks a key moment in cinematic discourse in its struggle to wrest signification from perception. The logic of plot develops only in a field of perceptual possibility with which it oscillates. The particular strategies and paths by which we move back and forth from picture to perception define the modes and genres of film. Eisenstein goes so far as to insist that only those representations that develop in deep struggle and difficulty can be deemed art.[23] Be that as it may, representation names that threshold at which viewers stand in their traversal of a film, a threshold that puts them not in control of the film, nor at the mercy of it, nor in a state of vertigo before its infinite openings (these are the reactions implied by realism, semiotics, and poststructuralism respectively); instead we find ourselves in a state of active ''listening'' to a world which might take shape and which, in this or that particular film, has taken a certain shape.

The irreducible perceptual manifold draws us of its own accord to test the adequacy of any given provisional organization that seems to arise from it as a representation. Such organizations narrate a version of a world in textualizing it. If such texts produce a single or myriad significations, it is only out of the skin of perception and the flesh of representation.

4

Signification

THE ASCENDANCY OF SEMIOTICS

The weening of modern film theory from Mitry's paternal embrace is named by a single term: semiotics. Mitry's lengthy ruminations on the rapport between language and cinema, together with Albert Laffay's *Logique du cinéma* and several other studies of the early 1960's, had evidently squeezed dry the fruits of gentlemanly speculation on the topic.[1] What seemed called for, and what arose, was a scientifically inspired investigation of the so-called language of cinema. Structural linguistics, advancing on the teachings of Hjelmslev, Benveniste, and Martinet and broadened by the use made of it by anthropologist Claude Lévi-Strauss, provided both the rigor and the model for such an investigation.

The semiotics of cinema was launched with a most heady optimism. Driven by an intuition that the intangible power of the cinema was knowable and that its mechanism was in fact only a mechanism, semioticians embarked on the requisite painstaking studies. In general these took the form of organizational outlines on the one hand and, on the other, of minute analyses of individual aspects of signification in film. The organic mystery of the movies was now thought to be a specific mélange or system of codes of meaning whose elements and interrelations could be detailed.

Some of these codes (for instance, visual punctuation and visual trick effects) could immediately be separated for analysis.[2] The success of such studies only fueled the hope that this new progressive kind of work would shortly replace mere speculation on the cinema and would ultimately deliver the entire medium into the hands of scholars for understanding if not for use.

The first task of semiotics was to put the cinema at its disposal by defining it in relation to "signs." Indeed, this turned out to be a polemical task because it flew in the face, or so it seemed, of Bazin, Morin, and even Mitry for whom the cinema's peculiar rapport with the lived world is its most primary characteristic. To state, as do semioticians, that the cinema is entirely made up of signs, and that it functions in our culture as a privileged sign vehicle, begins to remove from it its sanctimonious veneer of "revelation." As a sign system, the cinema can model but can never reveal actual experience.

The consequences of this position are more radical than one might at first suspect, for semiotics, based as it is on French rather than Anglo-American linguistics, specifically eliminates all discussion of sign-referral. Not only are film images and sounds no longer to be thought of as fragments of reality, they now do not even refer to the real.

The bracketing of the question of reality is a crucial step for semiotics and it is one that is very difficult for Americans to accept. The implicit semiotic model under which most of us have been raised stems from the Germans (especially Frege) through the British Cambridge School, notably through I. A. Richards. In the 1923 book he wrote with C. K. Ogden called *The Meaning of Meaning*[3] Richards outlined a theory of knowledge which consisted of referent, sign, and interpreter. In this situation the sign relates a state of affairs or object in the world to the psychic world of the interpreter. That psychic world itself consists of life experiences and of other signs.

The semiotician working within this Anglo-American tradition finds himself acting as a psycho-social therapist or as a kind of sign-repairman. I. A. Richards has indeed spent a lifetime helping to adjust our sign-life to the complexities of our world either by calling for changes in signs themselves or in our handling of them. He has invoked the activities of rhetoric, criticism, education, and poetry as the specific domain of semiotics in this task of creating a healthy and adequate sign-life.

Richards's workaday epistemological model suggests that we can be in touch with the "world out there" if we properly organize our interior impulses via signs. The infinitely complex relations of actual life (and Richards explicitly recognizes psychological as well as social and physical complexitites) are theoretically available to nearly infinite articulations of our signs if we are attentive to their subtle powers.[4] From this comes his interest in poetry as an exercise in ambiguity, complexity, and sign adjustment. From this too comes his own work as theorist of rhetoric, criticism, and hence education. For Richards, most psychological and social problems result from an inflexible or overly simple sign constellation by which a person or culture tries to fix permanently the myriad relations of life, relations which in reality flow in, around, and past such rigid systems. Madness and revolution express above all the inadequacy of the reigning sign system in the face of changing historical circumstances. Semiotics, as Richards envisioned and practiced it, would make us conscious of ourselves and our worlds by being attentive to the life of our signs in historical circumstances. Ultimately it could thus give us control if not over history, at least over its effect on our lives.

Now the French model, as it has come down to us from Saussure, is far more radical and in a way far more exhilarating. The semiotician has no privileged access to an understanding of lived life or of psychic life except through signs. We can adjust signs to one another but it is naïve to think of adjusting them to reality. Thus the semiotic model that reigns today, not only in France but throughout our culture, is one that involves a material signifier and the mental concept or signified which it instantaneously evokes.[5] Signs thus elaborate the contents of our mental worlds but they give us no assurance that this world is consonant with "things as they are." The dimension of meaning is an exclusively human dimension which we should not project onto the world. To alter signs is not to adjust humans to reality, as it is for Richards, but to alter ideology, the consistent pattern of significations subtending the experience of each human subject. Signs thus bear relations only to one another rather than relations to the world.

Reducing intelligible experience to signs, the semiotician has by no means denatured the variety of intelligible experiences we think of as our life. For although the prototypical sign in classical semiotics is the unambiguous conventional code (as in mathematics when we say, "Let y stand for any cone"), unquestionably there exist different sorts of signs demanding different attitudes from the interpreter. Not every experience of meaning in life can be reduced to the operation of an invariant algebra.

The late American semiotician and anthropologist Sol Worth liked to distinguish between arbitrary and natural signs following a tradition from St. Augustine to our own day.[6] Arbitrary signs occur only in thoroughly symbolic situations where we treat the signifier as an expressed intention of another human agent. In more existential situations, as Worth called them, we may treat the sign as natural (that is, as originating from the non-human, non-intellectual). In this case, we do not decipher the code so much as we attribute meaning to what we sense. The signs of spring, as we call them, or of a coming storm, or of an illness are all natural signs by which we read nature. Some people and some cultures may indeed decipher such symptoms as the language of God or of the gods, but for most of us they are mere symptoms habitually standing for a whole state of affairs which they inspire us to call up when they are present.

Semiotics omnivorously absorbs all of intelligible experience when it deals with such natural signs for insofar as the elements of our world are interconnected by space and time and by cause and effect, any element may serve as a sign for its near neighbors.[7] This would be true in private as well as social life. An entire culture may well sense the coming of spring in the warm winds or budding trees but only a single subject will bring to mind the trauma of, say, an automobile accident by a given smell or the birth of a love affair by the sight of a particular grove of trees. These private signs are existentially conjoined to the subject's peculiar historical experience either by contiguity (the grove in which the love was bonded) or by cause-effect (the odor that should have warned).

Between the thoroughly public symbolic sign and the potentially private natural sign lies a whole range of ambiguous signs about whose status we are unsure. The art-sign, especially in our culture, is an ambiguous sign for it speaks to us from potentially multiple sources. As a human creation using a conventional system, it certainly would seem to be an instance of intentional communication which we are meant to decipher directly. Yet as an expression of a world view, we are likely to treat it more as a symptom of the author, attributing to it more than the author ever intended. Finally, certain artworks might even cause us to attribute things to the world which it models. In this case, it is not an author speaking, nor even the artwork reavealing the author, but the world itself revealed through the "rightness" of the artwork. Such a view, while not popular among semioticians, was held in the nineteenth century by all those under the sway of romantic aesthetics for whom the organism of the artwork magically contains the spirit of organic processes in life. In quite another way, Bazin felt the same thing about the cinema. For him the interest of many documentaries was certainly not the message of the filmmaker. That only got in the way. Nor did the worldview of the filmmaker interest him, though this is what his followers latched onto in their auteur theory. No, he was fascinated by the possibility of learning more of nature through its photographic image on the screen.[8]

Every artwork demands that we come to terms with its status as a sign before adopting a strategy of interpretation. From this arises the debates critics have over such matters as authorial intention. An artwork obviously can be read as a direct communication but it can also be seen to exist as a symptom of the author or even as a privileged sign of nature whose meanings are not given by an *authority* but whose possible meanings we are invited, often irresistibly, to entertain. The cinema calls forth such differing interpretations in a special way. Its mechanically generated images and sounds can readily be treated as indices or traces left by nature on photographic emulsion and magnetic tape. This is the context within which Bazin felt we must always sense the difference of cinema from the other arts. But cinema is also a compilation of clearly ordered codes, giving us a message. It is a tool of Madision Avenue, of Hollywood ideology, of Marxist visions.

Sol Worth's interest in the way we treat signs is essentially a phenomenological interest. The semiotician, while recognizing that various signs address us differently, wants to describe the consistent way in which they function. In all cases a physical support brings to mind a mental concept. The mechanism of signification is uniform and can be designated by the term code. A code is a group of signs all operating according to the same rule of interpretation. While there are many codes and countless signs, all of them function by means of calculated variations (articulations) in some given material that produces in a consistent way different mental concepts.

Trenchant semioticians suggest that all knowledge derives from the mechanics of codes operating on different materials, and even lukewarm semioticians maintain that all artforms are fully coded since by definition they articulate meaning in delimited material forms (words, gestures, sounds, and so forth). If cinema escaped serious analysis for so long it was only because it presents a mélange of different codes so thoroughly intertwined that it might appear to operate beyond clear laws of signification. This is its claim to realism, that meaning flows from it along so many channels that we must attend to it as we attend to situations in ordinary experience. But semioticians have never shied away from complexity. They have eagerly attacked this illusion of cinema by disentangling the arbitrary codes (like speech) from the natural ones (codes by which we make inferences); more important, they have tried to show that every element of meaning in the cinema has been equalized, so to speak, by the mere fact of its presentation on the screen.[9] No one reaches for his umbrella upon hearing a thunderclap on the soundtrack. Instead one infers the *idea* of an approaching storm as a signification in the text on the screen. True, this is a different way of signifying a storm from one in which a character says, "I think a storm's brewing," and semiotics must take account of this difference. But it will do so by pointing to a difference of styles not to a difference of kinds of meaning. Thus the clichés of early theory that cinema is the language of reality run up against the modern assertion that reality is unavailable and that, through and through, cinema signifies in the manner of codes.

SEMIOTICS AND REALISM

Semiotics developed as a movement in criticism hand in hand with the modernist movement in literature. In an important way they have supported one another. Modernism's first task was to break the shackles of realism where art was obliged to reflect actuality. Modernism in all its forms preached the sovereignty of artistic construction, of truth to materials. It gloried in experimentation in new processes of signification, because it believed that the task of art is to liberate us from our preconceptions by forcibly rearranging our very ways of processing meaning.

Semiotics has supported modernism in its vicious attacks on realism. By demonstrating the illusory nature of realism, by treating it as a particular mode of signification which has no special rights or privileges, semiotics implicitly pays homage to the codes of art rather than to any of its effects. In the realism of literature, theater, and painting such attacks were consistent with the artistic practice of our age. Realism in those arts can readily be seen as a particular style (and even a period) that has come to an end. Before the realist age these artforms aimed at other effects with other stylistic strategies, and now, after realism, this can be the case again.

But the issue in cinema is not so easy, for this is an art born in, and as part of, the age of realism. It has known no other norm. Even today, despite the struggle of modernist filmmakers, realist cinema dominates our screens. Semiotics of cinema has, then, felt obliged to deal with this issue over and over. Film semiotics is virtually synonymous with the study of codes of illusion.

When a culture consistently pictures in some medium its version of reality and when these pictures are generally swallowed by the members of that culture *as* reality, we are in the midst of the workings of ideology. In trying to shatter this illusion, film semiotics thus joins an essentially political conflict. We have already seen that cinema's peculiar rapport with realism has two key aspects, that of perception and that of representation. Certain semioticians have sought to overcome the power of cinema at the basic moment of perception. This was the thrust of Eco's work on the multi-articulation of cinema, on the mechanically coded way in which light, color, and shadow build up molecular units which we recognize as shapes, and later which develop into images of objects and actions that we can identify as being in our world.[10] Even those semioticians who refuse to go this far agree that no medium ever reproduces reality. Its signs reproduce at best one aspect of the object as we conceive it. Since every society represents only those objects it has already come to know (already semiotized), an iconic sign like a photograph is really a sign of a sign, a partial duplication of a mental image which in its turn partially coincides with a phenomenon in lived life. We see according to the mental concepts which our language above all has isolated for us. We see what has been named, and what we see in a film is meaningful to the extent that it supports our semantic universe. This becomes all the clearer at the level of representation when the perceived objects of a film are built into a particular picture of a state of affairs, a story, or an argument. Distinct codes of organization here make use of our perception, channeling it into a single picture of things. Since we trust our eyes at the perceptual level, we are primed to trust the whole picture at the organizational level. This is where the semiotic task of untangling the myriad codes that make up the filmic system has been of such importance. Semiotics has enabled us to see the manner in which a representational picture is woven. It has at least enumerated the threads which go into making up the fabric. And this is an essential project, for never again can we accept this picture as the "seemless garment of reality"[11] when we have now been shown the seams, the threads, sometimes even the weave itself.

The realism of cinema has depended not just on its perceptual base and not just on the complexity of its representational schemata. It has also been the effect of certain codes designed for no other purpose than to promote the experience of realism. These are the codes of *vraisemblance,* the verisimilar or seeming-real, and they are common to literature as well as film. The comfortable feeling we have in many films that reality surrounds the significations of the images like a sea derives from these codes, specifically from from the code of the probable and from the code of the excessive detail. Literary critics Gerard Genette, Tzvetan Todorov, and Roland Barthes[12] have treated these codes in literature, arguing that an author is able to verify his tale by appealing to the common sense, or mores, of his time in explaining even the most bizarre action or statement. In the cinema filmmakers call on this code whenever they pan or cut to an object or character's expression, which motivates the scene we have just witnessed, indicating that the elements of the cinematic world are interlinked just as they are in the spectator's world. Thus, on the strength of few, we sense that the story, no matter how outrageous, is supported by a vast web of interrelations which we spare the filmmaker from detailing. This code of the probable, of the one supporting motivation, signifies our own moral world. For example, in the Rome episode of *Paisa,* Maria Michi's fallen state is not entirely the result of a feeble personal will. Rather, the decline of the whole Italian culture in the face of poverty and of the American military conspires to bring her down. Rossellini doesn't detail this fall or its complex causes. Instead he merely allows his camera to rest on the face of the concierge (or madame) after Maria Michi exits from the house of ill repute. The economic hierarchy alluded to in this shot carries enough moral overtones for us to imagine a complete cultural web; in this way we watch this melodramatic short story as coming directly out of an actual historic milieu which Rossellini has evoked with very few strokes.

The code of the probable is an ascetic code, excusing the director from providing more than minimal details to justify the event being presented and to insist that this event is lodged in a world we comfortably believe is actual. The code of the extraneous detail is, on the contrary, a profligate rendering of too many items and actions, but its effect is the same. Roland Barthes called attention to this code in dealing with Flaubert, that most careful of literary craftsmen. How was it, Barthes asked, that extraneous objects and acts seem to interrupt the otherwise airtight presentation of the world of Madame Bovary? In a notable example he pointed to Flaubert's description of a barometer in the drawing room where an important conversation is taking place.[13] Far from operating symbolically (as an index of the stormy relationship the conversationalists suffer through) and far from being an element of the plot (as an object about to be hurled to the floor, for instance), this interruptive description serves only to remind the reader that the event takes place in a world which he knows and can assent to. It puts the reader at ease, the uselessness of the detail being precisely what grounds the highly significant drama in the banality of everyday life, and of the ordinary familiar world.

Nor does this code always manifest itself on the picture track (as a pan away from the action to the objects in a room or in the street, for instance). The background music which we suddenly notice when a dramatic scene has run its course can do far more than provide a mood for that drama. It can serve as an opaque prop, situating this artificial fiction directly within a milieu we are familiar with. Because photographic and phonographic recordings are so indiscriminate, excessive details crowd the constructed fiction from all sides. When these are made the subjects of scrutiny, it is to put us at rest within a known world that surrounds the tale, even if that tale is highly unlikely, a fragile fiction.

Now these two methods of achieving verisimilitude are sophisticated stylistic constructions. They show the final triumph of signification as it brings into being a certain privileged form of representation, making us forget that it is a signification at all. Thus in its final narrative effects, as well as in its basic perceptual units, cinematic representation appears to the semiologist as a rule-governed exercise of codes.

To the semiologist, representation must be opposed to any conception of the truly real. Cinematic perception is a representation of our visible world; cinematic narratives are representations of situations in "real life." But clearly one function of art is precisely to dispute such normal and normative representations. Avant-garde filmmakers over the years have disrupted the codes of perception by altering the usual focus, framing, and even the speed and direction of visual recording. At the other, narrative end of the spectrum, nearly every important film artist and theorist has explicitly opposed "verisimilitude" (or conventional realism) to true realism, as surface is opposed to depth, as culture is opposed to nature.

Theorists as different as Eisenstein and Bazin have battled against verisimilitude and the ordinary presentation of "real life." Eisenstein argued for the expansion of the code of motivation, in order to go beyond the easy and familiar connections we always make to the complicated dialectical motivations underlying all historical units.[14] Bazin argued for suppression of motivational cutting and increased attention to nonsignifying details.[15] He too wanted to force spectators to confront a world beyond the one they were comfortable with, but unlike Eisenstein he wanted to confront them with the unincorporated facts provided by the camera to the side of the drama, forcing the spectator to try to make sense of the material before him.

Both Eisenstein and Bazin sought in particular and very different stylistic options a more authentic representation than that by which cinema customarily pictures reality. Semiologists would seemingly go further by rendering moot all questions of reality as such and speaking instead only about codes of style and their representational effects. By bracketing issues of value (and value-laden terms like reality) they appear ready for a precise and systematic description of the workings of cinema, whether actual or potential. This indeed was Metz's early hope,[16] that one branch of the field would progressively illuminate the logical codes that all films must draw on to signify anything, while another branch would investigate the particular interweaving of those codes in individual films, genres, or periods.

CRITIQUE OF SEMIOTICS

The grandiose designs of a complete semiotic description of cinema sustained film theorists in the late 1960's. By placing film semiotics within the framework of a theory of knowledge and a project of cultural criticism they sketched the full outline of this exhilarating endeavor. Metz's *Language and Cinema* is just such a sketch. Yet its extreme generality and epic scope were obviously troublesome. How should the *practical* work begin the task of filling in this outline?

Here Metz and his followers modestly retreated to the province of their expertise, the cinema. They willingly left to ideological critics the analysis of general cultural codes that crop up in films (codes of manners, speech, clothes, and cars) and to aestheticians that of untangling the various codes that have infiltrated the screen from the other arts (codes of classical music, of acting, design, and so forth). Instead, film semioticians concentrated on those codes peculiar to cinema, those aspects of filmic signification which are "cinema-specific." [17]

Did the semioticians really believe that the specifically cinematic codes discipline everything that appears on the screen, so that camera work, editing, optical effects, and so on would form a master grammatical system organizing filmic discourse? This would have been a happy situation but Metz soon retreated from the idea if he ever seriously entertained it. Too many of the cinematic codes are shared by other art forms (lighting belongs to theater, narrative to the novel, even editing, that cornerstone that makes of cinema a distinct art, supports the photo-roman as well). Besides, there is no logical necessity insisting that those codes that happen to be unique to an art should also be the ones that dominate the practice of that art.

While failing to anchor a complete study of cinema, the issue of specificity has proved important for organizing the taxonomy of the primary means of signification available in this medium. Armed with an ordered list of codes, the analyst can clearly distinguish different periods of film from one another, showing, for example, that the function of expressing interior states of characters was served in the silent French cinema by means of *trucage*, or the plastic deformation of the image itself, whereas the Italian cinema of the later 1950's sought similar effects entirely within the design of the decor. [18] Here a mixed code (mixed because decor operates in opera, theater, and ballet as well as in cinema) replaced a specific code (*trucage*). This kind of precise observation, and countless others like it, was made possible by the fragmenting of the cinematic mystery into bundles of codes, yet the mere listing of such codes is a convenience, not a rule. Even the identification of the codes operating in such and such a film is far from an account of the work of signification in the cinema or in that film. The first critique of semiotics stressed exactly its inability to account for the syntax of films, that is, its organized production of meaning.

As is well known, the early dream of semioticians to establish a grammar of the cinema was quickly dashed by Metz's first essays.[19] Cinema simply does not exist as a system outside of all use, as does English, or French, or the Morse code. We cannot even create examples of unintelligible cinematic sequences the way we can with sentences. Cinema exists as a set of films and their history, all drawing in various ways on the list of codes semiotics has enumerated, but intertwining them, exchanging their functions, and inflecting them in ways impossible to specify by a semiotic rule. Indeed, we must begin to conceive of cinema not so much as a *system* of signification as a *place* where various codes come together to create meaning. It is therefore fully consistent for semioticians to have moved to film history and criticism, the place and places of signification. Even Metz's *Grande Syntagmatique,* which for so long seemed like cinema's best chance for an abstract grammar, even this master code was shown not to be abstract at all but to be tied to the classic cinema, 1933–55.[20]

Semioticians by and large have not felt defeated by the looseness of the cinematic system; instead they have quite properly sought larger systems of force which might be shown to organize the texts of cinema where semiotic codes failed to do so. The primordial forces of society, the psyche, and their interaction in the history of ideology all give shape to texts. The fact that in our day these forces are themselves described as coded (the text of society, the text of the psyche, and the specifically representational character of ideology) permits the film semiotician to feel fully engaged in a unified materialist analysis of human and cultural processes. Once again it is the notion of "work" that is the basis of this analysis, the work of the unconscious and of ideology replacing the work of language as the key to explaining the shape of films and of our response to them. The language of cinema henceforth must be considered as material worked upon by these greater forces that give structure not just to our films but to every domain of public and private life. The film semiotician details this work of signification as it transpires in the codes of cinema. If we have returned to a murkiness here, it is no longer the murkiness of an ambiguous surrounding reality; instead it is the murkiness of psychological and sociological processes which cultural critics are at last learning how to analyze. Film semioticians feel themselves in the forefront of this materialist analysis. [21]

If the first critique of semiotics berated its problems with filmic syntax, the organization of codes, the second critique goes deeper, directly to the heart of semiotics, to the notion of the code itself. Once again, Metz had an early premonition of the difficulties in store for the field when he pointed to the heterogeneity of the cinematic signifier.[22] Whereas the dictionary is composed only of graphemes, arranged alphabetically and interrelated via synonym, antonym, etymology, and verbal example, a cinematic dictionary would have to be capable of interrelating signifiers of various sorts: spoken words, music, sound effects, graphic signs which appear on the image track, representational images, image deformation, and so on. Moreover, the snugness with which signifier and signified are bound to one another in this iconic medium makes the issue of synonymy ridiculous. The picture of a six-gun looks only slightly different from the picture of a derringer, whereas the words "gun," "derringer," "gat," "pistol," and "revolver," though calling up quite related clusters of mental concepts, are patently different in sound and in print. We say that these verbal synonyms have substantially the same denotation but differ in connotation— "derringer" suggesting a sleak, concealed, elegant weapon, "gat" one wielded by a gangster, and so forth.

What do we say of iconic signifiers like pictures? What rule tells us how to arrive at the proper signification of a picture? Without such a rule the entire thrust of the concept *code* is blunted. If we say that a picture signifies what it depicts then we are really stuck within the realm of realism, and for all practical purposes the medium would be a language of fragments of reality. Semioticians expected the concept of connotation to save them from this crass realism. Pictures signify, they suggested, *by means of* likeness, but they do not always signify the *content* of likeness.

In classical semiotics the denotative function of a sign is considered the standard form of signification. Here a given signifier is tied to (or ties down) a particular and singular mental concept. Moreover, this union is immediate, with the bar (/) in the formulation S^r/S^d suggesting that both elements in the sign are present simultaneously. Saussure and his followers felt that all significations were of this form or derivatives of this form. The major derivative certainly is connotation, a type of compounded denotation wherein a single signifier generates several related signifieds in succession. In a brilliant formulation Roland Barthes, following on the work of Louis Hjelmslev,[23] composed the rule for connotation, diagramming it thus:

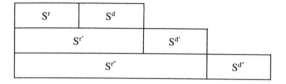

In connotation the single material signifier produces a series of related signifieds. In such cases the immediate mental concept as given by the signifier is not what we attend to; rather it becomes a signifier itself of a more distant concept which, in its turn, can also function as a signifier triggering a still more distant (and generally more abstract) concept. The scripted signifier ''collaboration'' denotes an image of ''working together or participating.'' But in France during World War II this sign became a signifier invariably calling up the image ''friendship with the Nazis.'' Readers skipped past the denotation in the automatic process of arriving at the important, connotative sense of the sign. Any naïve writer hoping to communicate the concept ''participation'' pure and simple would surely find that purpose derailed as in the sentence, ''Etienne Olivier at the violin collaborated with the State Orchestra in this recording of the Beethoven concerto.''

Connotation is always sensitive to context; in the above example the context is World War II France. Dictionaries frequently cite major connotations of words by indicating the context within which the reader must attend not to the first concept but to the inevitable connotation that the situation drives the sign to engender. The term ''cross'' signifies the graphic shape + but, as the dictionary is quick to point out, this shape connotes the crucifixion of Christ and by extention (that is, by connotation) the Christian religion in general. Given a slightly different context, the same signifier could arrive by a slightly different path at the connotation ''burden'' as in ''he had an awful cross to bear.''

Beyond these lexical connotations, which, in the cases cited above, have become formalized enough to be thought of as belonging to the realm of denotation (so that ''burden'' is listed as the sixth denotation of the signifier ''cross'') there exist the epi-significations of style and expression which are so snugly bound to the speaking situation that they could never be listed in a dictionary as part of the signifier they accompany. Here we might mention the connotation of educational level or social class betrayed by the speaker who uses the term "crimson" in place of "red" or who speaks with a Harvard accent. Such connotations begin to cloud the distinction made earlier between arbitrary and natural signs, for a speaker's accent is a symptom rather than a signifier of his place of origin. Psychoanalysis of course trades precisely on this murky zone between conscious signifier and repressed symptom, seeking the unconscious paths by which certain signs betray their true (natural) motivation, even when the speaker contends that those signs are used denotatively.

Altogether, then, connotation seriously muddies the cleanliness of Saussurean semiotics, this despite the seemingly mechanical way one signified generates its successor and, in Barthes's model, the way all these signifieds derive from a denotative base. Connotation introduces the problem of the interpreter who stops the flow of multiple significations at the appropriate mental concept by scanning the context within which the sign appears. Indeed, connotation puts in question the notion of a proper meaning, undermining the priority of denotation once and for all.

Nowhere is this trauma of semiotics more evident than in the cinema, where the process leading from sensation through perception to signification is one that demands the activity and the time of interpretation. Moreover, so many of cinema's codes are iconic that the so-called denotation (that which the signifier depicts) is generally a threshold to the truly appropriate signification of the sign (+ signifying not a cross but Christianity or a burden; a picture of a car signifying not a Ford but a social class, and so forth).

Of all theorists, once again it has been Christian Metz who was most intrigued and troubled by this problem.[24] He recognized that the seeming split between denotation and connotation in most cinematic codes aligned this medium with narrative literature and opposed it to such systems as music and architecture, which are systems of pure connotation and expressivity. In all cinema, except the marginal genre of the non-representational experimental film, there appears to be a denotative base whereby we recognize a signified before attending to the epi-significations (crucial for art) which these evoke by the manner of their presentation.

Metz's dependence on Mitry is quite evident in this mixture of phenomenology and semiotics, for we can readily consider denotation to be the equivalent of the perceptual and narrative levels of Mitry's schema, narrative organizing the denoted objects and actions into a represented world. Connotation would then develop Mitry's higher, poetic level both in the way in which perceptions are given (lighting, focus, angle) and in the symbolic ramifications of their narrative organization.

Metz found himself locked within a classical dilemma when he felt compelled to assert that there exist separate codes for denotation and for connotation. Those codes that enable the recognition of an object or action he termed denotative, whereas all codes launching themselves from these represented objects, proceding toward more abstract significations, would be in the realm of the connotative.

Despite the sophistication of this formulation, it nevertheless returns semiotics to the form/content split which it has been modern theory's announced project to dissolve. Metz could not, as a modern theorist, maintain that there actually exist connotators added to denotation like sugar to a pill or decoration to a building. Instead he argued that connotation was "the form of denotation," responding to the fact that when we discuss the contents of an image we are speaking at the first level of meaning, that is, at the level of denotation, but when we pass to the form under which it appears (the light surrounding it, its disposition in the frame, the timbre of the sound accompanying it), we are speaking of the connotations of the image.

Metz implicitly recognized that denotation and connotation are categories pertaining not to the functioning of the system or of the sign, but to the activity of the analyst dealing with the sign. All levels of meaning are present under the same material form, the rendered object and the expressiveness of the rendering coming to us simultaneously. Analysts, and even ordinary viewers, have the option of halting their interest at the point where an object or action is recognized (and this we may term the denotation); more often the analyst will entertain the open-ended realms of signification which every image seems able to imply or call up.

Cinema has no dictionary specifying common denotations like a Webster's. The common meaning of a cinematic signifier can only be determined by the context which not only modifies the sign but instructs us to read it at such and such a level. In a comedy of manners, a character's refusal of a marriage proposal may be signified by her walking out of a room and slamming the door behind her, but this mental concept (the obvious denotation in this genre) is available to us only after we recognize the acts of turning, stepping, and slamming as related to the recognizable image of a woman. In turn these acts can be broken into minimal gestures and forms. The denoted signification (refusal) is in this case the highest reach of connotation.[25] Other sorts of viewers might arrest this flow of signification at an earlier point. A physiologist or behavioral psychologist might find the minimal gestures to be denotative in the context of their interest. Furthermore, another sort of filmmaker working in another genre might instruct us to glean from the signifiers only perceptual signifieds and not make the leap toward narrative context. I'm thinking here of an experimental film like *Tom, Tom the Piper's Son* which specifically reworks an early narrative film (a 1905 melodrama) in a way that focuses our attention on the objects, movements, and recording strategies themselves, rather than on the story they were originally intended to deliver to us.

Here, as always in the cinema, the context of our interest (and of the genre of the film, which is only a name for normative interest) determines the sign, making the arts of rhetoric and criticism rather than those of linguistics the ones we need to call into play. As the science of signification, semiotics is as essential here as ever, but we must no longer think of it as based in a privileged linguistic model, as Barthes once claimed in his *Elements of Semiology*.[26] Instead we must treat filmic significations as elements of representations with which we must struggle case by case.

Connotation has thus taught us the primacy of the whole text over the mechanism of its parts and of interpretation over analysis. For the film image as signifier is so finely graded that only interpretation can serve to complete it. We may describe the structure of connotation, to be sure, but we cannot predict its workings because these depend on the context of the genre and the situation of the viewer.

Thus the semiotic endeavor which constructed so many codes of cinema has given way to interpretive strategies engaging cinematic discourse. This was already signaled at the end of Metz's *Language and Cinema* when he turned suddenly to the issue of *écriture*,[27] to the work by which the haphazard codes of a film are sytematized in a specific sense-producing text. Every text is an instance of discourse, a product of such work across codes. It is a stopping place where the always-available codes and processes of signification are fixed in a particular configuration which we honor as a privileged sign and from which we take our interpretive cues. In this view, a text is a representation, containing but not reducible to the significations which comprise the fabric of its weave; and film theory must be about the task of studying the interplay between texts and codes, using the vocabulary and analytic instinct of semiotics but always in dialogue with the texts of cinema which continue to interest us. For our field is made up of texts and not of codes, so that we construct codes only the better to understand texts. It is the texts of cinema that engage us and ask for our attention. In film theory we respond with a very special form of attention.

5

Narrative Structure

NARRATIVE AND CINEMA

Cinema is a medium of excess. Meaning in the cinema comes by way of calculated or ideological limitation of this excess. This we have seen three times over in each of the preceding chapters. In the first place, perception results from the borders we put on the super-flux of sensation, borders which allow us to rely on the stability of a certain sensory arrangement. Both the machinery of cinema and the rhetorical strategies it employs turn the flow of light and color into recognizable images.

At the next level, that of the comprehension of a complete film, a similar bridling takes place. Percepts are shaped into representations of a state of affairs by processes which effectively choose those aspects of our perceptions which are qualified to participate in some higher organization. As we have seen, genres are, first and foremost, habitual ways of dealing with perceptions to filter out specific ''states of affairs.''

Thirdly, the issue of excess arises even when we adopt a semiological perspective and attempt to treat significance as a cumulative process whereby minute differences in the signifying materials articulate elements of mental concepts until large units of significance (signs) are recognized or begin to function. For, despite the utopian clarity envisioned for them by Saussure, signs are not the terminus of the process of signification, but rather are intermediate points of coagulation which go on to call up a plethora of mental concepts in the limitless play of connotation.

Denotations, we found, are the final step in a particular trajectory of connotation and they are ruled by a guiding principle of genre and context. It is context and genre that tell us to respond to the orchestra finale of Hitchcock's *The Man Who Knew Too Much* not as we would in a documentary on Beethoven, or even one on Toscanini, but as a dramatic indicator of temporality, with each wave of the baton, each measure of music bringing us closer to the crisis.

Over and over in the study of cinema the issue of narrative arises not simply because it has been the historically dominant mode of cinematic production, but because it is above all a tool for contextualizing, a logic for delimiting meaning. Since cinematic signification appears on all counts to depend on delimitation, narrative (or some grander schema of which narrative is the dominant subset) is a necessity, a rule, not an option. In the representational cinema it can be flaunted, observed, or ridiculed, but narrative can never be absent. Long ago Mitry made this very point. "A film is a world which organizes itself in terms of a story," he said in order to differentiate it from the novel, "which is a story organizing itself in a world."[1] While literary artists may work in non-narrative modes, the cinéaste seems condemned to some form of narrative just to rein in the galloping connotations of images.

Cinema has confirmed that narrative is more than a set of texts or even a certain kind of text. It is first of all an innate capability, like language itself, which surfaces in many areas of human life and is dominant in some of these. Narrative competence holds our significations in place to give them an order and a thrust. We sense its power in our daily conversations and in nearly every form of communication. It has its impact in a host of art forms, in painting, dance, opera, and mime. It is celebrated in literature and, as we have seen, it is nearly synonymous with the word "cinema."

The study of cinema has consequently been bound up with theories of narrative, so much so that its modern phase might be said to have been triggered by the structuralist wave which overran narrative theory in the early 1960's. Specifically, Christian Metz formulated his *Grande Syntagmatique* in the atmosphere of Paris's Ecole Pratique des Hautes Etudes where he daily encountered Roland Barthes, A. J. Greimas,

Gerard Genette, Tzvetan Todorov, and Claude Bremond. His first essays could not help but concern themselves with narrativity. A survey of these structuralist approaches to narrative, together with a chronicle of the rise and fall of structuralism in general, thus goes far in explaining the kinds of film theory and the methods of film analysis which have dominated our field.

The study of narrative, like that of language, has gone through a genetic phase toward a structuralism which, in its turn, has recently given way to what I would term "functional analysis." The genetic approach, exemplified by Scholes's and Kellogg's *The Nature of Narrative,* seeks to understand storytelling by examining its origins and the different forms it has assumed in history. The evolution of genres is thus traced by a chronological survey of extant texts.

Though genetic analysis is doubtless the most accessible and widely adopted sort of inquiry into the world of stories, it has been challenged by structuralism and labeled a remnant of the nineteenth-century Darwinian impulse to classify and interrelate species. Structuralism has sought to replace this impulse in all fields. The history of linguistics is most clearly marked by a dramatic shift from the study of linguistic origins and linguistic change to the study of universal laws and the fundamental structures of language competence. Instead of the specific cultural differences between languages, the striking similarity among all languages became after Saussure the central phenomenon to be explained. No longer did scholars pursue those fleeting events and situations that shape the development of particular languages; now they looked baldly at the fact that language, far from being a wondrous, fragile gift obtained at great expense and subject to the ravages of history, is the one changeless and unquenchable aspect of human life. Although history may shape the form of any particular language to some degree, the laws of language itself will impose their ineluctable logic on all activities called "human." The differences among the many languages pale before this astounding fact. What is this irrepressible capability? What are its laws?

Narratology, the structural study of narrative, as another, although related, capability, descends directly from modern linguistics, from Saussure in France and from the Russian and Prague schools of linguistics and poetics championed most notably by Roman Jakobson. Its roots grew through Claude Lévi-Strauss, whose encounter with Jakobson in America proved decisive for structural anthropology and, because of Lévi-Strauss's multivolume opus on the mythology of American Indians, for the study of narrative as well. Inspired by Lévi-Strauss, Roland Barthes in 1963 went directly to Saussure as a source for his general semiology and for his crucial 1966 essay "Introduction to the Structural Analysis of Narrative." At about the same time Tzvetan Todorov made available in French translation much of the structural poetics of the Russian and Prague schools, generating a flurry of analyses at the Ecole Pratique des Hautes Etudes. Narratology in the 1960's was unquestionably one of structuralism's greatest achievements, of which the following outline will provide at least some indication.

A SURVEY OF NARRATOLOGY

Like language, narrative invites two great domains of inquiry, semantics and syntactics. Curiously, it was anthropology that provided the first important models for the structural study of both domains. Vladimir Propp's *Morphology of the Russian Folktale* (1927) is the syntactic counterpart of Lévi-Strauss's "Structural Study of Myth" (1955). Significantly, both of these methods downplay, even eliminate, the artistic or privileged formulation of a story. Both seek to explain the proliferation of popular narratives and in this way address themselves to the general human capacity to tell and to understand stories.

For Lévi-Strauss narrative is equivalent to mythmaking, which, along with totemism and kinship, provides cohesion and stability for every social group. Mythology is part of a larger system which it mirrors and participates in. Myths are systems of concepts placed in binary opposition and repeated in countless variations. They are, by definition, stories that have no teller. They are made up entirely of character and action. Lévi-Strauss even maintains that there is no privileged *énonciation* or telling of a myth, that from the point of view of myth proper, Sophocles is no better a source than a crude singer or reinterpreter. He maintains that even Freud provides a legitimate version of the Oedipus myth.[2]

Lévi-Strauss's methodology of reading every version of a myth like a musical score (horizontally and vertically) is well known, as is his practice of stacking all versions of a myth on cards to yield a three-dimensional reading. His methodology unearths what must be thought of as a chemistry of myth. He finds the values of various mythical elements and measures the overall energy level of the relationships between particles. It can be argued that Lévi-Strauss disrespects stories, seeing them only as structures to be broken down until they speak directly to the ethnographer. It is true at least that he has no interest in, or use for, what literary critics would call the formal aspects of narrative. He has worked at building something like an atomic chart of mythemes, recording atomic weights, stability, and valence.

Although his work is definitely in the domain of narrative semantics, an "atomic chart" rather than a "dictionary" or "thesaurus" seems the most appropriate metaphor to describe it. Genetic mythographers like Frazer and even Frye build dictionaries of terms, characters, and situations, specifying the symbolic import of various motifs down through the ages. But for Lévi-Strauss the world of stories is solely a mechanism of forces and relations. Just as the physicist studies the elements (oxygen, neon, even gold) for their structural import, paying no attention to their geological, economic, not to mention poetic aspects, so Lévi-Strauss discounts the historical weight of mythical motifs as he writes the formulas that account for their presence and function.

This purely structural attitude toward narrative has been pushed to the limit by A. J. Greimas in his *Sémantique structurale* (1966) and especially in the section of *Du Sens* (1970) called "Le récit." Whereas Lévi-Strauss had calculated his abstract system from a study of numerous examples of stories, Greimas disposes of examples altogether in order to treat the pure logic of semantic variables in any possible story. Every positive narrative value (a hero, for instance) attains its position only in relation to its opposite on the one hand and its negative on the other. Stories put into play various combinations and compounds of such values and achieve their power through exchanges and reversals. Oedipus, for example, is honored at the outset over and above his negative (the common citizens of Thebes) and his opposite (the unknown source of evil). The drama then contrives to reverse the situation, making him the unexpected source of evil, his own opposite.

The formal logic this sort of study depends upon has little in common with the method of erudition practiced by Northrop Frye, whose work was once thought to be structuralist. Frye explicitly invokes biology and botany rather than atomic physics to characterize this work of cataloguing, differentiating, and characterizing the species of literature.[3] In this respect his explanation of narrative patterns is genetic rather than structural. But the Anglo-American tradition did produce at least one important proto-structuralist in Kenneth Burke, whose *Rhetoric of*

Motives (1946) can be considered a precursor of Greimas's more rigorous logical inquiries.

Because of structuralism's concern with the abstract, purely formal mechanism of stories, the linguistic analogy has been more vigorously applied to the syntactic rather than to the semantic domain. There are several reasons for conceiving of literature and especially narrative as part of linguistics. Barthes gives us the most persuasive of these reasons.[4] Faced with countless stories, how can we find the general laws which produce them and make them intelligible? This situation is precisely the one Saussure faced in linguistics. Since literature is and can be nothing more than a kind of extension and application of certain properties of language, the system of narrative must be viewed as a system analogous to language and individual stories must be viewed as "paroles."

Structural linguistics usually stops its analysis at the level of the sentence. The sentence is an order, not a series, and cannot be reduced to the terms that compose it. How could linguistics proper approach the study of a series or group of sentences? Barthes says, "Having described the flower, the botanist need not bother to describe the bouquet."[5] What Barthes seeks is to go beyond the sentence, in order to learn the laws of sentence linkage, or the laws of discourse. Now narrative is nothing other than a particular kind of discourse, and the narrative analyst will therefore examine the particular order of sentences in this discourse which creates a meaning greater than the sum of those sentences.

Narrative discourse is an ensemble of sentences organized according to laws higher than those of linguistics but homologous to them. Narrative is a secondary system—a "Giant Sentence" built as an order of smaller sentences— whose sense is not reducible to these sentences. In anthropology such double systems are common: incest taboo systems create kinship systems; tools create other tools, and so forth.

Thus we must examine the purely formal homology between the character of language and that of narrative. Barthes points out that the principal categories of the verb (time, person, aspect, and mood) apply to narrative discourse and that narrative subjects readily form a grammar of predicates as well.[6] For Barthes this homology is not merely heuristic. Language is the mother sign system of all sign systems and is especially related to narrative.

From the beginning and largely independent of Saussure, the East European formalists saw narrative in this light. Boris Eichenbaum, for instance, compared the short story to the anecdote and implicitly to a particular sentence structure.[7] Inheriting this tradition, Tzvetan Todorov pursued a minute examination of the "grammar" of the *Decameron,* and found its stories to be expanded but homologous forms of diverse sentence patterns.[8]

The linguistic analogy permits the decomposition or "parsing" of the narrative complex into functional units. Structuralists have worked to describe these units and to account for the effects of their interrelation based on the following skeletal definition: a narrative is a discourse wherein a teller relates an event containing both actions and agents. Every narrative, therefore, is a mélange of four basic components: speaker, speech event, agents, and narrated event. As such it is structurally equivalent to instances of daily discourse in which someone reports something.

Roman Jakobson elaborated the category of "verbal shifters" to help describe the structure of such discourse. Shifters are those special linguistic signs that are fully conventional yet change according to the speech event in which they participate. The personal pronouns are the paradigm example of this category, but demonstrative pronouns ("this" and "that") as well as allocutionary adverbs ("here" and "now") are also common shifters. In essence the shifter is any sign whose *reference* changes from case to case even though its *meaning* always remains the same. "Here" has but one meaning, "at this place," even though it refers to quite different places depending on where and by whom the word is uttered. Jakobson, whose importance for structuralist studies of film and literature has been incalculable, articulated an analytic grid on the basis of the category of shifters that was capable of logically differentiating such verbal descriptors as mood, voice, tense, aspect, dependency, person, and number.[9] Such descriptors are common to all grammars, he averred, encouraging us to apply his grid (in a slightly modified form) to the grammatical properties of narratives. Indeed, Jakobson's grid can help us organize not just the principal elements of narrative but the kinds of structural studies to which narrative has been subject. In the accompanying table, the narrated part of a discourse, "n," has been separated from "s," the speech part, while the letter "p" refers to participants or agents, and "E" refers to events.

	Actions		Agents	
	The term	Term in its relation	The term	Term in its relation
Non-shifter	E^n	$E^n E^n$	p^n	$p^n E^n$
Shifter	$E^n E^s$	$E^n E^{ns}/E^s$	p^n/p^s	$p^n E^n/p^s$

Every narrative, like every discourse, possesses values for each of the above categories. Structural studies of narratives generally examine the possibilities contained within a single category. An analysis of narrative "tense," for instance, would focus on the category $E^n E^s$, where the shifting possibilities of temporal relation of the tale to the telling can be logically broken down (present, past, progressive, and so on). This grid would be used differently, however, by historians and critics who might instead find values in all the categories for a body of works which seem to have something in common (genre, epoch, style). At a glance the historian or critic could then discover which categories of variables individuate the genre or period, since identical values would appear in such categories for every work considered. Thus an analysis of countless detective stories might show that each one is characterized only by the same type of event structure ($E^n E^n$), or the "Spaghetti Western" might be found to differ from other Westerns primarily with regard to its way of burying stories within stories ($E^n E^{ns}/E^s$). Taken altogether, structural studies try to define literary possibilities on the one hand and account for literary actualities (types, genres, periods) on the other. There exist at least rudimentary structural analyses dealing with each of the above categories of variables; following is a survey of some of these.

1. E^n (type of action): The simplest categories are the non-shifters and, among these, those where no agents are involved. One can classify the possible types of stories by logically deducing the sorts of actions modeled by verbs and verbal structures.

The "mood" of the action is here under scrutiny as we differentiate actions which are affirmed, denied, optative, exhortative, conditional, and so forth. This yields the primary "modes" of myth, legend, fairy tale, and so on, as can be seen in the pioneering work of André Jolles.[10] At the same time the "aspect" of the event can be determined. "Aspect," which describes the state of the action (whether it is ongoing or completed), is indicated in English literary narratives by the use or neglect of the progressive forms of the verbs.

2. E^nE^n (subordination of actions): A more complex category is that of narrative syntax or sequential relations. Preliminary to any study involving this category is the indentification of the unity of narrative action, the separation of bound motifs from free motifs.[11] The bound motifs, which Barthes prefers to call "hinge functions,"[12] are those smallest units of a story that create the event linkage without which we would have another story.

Propp's *Morphology of the Folktale,* the most influential of all structural analyses of narratives, proceeds by assigning code terms to each kind of bound function (that is, "M: a difficult task is proposed to the hero")[13] found in Russian fairy tales. Propp then examines the kinds of linkage which make up each tale, comparing the formulas derived from each. Propp discovered that in the 100 fairy tales he examined, only 31 functions (kinds of actions) were represented. More startling, he found that any function will always appear in the same place of a sequence of functions if it does in fact appear at all.[14] If function T occurs, its position in the story will be before U and after S. Given the morphological rules he discovered, a computer could generate a tale which would be at least formally correct. Over 1,000 Russian tales have since been analyzed, and Propp's thesis holds up.

Claude Brémond has tried to apply Propp's methodology to more complex narratives.[15] He has asserted that every event exists in a triadic form: a possibility conceived, a carrying out of that possibility (successfully or not), and a resultant state. Any such event may be interrupted at any of these three points to make room for another event that may leave the initial one in suspense or bear on that initial event. An example Brémond gives of this latter case is

interdiction given		
temptation accepted	=	possibility of trickery
		the dupe falls in the trap
violation of interdiction	=	trickery succeeds

Here an initial event (the interdiction) is completed in a virtual sense when another event (the trickery) is carried to completion explicitly.

The resultant state, the successful trickery and the violation, then becomes the initial state for a new triad which might be labeled revenge or punishment, and which would undoubtedly contain other embedded triads as it worked itself out.

Brémond's schema is capable of ascertaining the type of plot construction in even a complex narrative. His work deals with causal syntax personified by the arrow that winds its way vertically and horizontally through his graphs. But other kinds of analysis can deal with syntax also. Todorov examines repetitions of various sorts, seeking a "spatial relation" of events rather than a causal one; and he allows for a sheerly temporal syntax as well, though this seemingly could be analyzed by Propp's end-to-end system.[16] At a higher level, of course, the relation of events to one another produces a general movement of sequences. Brémond claims that all such movements can be defined as either amelioration or degradation of a situation.[17] Here he is operating under Todorov's definition of plot.

> Every narrative is a movement between two states of equilibrium, which are similar but not identical. At the beginning there is always a balanced situation; the characters form a configuration which may be in movement but which nevertheless preserves unaltered a certain number of fundamental traits . . . then something comes along to break the calm and creates an imbalance . . . the equilibrium is then restored, but it is not the same as at the beginning; the basic narrative therefore includes two types of episodes: those which describe a state of balance or imbalance, and those which describe the transition from one to the other. The first type contrasts with the second as stability with change, as adjective with verb.[18]

In a postface to the recent English translation of his work, Brémond stresses the counterforces which act to preserve the status quo against change and movement. "Frustration" and "protection" round out the terms in his "Logic of Possible Narratives," an essay that enumerates exhaustively the general forms of action, using as his agents such abstract terms as "adversary" and "ally" in situations such as "completion of a task," "undergoing a punishment," and so on.[19] Brémond concludes that the elementary laws of narrative movement correspond to general laws of human comportment and that a valuable narrative is one that uses these in the construction of a clever and revealing pattern. Following Propp he specifically ties his work to the field of anthropology.

As we have noted, different kinds of stories are variations of different narrative algorithms. Todorov has shown that the difference between an Agatha Christie thriller and a Sherlock Holmes mystery is less a matter of style and mores than of sheer event pattern.[20] These stories, when diagramed, immediately reveal at the level of plot the difference an alert reader feels as he or she reads them.

3. p^n (characters): A classification of the agents of an action has been outlined by Todorov, using *Les Liaisons dangereuses* as his example.[21] Core predicates are abstracted to isolate the major kinds of relations possible among the participants (in the example, he finds desire, communication, and participation). Todorov then derives other possible relationships by employing two linguistic laws, that of opposition, which creates a negative of any relation, and that of passivity, permitting the interchangeability of agents within any given relation: thus *A* may desire *B* and be desired by *B*. Once again, such relations are quite dependent on laws of human comportment. This time, these laws are far more provincial, so that the cataloguing of relations in the Laclos novel will be quite different from a catalogue derived from a Faulkner or even a Dickens novel. But it will have much in common, no doubt, with one derived from Richardson.

4. p^nE^n (character interrelations): We complicate this situation only slightly when we connect the agents and the event. Characters are interrelated by opposition (desire, hate), by reciprocation (to desire, to be desired), and by dissimulation (hating, while appearing to desire). The events of the tale force transformations within characters and among them according to a limited set of rules. In his study of Laclos's *Les Liaisons dangereuses* Todorov has constructed four axioms to account for all character transformations. Obviously these axioms appear ludicrously reductive, especially since Todorov does not shy away from presenting them in the idiom of logic or geometry. For example, "Rule 1. Given A and B, two agents, and A loves B. Then A acts in such a way as to effect the reciprocal of this predicate (that is, the proposition 'A is loved by B')."[22] Under this law are played out Valmont's actions in relation to Tourvel, Danceny's seduction of Cécile, and so on. While this rule is doubtless universal, other rules are specific to eighteenth-century mores. Todorov aspires to define periods by these axioms, again mixing the study of literature with anthropology.

By outlining the kinds of categories applying to agents and narrated actions, we have surveyed that part of narrative called in French *l'his-*

toire or *l'énoncé*. It can be rather precisely delimited on the syntactic level by the kinds of analyses indicated above. But the definition of narrative includes also the act of narration, and this fact confronts us with the complexities of the teller's relation to the tale. In Jakobson's schema we find ourselves in the realm of shifters. As Jakobson points out, this is one of the last features of language to be acquired and, in aphasia, one of the first to be lost.[23] It is very complex, involving a constant interplay between code and message, or, in our terms, between the speech event and the narrated event.

Anglo-American critics have been in the forefront of the study of the narrator since Henry James and Percy Lubbock. Wayne Booth's *Rhetoric of Fiction* (1961) is still the most powerful such study. Nonetheless the East European formalists and French structuralists promise to bring far more system to this kind of study. Where Americans, even those as systematic as Booth, belabor description, groping through the problem by means of the examples that have occurred to them, their European counterparts go right to the heart of narrative capability via taxonomy and permutation. While the erudite Booth can think of many instances of certain narrative traits, the linguistically oriented Todorov exhaustively lists all the possible kinds of narration and narrative. Within all four categories of enunciation, one theorist dominates, and one book, Gérard Genette's *Narrative Discourse* (1980). Genette has minutely examined that most complex of narrators, the one created by Marcel Proust, to derive a general rhetoric of narration. Genette retraces the "figures" by which Proust organized his tale, figures of time, mode, aspect, and voice. This justly influential study is related to earlier work on topics in these categories, work carried out not in France so much as in Russia, England, and America.

5. E^n/E^s (type of discourse): To begin once more with categories not involving agents, we must deal at once with the bare relation of the speech event to its narrated content. The primary variable here is tense, the temporal distance of the narrated event from the point of narration. Other shifters of allocution (time and place) locate the narrated event in relation to a narration *here and now*. This category includes as well the "register" of the speech act, that is, the linguistic style of the narration in relation to its object. Primary types of register are referential language, stylized language, evaluative language, parodic language, and so on. Finally we are dealing in this category not merely with the temporal, spatial, or stylistic distance of the narrated

event from the narration but with the implication of the narration in the narrated event itself. Henry James's and Percy Lubbock's famous opposition of "telling versus showing" would fill out this category.

6. E^nE^{ns}/E^s (subordination of tales): The static category designating the relation of speech event to narrated event which we have just covered must give way now to the more active category of the "evidential." Here the shifting import of the narrated event is accounted for by cataloguing the relation of the report about that event to the primary speech act itself. Of greatest interest here is the study of stories within stories and direct versus indirect narration. The East Europeans have dominated in the research covering this field. V. N. Voloshinov's essay on "Reported Speech"[24] and Mikael Bachtin's "Discourse Typology in Prose"[25] present lengthy and complete catalogues of the kinds of relations possible together with their usual effects. Both treat literary discourse as dialogue with the reader on the one hand and with other literary works on the other. Needless to say, such features as imitation, parody, stylization, and reinforcement are fully analyzed in these essays, which are far too dense to summarize here.

7. p^n/p^s (narrator): Finally we reach the tale's narrator, first without relation to the narrated event. The narrator may be related to or isolated from the participant(s) of the tale; and may have greater vision than the hero, vision more restricted than that of the hero, or vision which coincides with that of the hero. In determining these values we are dealing with the person and aspect of the narrator, both very common topics in English criticism.

8. p^nE^n/E^s (narrative distance): In the final category we can advance the important notion of point-of-view, for here we must account not simply for who the narrator is but for that narrator's relation to the actions spoken of. Lubomír Doležel, another East European by birth, has constructed a permutation table on the model of a phonetic chart to catalogue narrators in his "Typology of the Narrator."[26] He reduces his table to three major subdivisions: first- and third-person speakers; active and passive speakers; and speakers as characters or narrators. This yields eight possible narrators of which six exist in Western literature: the objective, the rhetorical, the subjective third person, the observer, the auctorial first person, the personal first person. Actually each of these categories is discussed in Norman Friedman's much quoted essay, "Point of View in Fiction," and Doležel is careful to acknowledge this article.[27] Once again, the advance to

which structural analysis lays claim is the deductive and morphological nature of its inquiry, whereas Friedman and even Booth work essentially inductively.

All these kinds of studies have in common a strong belief in scientific methodology. Todorov has provided a brief rationale and defense of this method.[28] Most of his remarks echo the familiar "Polemical Introduction" to Frye's *Anatomy of Criticism*. The purpose of structural analysis is not the description or intricate knowledge of a single text. Nor is it the understanding of literature within the scope of another discipline like economics, psychology, or philosophy. The object of structural analysis is literary discourse itself, "literature that is virtual rather than real." Naturally it thrives on actual cases, but once analysis has yielded a proven hypothesis, structuralism will not reapply this hypothesis to every case it comes in contact with. On the contrary, it will seek further laws and try "to present a spectrum of literary possibilities in such a manner that the existing works of literature appear as particular instances that have been realized."[29]

Todorov meets the common objections of organicists and skeptics by appealing to their own biological analogy. Whereas with a living body one can never find any element operating alone (for example, the circulatory system), nevertheless biologists isolate such elements for purposes of analysis. They create a scientific model, what Barthes calls a "simulacrum," of the organism which is comprehensible and calculable. And again the biologist does no disservice to the living body by studying its properties and abstracting its laws. This is the science of human life in general just as poetics is the science of literary discourse in general. While other sciences may seek to study man (economics, sociology, and so on), biology is the most primary study. Similarly, the structuralists welcome other kinds of studies of literature but proclaim poetics to be in the first place of a hierarchy of such studies because, like biology, it is a general yet internal study of the phenomenon in question.

BEYOND THE LIMITS OF STRUCTURALISM

From the outset there have been strident defamations of the structuralist approach to literature. Most of these have come from those who have misunderstood its aim. The structuralists, on the whole, are content to leave individual works alone. Those scholars and teachers who feel such works need to be squeezed, strained, and moved in and out of all sorts of contexts may go on ahead with their work. Structural poetics will skirt the facticity of literature in search of "literariness." Neither do the structuralists feel inclined to employ literature for the better understanding and appreciation of culture. They are scientists, pure and simple, investigating a phenomenon found in culture.

There are, however, more serious charges to be leveled at the structuralists. While their aim at scientific methodology is admirable and necessary, they have constantly overreached the limits of their methodology, forging blindly into areas more proper to philosophy. Let me list some structuralist ideas pertaining to literature which essentially are outside the realm of methodology:

1. Roland Barthes claims that criticism is part of the object it seeks to explain.[30] Criticism makes the structural relations of the work clear by introducing abstract symbols for the terms the work deals with. Barthes is claiming that the work *is* the structural pattern, and all discourse about it that represents that pattern is a variant of the work. It was this kind of logic which made Lévi-Strauss equate the versions of Oedipus produced by Sophocles and Freud. It should be pointed out here that Jakobson long ago listed the dangers of applying to literature concepts that govern folklore and myth.[31] The one defines itself in relation to cultural codes; the other is a cultural code *per se*. In seeking to equate all discourse about a work with the work itself, Barthes is really making a statement about culture, not about literature, and it is this kind of statement that his methodology is finally unable to support.

2. Having equated the scientific study of literature with literature, Barthes goes all the way and suggests that science is closely related to literature in form.[32] He sees both as closed semiotic systems, so that neither can possibly hold a privileged view of reality. For Barthes, the criterion of truth is replaced by that of the "validity" of the sign system and the operations under analysis. He calls for the demise of science's present status as the "theology of our century" and asks for a playful science whose aim is imaginative pleasure, not truth. Science would then be a kind of literature, employing a special code.

3. Some of the structuralists have hinted that future literature should model itself in some ways after the new novel as practiced by Sarraute and Robbe-Grillet. Once again the reason stems from Barthes's vision of literature as a combination game in which both the elements and the laws of permutation are limited. He feels that literature always and only

refers to itself and that we should emphasize this self-reflexiveness as Robbe-Grillet has done.[33] The novel is not the book of life but of literary codes and terms.

4. The structuralists are concerned not with any instance of speech but with the system of language. Insofar as they are able, they show that every speech act merely "speaks the system." A description of the system or language of literature is for Barthes a description of human thought and emotion as well. Perhaps now we can see why Barthes is so fond of turning every human activity into the category of myth, for myth is a speakerless instance of language. It is a system that always speaks itself, so much so that it cannot be harmed by an impoverished telling. Barthes would have all literature strive for mythical status. He would remove from readers the experience of being "one down" before a privileged user of language.

5. Italo Calvino goes so far as to propose an elimination of writers altogether.[34] Given the rules of literariness on the one hand and the lexicon of mythical paradigms which Lévi-Strauss and his colleagues are unearthing on the other, a computer could generate countless correct stories. Some of these would move us as readers very deeply by making us perceive the system in a new and valuable way. This, then, would be the goal of literature: the playful celebration of a system that can occasionally startle us in making us take a new stance toward the system. For the structuralists, this means taking a new stance toward ourselves.

Now each of the above ideas is essentially a vision of the world based on the methodology employed in understanding that world. When Barthes claims man to be nothing other than a "structuralist activity,"[35] he has defined man and culture in terms of a methodology developed to study man and culture. The circularity here is disconcerting. Furthermore, structuralism glories in the sense-giving powers of man while dooming man to a groundless and ceaselessly self-reflecting sense. It thereby discourages hope in revolution, whether public or private, seeing in all change not a new order but a transformation of terms within a closure of immutable laws. "Man is language," it declares; language, that is, which refers only to itself.

The confidence with which structuralism undertook its narratological projects flowed on the one hand from its scientific, progressive method, and on the other from its implicit world view, which, though pessimistic in its anti-humanism, nevertheless afforded the kind of satisfaction always open to those who feel they have seen to the end of things. But such self-possession is clumsy to maintain in our epoch and, soon enough, various mutations, defections, and outside attacks were to break the very spirit of this essentially 1960's movement.

Roland Barthes, who pioneered structural narratology, pioneered also some of its poststructuralist alternatives. The trajectory from his 1966 essay on the structural study of narrative to his 1970 *S/Z* and on to the 1973 *Pleasure of the Text* traces the flight of a whole generation away from the closed world of structuralism and toward the "anarchic" readings of psychoanalysis and intertextual analysis.

Essentially, the decade of the 1970's brought with it an interest in the processes of structuring rather than in the *fait accompli* of structure. Lévi-Strauss was a primary casualty of this shift since he has always sought to expose structures and their meanings, being indifferent to the psychological and sociological play which goes into the construction of any story or myth. *S/Z,* in contradistinction, is concerned entirely with the process by which a text calls out to the reader (the five levels or codes which interest the reader) and the corresponding acts of investment and interpretation by which the reader rewrites the text. For Barthes a text is an intersection of processes which may produce different structures of meaning on every occasion of its being read. Only the bourgeois realist text strives to control and thoroughly discipline its own reading so that it can appear invariable as a solid, unalterable object. To this Barthes opposes the modernist texts of Butor and Robbe-Grillet, which explicitly invite various, perhaps infinite, types of readings and structurings. But he argues equally for a modernist criticism which, in its readings of classical texts, will not slavishly track down some single meaning or dominant structure but, rather, play with the signifiers so as to produce the text anew.[36]

In practice this attitude has produced two types of critical writing: "free readings" of texts and metacritical studies of the processes of writing and reading. The seemingly free or even anarchic readings have, of course, never been fully free. Indeed, one can see vestiges of the scientific rigor of structuralism in the deconstructive textual analyses of stories (for example, in *Glyph*) and of films and paintings, by critics such as Stephen Heath,[37] Raymond Bellour,[38] and Louis Marin.[39] In all these examples a text or fragment is challenged by the analyst who seeks in its array of signifiers traces of the lost battle for closure, fi-

nality, reification. Precise, minute dissection (Ropars's work on Res-
nais's *Muriel* is book-length, Bellour's study of the cornfield sequence
in *North by Northwest* is forty pages) permits freewheeling speculation
on the project of the text, as the analyst discloses the fissures in the
work, the countercurrents and unscripted backdrops which surround and
penetrate every text. Most recently the key role played by sexual difference in narrative has been lifted into focus, [40] not so much to show
the repressive ideology at work in most stories, but more generally to
indicate the dynamics of sexual markings within the smallest units of
narrative. This is the subatomic physics of narratology, a science of
stories as far from classical structuralism as is modern physics from
Newton. In both science and aesthetics we live now in a world of partial systems, of gaps and holes, where the act of analysis alters the
object under study so that it is hardly possible to speak of "objects"
anymore at all.

The practical work of close textual analysis has been undergirded by
the theories of Jacques Derrida and Julia Kristeva. Derrida's critique
of Saussure and Lévi-Strauss has oozed into every branch of cultural
criticism. No longer is the sign conceived as an invariable relation of
signifier and signified (Saussure's famous "recto and verso" of a sheet
of paper). In the tradition of Nietzsche, Freud, and Heidegger, Derrida
has pointed to the inevitable distance between signifier and signified
and to the resultant instability of signification. This instability is not
confined to a style or an epoch but is congenital and universal. Every
epoch deals with this trauma in its own way, leaning on or rearranging
earlier texts to create a veritable house of cards.

The fragility yet durability of narrative structures has been the subject of much of Kristeva's criticism. The process by which texts arise
from other texts in response to and in the service of ideology widens
the inquiries of narratology beyond the closed world of the tale. From
now on the tale can only be seen as an unstable organization of motifs
(most of which derive from, or deform, earlier motifs) which mediate
the necessities of a particular social order and the desires of its readers
via a play of signs which desperately scratch for solid ground.

Kristeva has been in the forefront of a movement forcing psychoanalytic and ideological concerns into the complex of narrative and
blasting the hope for a clear narrative grammar. It would seem that in
this expanded sphere of work narrative might be reduced to a mere

example or single cog in the larger systems which govern the psyche and society. But the subtler textual analysts as well as the theorists supporting them see narrative (and aesthetic activity in general) as quasi-autonomous, developing in relation to social and psychological systems but developing in its own "textual" way. Narrative can even provoke events in the psyche and in ideology; it does not simply respond to these systems in mechanical fashion. Here lies the openness of the text and of history. Current narrative analysts find themselves playing with the text, forging new and provisional structures, often with a shudder of anarchic *jouissance* which compensates for the loss of the sense of stable signification.

Structuralism's chief antagonists have invoked both traditional humanist philology (Auerbach, Spitzer, Abrams, and so forth) and phenomenology (Bachelard, Dufrenne, and Poulet). As for the former, structuralism has always considered itself immune from the attacks of philology because those attacks depend on an outmoded belief in stable, recoverable meanings and in the priority of some original creative mind operating in a recoverable historic moment. As the Barthes-Picard exchange illustrated, there is simply no common ground for discussion. In contrast, structuralism was to engage in an eventful dialectic with phenomenology, the philosophical school it supplanted in the 1960's, partly because the phenomenological roots of key deconstructionists like Derrida and Lacan are unmistakable. In his essay, "The Two Languages of Criticism," Eugenio Donato sums up the opposition this way.[41] One can either examine a phenomenon at a distance or up close. One can either be dispassionate in one's analysis or engaged. One can consider one's object of study as a spatial system or as temporal, as structure or process. The phenomenologist chooses the latter term in each of these oppositions.

Georges Poulet and the Geneva School of existential criticism have always focused on the temporal aspect of literary works. They have tried to write about the *act* of writing and the *act* of reading rather than the static laws of discourse. Their work derives its theoretical impulse from Merleau-Ponty's philosophy of language, which sees every speech act as bifurcated into an expressive and a communicative impulse. The structuralists believe that a study of the communication process of language exhausts the system, while Merleau-Ponty holds that communication exists in inverse proportion to expression. Thus, insofar as I properly convey a message, I remain at the conventional level and hardly express myself at all; insofar as I deform the system to express myself, my ability to communicate decreases.[42]

Merleau-Ponty unfortunately died just as structuralism supplanted phenomenology. While most of his colleagues, especially Mikel Dufrenne, have reacted in a hostile manner to the anti-humanism of structuralism, Paul Ricoeur is representative of a more healthy reconciliation between these methods. His hermeneutics makes structural analysis a crucial step in our confrontation with any text. Structuralism reminds us that every text is comprehensible only because of a system (grammar) that gives us access to it and inevitably limits what the text can say. But Ricoeur would go beyond the structural approach to a functionalism which seeks to show the place of narrative texts in human life.

Ricoeur centers, oddly enough, on the linguistic category of shifters in his attempt to open up the closed systems of language which the structuralists have described.[43] Shifters comprise a verbal category which is embarrassing to the structuralists because it is a group of signs that have as their function a relation to given speech acts. Shifters are available to mold the whole language around any given personal situation. Any speaker may adopt the shifter "I," may use a tense structure, allocutionary demonstratives ("here" or "now"), and so forth. In so doing the whole system of language is oriented toward self-expression on the one hand and toward a reference "in the world" on the other. The speaker thus uses, rather than speaks, the system.

Ricoeur's hermeneutics has led him to an interrogation of three related aspects of texts: word, metaphor, and discourse.[44] While structuralism diminished the importance of semantics and made the sentence supreme over the words which constitute it, hermeneutics reminds us that words carry within them the traces of earlier acts of signification. They are stopping places between the indiscriminate flow of the system and historical, highly specific moments of meaning. A look at the Oxford English Dictionary confirms this, as every word is shown (through literary examples) to bear within it the scars of earlier uses.

Metaphor is an explicit act of transgression against the system in search of new meaning in specific historical circumstances. While it depends on a certain structure of nomination and predication (a structure which rhetorical schools such as the Liège group have been subtly able to determine, working in the tradition of structuralism),[45] it succeeds in rewriting the dictionary in a specific event of language. For Ricoeur a fictional narrative may function as an expanded metaphor by proposing a possible world the reader is invited to traverse. The metaphorical text (be it a simple trope or a lengthy novel) becomes precious in its singularity as an achievement of meaning in relation to a system that does not swallow it up but adjusts itself to this new usage (as the dictionary expands with new words and with new acceptances of old words).

Ricoeur's attention to the function of words and of metaphors, that is, to the historical uses of the structured system, has led him ultimately to a theory of discourse and to his current examination of narrative discourse in particular. Whereas his philosophical orientation is radically different from that of the deconstructionists, his critique of structuralism hinges, as does theirs, on the role of interpretation and on the complex rereading of key texts in our culture.

This, I would say, has been the mark of the 1970's, to contaminate a limpid structuralism with the living processes of interpretation and to thwart the egalitarian ideal that made all texts equal as versions of the same structure (the same myth). Instead, poststructuralism has upheld the priority of texts that question themselves and thereby seem to rewrite themselves for every epoch. The actual readings of such texts has included the flagrantly personal flights of Roland Barthes as well as the "translations" of George Steiner, who, in the spirit of Ricoeur's hermeneutics,[46] tries to flesh out the hints of a text as it confronts us in our era and in our place. In both these cases narrative is treated as open to new readings, as demanding new readings. In both cases the heritage and vocabulary of structuralism has been used to separate us from the text, to clarify the systematic operation of the text so that we can respond to the forces present in writing itself rather than to some image of what an author had in mind. Structuralism has been surpassed because our era has allowed those forces to bleed out of the neat textual grammars envisioned in the 1960's. The rampant, quasi-independent power of narrative writing which structuralism helped display is now what interests all those concerned not simply to explain culture and meaning but, in both anarchic, ironic deconstruction and in progressive hermeneutics, to produce cultural meaning.

6

Adaptation

THE SOURCES OF FILMS

Frequently the most narrow and provincial area of film theory, discourse about adaptation is potentially as far-reaching as you like. Its distinctive feature, the matching of the cinematic sign system to prior achievement in some other system, can be shown to be distinctive of all representational cinema.

Let us begin with an example, *A Day in the Country*. Jean Renoir set himself the task of putting his knowledge, his troupe, and his artistry at the service of a tale by Guy de Maupassant. No matter how we judge the process or success of the film, its "being" owes something to the tale that was its inspiration and potentially its measure. That tale, "A Country Excursion," bears a transcendent relation to any and all films that adapt it, for it is itself an artistic sign with a given shape and value, if not a finished meaning. A new artistic sign will then feature this original sign as either its signified or its referent. Adaptations claiming fidelity bear the original as a signified, whereas those inspired by or derived from an earlier text stand in a relation of referring to the original.

The notion of a transcendent order to which the system of the cinema is beholden in its practice goes well beyond this limited case of adaptation.[1] What is a city symphony, for example, if not an adaptation of a concept by the cinema?[2] A definite notion of Berlin preexisted Walter Ruttman's 1927 treatment of that city. What is any documentary for that matter except the signification by the cinema of some prior whole, some concept of person, place, event, or situation. If we take seriously the arguments of Marxist and other social theorists that our consciousness is not open to the world but filters the world according to the shape of its ideology, then every cinematic rendering will exist in relation to some prior whole lodged unquestioned in the personal or public system of experience. In other words, no filmmaker and no film (at least in the representational mode) responds immediately to reality itself, or to its own inner vision. Every representational film *adapts* a prior conception. Indeed the very term "representation" suggests the existence of a model. Adaptation delimits representation by insisting on the cultural status of the model, on its existence in the mode of the text or the already textualized. In the case of those texts explicitly termed "adaptations," the cultural model which the cinema represents is already treasured as a representation in another sign system.

The broader notion of the process of adaptation has much in common with interpretation theory, for in a strong sense adaptation is the appropriation of a meaning from a prior text. The hermeneutic circle, central to interpretation theory, preaches that an explication of a text occurs only after a prior understanding of it, yet that prior understanding is justified by the careful explication it allows.[3] In other words, before we can go about discussing and analyzing a text we must have a global conception of its meaning. Adaptation is similarly both a leap and a process. It can put into play the intricate mechanism of its signifiers only in response to a general understanding of the signified it aspires to have constructed at the end of its process. While all representational films function this way (as interpretations of a person, place, situation, event, and so forth), we reserve a special place for those films which foreground this relation by announcing themselves as versions of some standard whole. A standard whole can only be a text. A version of it is an adaptation in the narrow sense.

Although these speculations may encourage a hopelessly broad view of adaptation, there is no question that the restricted view of adaptation from known texts in other art forms offers a privileged locus for analysis. I do not say that such texts are themselves privileged. Indeed, the thrust of my earlier remarks suggests quite the opposite. Nevertheless, the explicit, foregrounded relation of a cinematic text to a well-constructed original text from which it derives and in some sense strives to reconstruct provides the analyst with a clear and useful "laboratory" condition which should not be neglected.

The making of film out of an earlier text is virtually as old as the machinery of cinema itself. Well over half of all commercial films have come from literary originals—though by no means all of these originals are revered or respected. If we confine ourselves to those cases where the adaptation process is foregrounded, that is, where the original is held up as a worthy source or goal, there are still several possible modes of relation between the film and the text. These modes can, for convenience, be reduced to three: borrowing, intersection, and fidelity of transformation.

BORROWING, INTERSECTING, AND TRANSFORMING SOURCES

In the history of the arts, surely "borrowing" is the most frequent mode of adaptation. Here the artist employs, more or less extensively, the material, idea, or form of an earlier, generally successful text. Medieval paintings featuring biblical iconography and miracle plays based on Bible stories drew on an exceptional text whose power they borrowed. In a later, secular age the artworks of an earlier generation might be used as sacred in their own right. The many types of adaptations from Shakespeare come readily to mind. Doubtless in these cases, the adaptation hopes to win an audience by the prestige of its borrowed title or subject. But at the same time it seeks to gain a certain respectibility, if not aesthetic value, as a dividend in the transaction. Adaptations from literature to music, opera, or paintings are of this nature. There is no question of the replication of the original in Strauss's *Don Quixote*. Instead the audience is expected to enjoy basking in a certain pre-established presence and to call up new or especially powerful aspects of a cherished work.

To study this mode of adaptation, the analyst needs to probe the source of power in the original by examining the use made of it in adaptation. Here the main concern is the generality of the original, its potential for wide and varied appeal; in short, its existence as a continuing form or archetype in culture. This is especially true of that adapted material which, because of its frequent reappearance, claims the status of myth:

Tristan and Isolde for certain, and *A Midsummer Night's Dream* possibly. The success of adaptations of this sort rests on the issue of their fertility not their fidelity. Frank McConnell's ingenious *Storytelling and Mythmaking* catalogues the garden of culture by examing borrowing as the history of grafting and transplantation in the fashion of Northrop Frye or even Carl Jung.[4] This direction of study will always elevate film by demonstrating its participation in a cultural enterprise whose value is outside film and, for Jung and others, outside texts altogether. Adaptation is the name of this cultural venture at its most explicit, though McConnell, Frye, and Jung would all immediately want to extend their theories of artistic fertility to "original" texts which upon inspection show their dependence on the great fructifying symbols and mythic patterns of civilization.

This vast and airy mode of borrowing finds its opposite in that attitude toward adaptation I choose to call "intersecting." Here the uniqueness of the original text is preserved to such an extent that it is intentionally left unassimilated in adaptation. The cinema, as a separate mechanism, records its confrontation with an ultimately intransigent text. Undoubtedly the key film exhibiting this relation is Robert Bresson's *Diary of a Country Priest*. André Bazin, championing this film and this mode,[5] claimed that in this instance we are presented not with an adaptation so much as a refraction of the original. Because Bresson featured the writing of the diary and because he went out of his way to avoid "opening up" or in any other way cinematizing the original, Bazin claims that the film *is* the novel as seen by cinema. To extend one of his most elaborate metaphors,[6] the original artwork can be likened to a crystal chandelier whose formal beauty is a product of its intricate but fully artificial arrangement of parts while the cinema would be a crude flashlight interesting not for its own shape or the quality of its light but for what it makes appear in this or that dark corner. The intersection of Bresson's flashlight and the chandelier of Bernanos's novel produces an experience of the original modulated by the peculiar beam of the cinema. Naturally a great deal of Bernanos fails to be lit up, but what is lit up is only Bernanos, Bernanos however as seen by the cinema.

The modern cinema is increasingly interested in just this sort of intersecting. Bresson, naturally, has given us his Joan of Arc from court records and his *Mouchette* once again from Bernanos. Straub has filmed Corneille's *Othon* and *The Chronicle of Anna Magdalena Bach*. Pasolini audaciously confronted Matthew's gospel with many later texts (musical, pictorial, and cinematic) which it inspired. His later *Medea, Canturbury Tales,* and *Decameron* are also adaptational events in the intersecting mode. All such works fear or refuse to adapt. Instead they present the otherness and distinctiveness of the original text, initiating a dialectical interplay between the aesthetic forms of one period with the cinematic forms of our own period. In direct contrast to the manner scholars have treated the mode of "borrowing," such intersecting insists that the analyst attend to the *specificity* of the original within the *specificity* of the cinema. An original is allowed its life, its own life, in the cinema. The consequences of this method, despite its apparent forthrightness, are neither innocent nor simple. The disjunct experience such intersecting promotes is consonant with the aesthetics of modernism in all the arts. This mode refutes the commonplace that adaptations support only a conservative film aesthetics.

Unquestionably the most frequent and most tiresome discussion of adaptation (and of film and literature relations as well) concerns fidelity and transformation. Here it is assumed that the task of adaptation is the reproduction in cinema of something essential about an original text. Here we have a clear-cut case of film trying to measure up to a literary work, or of an audience expecting to make such a comparison. Fidelity of adaptation is conventionally treated in relation to the "letter" and to the "spirit" of the text, as though adaptation were the rendering of an interpretation of a legal precedent. The letter would appear to be within the reach of cinema for it can be emulated in mechanical fashion. It includes aspects of fiction generally elaborated in any film script: the characters and their inter-relation, the geographical, sociological, and cultural information providing the fiction's context, and the basic narrational aspects that determine the point of view of the narrator (tense, degree of participation and knowledge of the storyteller, and so on). Ultimately, and this was Bazin's complaint about faithful transformations, the literary work can readily become a scenario written in typical scenario form. The skeleton of the original can, more or less thoroughly, become the skeleton of a film.

More difficult is fidelity to the spirit, to the original's tone, values, imagery, and rhythm, since finding stylistic equivalents in film for these intangible aspects is the opposite of a mechanical process. The cinéaste presumably must intuit and reproduce the feeling of the original. It has been argued variously that this is frankly impossible, or that it involves the systematic replacement of verbal signifiers by cinematic signifiers, or that it is the product of artistic intuition, as when Bazin found the pervasive snowy decor in *Symphonie Pastorale* (1946) to reproduce adequately the simple past tense which Gide's verbs all bear in that tale.[7]

It is at this point that the specificity of these two signifying systems is at stake. Generally film is found to work from perception toward signification, from external facts to interior motivations and consequences, from the givenness of a world to the meaning of a story cut out of that world. Literary fiction works oppositely. It begins with signs (graphemes and words) building to propositions which attempt to develop perception. As a product of human language it naturally treats human motivation and values, seeking to throw them out onto the external world, elaborating a world out of a story.

George Bluestone, Jean Mitry, and a host of others find this opposition to be most graphic in adaptations.[8] Therefore they take pleasure in scrutinizing this practice even while ultimately condemning it to the realm of the impossible. Since signs name the inviolate relation of signifier to signified, how is translation of poetic texts conceivable from one language to another (where signifiers belong to different systems); much less how is it possible to transform the signifiers of one material (verbal) to signifiers of another material (images and sounds)? It would appear that one must presume the global signified of the original to be separable from its text if one believes it can be approximated by other sign clusters. Can we attempt to reproduce the meaning of the *Mona Lisa* in a poem, or of a poem in a musical phrase, or even of a musical phrase in an aroma? If one accepts this possibility, at the very least one is forced to discount the primary articulations of the relevant language systems. One would have to hold that while the material of literature (graphemes, words, and sentences) may be of a different nature from the materials of cinema (projected light and shadows, identifiable sounds and forms, and represented actions), both systems may construct in their own way, and at higher levels, scenes and narratives that are indeed commensurable.

The strident and often futile arguments over these issues can be made sharper and more consequential in the language of E. H. Gombrich or the even more systematic language of semiotics. Gombrich finds that all discussion of adaptation introduces the category of "matching."[9] First of all, like Bazin he feels one cannot dismiss adaptation since it is a fact of human practice. We can and do correctly match items from different systems all the time: a tuba sound is more like a rock than like a piece of string; it is more like a bear than like a bird; more like a romanesque church than a baroque one. We are able to make these distinctions and insist on their public character because we are matching equivalents. In the system of musical instruments the tuba occupies an equivalent position to that enjoyed by the romanesque in its system of architectural styles. Nelson Goodman has treated this issue at length in *The Language of Art* pointing to the equivalence not of elements but of the position elements occupy vis-à-vis their different domains.[10] Names of properties of colors may thus metaphorically, but correctly, describe aspects of the world of sound (a blue note, a somber or bright tone). Adaptation would then become a matter of searching two systems of communication for elements of equivalent position in the systems capable of eliciting a signified at a given level of pertinence, for example, the description of a narrative action. For Gombrich adaptation is possible, though never perfect, because every artwork is a construct of elements built out of a traditional use of a system. Since humans have the general capacity to adapt to new systems with different traditions in achieving a like goal or construct, artistic adaptation poses no insurmountable obstacles. Nevertheless attention to such "proportional consistencies" demands that the study of adaptation include the study of both art forms in their proper *historic* context.

Gombrich and Goodman anticipated the more fashionable vocabulary of semiotics in their clarification of these issues. In *Film and Fiction, The Dynamics of Exchange,* Keith Cohen tries to justify this new, nearly scientific approach to questions of relations between these arts; he writes, citing Metz:

> A basic assumption I make is that both words and images are sets of signs that belong to systems and that, at a certain level of abstraction, these systems bear resemblances to one another. More specifically, within each such system there are many different codes (perceptual, referential, symbolic). What makes possible, then, a study of the relation between two separate sign systems, like novel and film, is the fact that the same codes may reappear in more than one system. . . . The very mechanisms of language systems can thus be seen to carry on diverse and complex interrelations: "one function, among others, of language is to name the units segmented by vision (but also to help segment them), and . . . one function, among others, of vision is to inspire semantic configurations (but also to be inspired by them)."[11]

Cohen, like Metz before him, suggests that despite their very different material character, despite even the different ways we process them at the primary level, verbal and cinematic signs share a common fate: that of being condemned to connotation. This is especially true in their fictional use where every signifier identifies a signified but also elicits a chain reaction of other relations which permits the elaboration of the fictional world. Thus, for example, imagery functions equivalently in films and novels. This mechanism of implication among signs leads Cohen to conclude that "narrativity is the most solid median link between novel and cinema, the most pervasive tendency of both verbal and visual languages. In both novel and cinema, groups of signs, be they literary or visual signs, are apprehended consecutively through time; and this consecutiveness gives rise to an unfolding structure, the diegetic whole that is never fully *present* in any one group yet always *implied* in each such group." [12]

Narrative codes, then, always function at the level of implication or connotation. Hence they are potentially comparable in a novel and a film. The story can be the same if the narrative units (characters, events, motivations, consequences, context, viewpoint, imagery, and so on) are produced equally in two works. Now this production is, by definition, a process of connotation and implication. The analysis of adaptation then must point to the achievement of equivalent narrative units in the absolutely different semiotic systems of film and language. Narrative itself is a semiotic system available to both and derivable from both. If a novel's story is judged in some way comparable to its filmic adaptation, then the strictly separate but equivalent processes of implication which produced the narrative units of that story through words and audio-visual signs, respectively, must be studied. Here semiotics coincides with Gombrich's intuition: such a study is not comparative between the arts but is instead intensive within each art. And since the implicative power of literary language and of cinematic signs is a function of its use as well as of its system, adaptation analysis ultimately leads to an investigation of film styles and periods in relation to literary styles of different periods.

We have come round the other side of the argument now to find once more that the study of adaptation is logically tantamount to the study of the cinema as a whole. The system by which film involves us in fictions and the history of that system are ultimately the questions we face even when starting with the simple observation of an equivalent tale told by novel and film. This is not to my mind a discouraging arrival for it drops adaptation and all studies of film and literation out of the realm of eternal principle and airy generalization, and onto the uneven but solid ground of artistic history, practice, and discourse.

THE SOCIOLOGY AND AESTHETICS OF ADAPTATION

It is time for adaptation studies to take a sociological turn. How does adaptation serve the cinema? What conditions exist in film style and film culture to warrant or demand the use of literary prototypes? Although adaptation may be calculated as a relatively constant volume in the history of cinema, its particular function in any moment is far from constant. The choices of the mode of adaptation and of prototypes suggest a great deal about the cinema's sense of its role and aspirations from decade to decade. Moreover, the stylistic strategies developed to achieve the proportional equivalences necessary to construct matching stories not only are symptomatic of a period's style but may crucially alter that style.

Bazin pointed to an important instance of this in the immediate postwar era when adaptations from the stage by Cocteau, Welles, Olivier, Wyler, and others not only developed new ways for the cinema to be adequate to serious theater, but also developed a kind of discipline in *mise-en-scène* whose consequences go far beyond the production of *Macbeth, Les Parents terribles, The Little Foxes,* and *Henry V.*[13] Cocteau's film, to take one example, derives its style from Welles's use of interior shooting in *Kane* and *Ambersons,* thus responding to a new conception of dramatic space; but at the same time his film helped solidify a shooting style that would leave its mark on Alexandre Astruc and André Michel among others. Furthermore his particular cinematic *écriture* would allow Truffaut to set him against the cinema of quality in the famous 1954 diatribe.[14] It is instructive to note that while Truffaut railed against the status quo for its literariness and especially for its method of adaptation, the directors he praised were also working with literary originals: Bresson adapting Bernanos, Ophuls adapting Maupassant and Schnitzler, and Cocteau adapting his own theater pieces. Like Bazin, Truffaut looked upon adaptation not as a monolithic practice to be avoided but as an instructive barometer for the age. The cinema *d'auteur* which he advocated was not to be pitted against a cinema of adaptation; rather one method of adaptation would be pitted against another. In this instance adaptation was the battleground even while it prepared the way for a stylistic revolution, the New Wave, which would for the most part avoid famous literary sources.

To take another sort of example, particular literary fashions have at times exercised enormous power over the cinema and, consequently, over the general direction of its stylistic evolution. The Romantic fiction of Hugo, Dickens, Dumas, and countless lesser figures originally set the stylistic requirements of American and mainstream French cinema at the end of the silent era. Similarly Zola and Maupassant, always of interest to French cinéastes, helped Jean Renoir muscularly reorient the style of world cinema in the 1930's. Not only that, through Luchino Visconti this naturalist impulse directly developed one strain of neorealism in his adaptations of Giovanni Verga (*La Terra Trema*) and James M. Cain (*Ossessione*).

This latter case forces us to recall that the "dynamics of exchange," as Cohen calls it, go both ways between film and fiction. Naturalist fiction helped cinema develop its interest in squalid subjects and a hard-hitting style. This in turn affected American hard-boiled novelists like Cain and Hammett, eventually returning to Europe in the film style of Visconti, Carné, Clouzot, and others. This general trading between film and literature in the currency of naturalism had some remarkable individual incidents associated with it. Renoir's adaptation of *The Lower Depths* can serve as an example. In 1881 Zola had cried out for a naturalist theater [15] and had described twenty years before the time precisely the sort of drama Gorki would write in *The Lower Depths:* a collection of real types thrown together without a domineering plot, the drama driven by the natural rhythms of little incidents and facts exposing the general quality of life in an era. Naturalism here coincided with a political need, with Gorki's play preceeding the great uprisings in Russia by only a few years.

In another era and in response to a different political need, Renoir leapt at the chance to adapt the Gorki work. This was 1935, the year of the ascendancy of the Popular Front, and Renoir's treatment of the original is clearly marked by the pressures and aspirations of that moment. The film negotiates the mixture of classes which the play only hints at. Louis Jouvet as the Baron dominates the film, descending into the social depths and helping organize a collective undoing of Kastylylov, the capitalist landlord. Despite the gloomy theme, the murder, jailing, deaths by sickness and suicide, Renoir's version overflows with a general warmth evident in the airy setting by the Marne and the relaxed direction of actors who breathe languidly between their lines.

Did Gorki mind such an interpretation? We can never know, since he died a few months before its premier. But he did give Renoir his imprimatur and looked forward to seeing the completed version, this despite the fact that in 1932 he declared that the play was useless, out of date, and unperformable in socialist Russia. Perhaps these statements were the insincere self-criticism which that important year elicited from many Russian artists. I prefer, however, to take Gorki at his word. More far-sighted than most theorists, let alone most authors, he realized that *The Lower Depths* in 1932 Russia was by no means the same artwork as *The Lower Depths* in the France of the Popular Front. This is why he put no strictures on Renoir assuming that the cinéaste would deal with his play as he felt necessary. Necessity is, among other things, a product of the specific place and epoch of the adaptation, both historically and stylistically. The naturalist attitude of 1902, fleshing out the original plans of Zola, gave way to a new historic and stylistic moment, and fed that style that Renoir had begun elaborating ever since *La Chienne* in 1931, and that despite its alleged looseness and airiness in comparison to the Gorki, would help lead European cinema onto the naturalist path.

This sketch of a few examples from the sociology of adaptation has rapidly taken us into the complex interchange between eras, styles, nations, and subjects. This is as it should be, for adaptation, while a tantalizing keyhole for theorists, nevertheless partakes of the universal situation of film practice, dependent as it is on the aesthetic system of the cinema in a particular era and on that era's cultural needs and pressures. Filmmaking, in other words, is always an event in which a system is used and altered in discourse. Adaptation is a peculiar form of discourse but not an unthinkable one. Let us use it not to fight battles over the essence of the media or the inviolability of individual art works. Let us use it as we use all cultural practices, to understand the world from which it comes and the one toward which it points. The elaboration of these worlds will demand, therefore, historical labor and critical acumen. The job of theory in all this is to keep the questions clear and in order. It will no longer do to let theorists settle things with a priori arguments. We need to study the films themselves as acts of discourse. We need to be sensitive to that discourse and to the forces that motivate it.

7

Valuation
(of Genres and Auteurs)

FROM FORMALISM TO GENRE STUDY

When contemporary film theory rose to power in the mid-1960's, it brought with it not just a new approach to film, but new types of films to value and absolutely new reasons for valuing films in the first place. The distance from the humanism of the 1950's to the post-structuralism of our day is perhaps best seen in the changing attitudes toward various types of films and toward whatever is thought to be the source of interest or power in any given film. In this chapter we will observe the replacement of creativity and art by ideology and system as the perceived source of value in the cinema.

In America film theory grew up under the reign of that brand of formalism known as ''the new criticism'' and in Europe under the sign of the first structuralism. These systems of inquiry have in common rigorously delimited attention on the artwork as object. Their sense of the type and function of this object may differ one from the other, but in practice both systems exclude questions which do not further an explanation of the semiotic makeup of the individual work. In practice this means showing the mutual interaction of parts as they thickly and redundantly speak a message meant for no one and no occasion in particular.

The insufficiency of this brand of criticism and the theory underlying it was quietly recognized throughout. An intermittent appeal was sounded to historicize structuralism and to build a context for the poems and films minutely analyzed by disciples of American new criticism.[1] Although films may operate logically and self-sufficiently, they nevertheless rise out of situations in a process no semiotic formula is able to account for.

Conscientious film theorists like Metz, Eco, and the editors of *Cahiers du cinéma* recognized as indispensable, alongside their semiotic and structural base, a study of the process of textual production and reception.[2] True to its methodological heritage, this expansion of concern has been carried out structurally, so that we can speak of film theory in the 1970's as developing a structural theory of spectator dynamics on the one hand and a structural theory of textual production on the other.

This development might best be thought of as progressing from an interest in "structure" to one in "structuration" and these in fact have been the nouns employed in contemporary theory. Instructively the substantive "structuration" was selected over the gerund "structuring" indicating that modern theory, despite its interest in process, still seeks to comprehend process with a stable theoretical system. It is my hope, in this chapter as elsewhere, to release a more dynamic theory, one taking its cue from films and history rather than dominating these.

The itinerary from humanism to formalism to structuralism and poststructuralism, is not without its continuities. The most significant of these for our purposes is the category of "genre" because in all these phases it has drawn attention to the peculiar relation between art and system, experience and knowledge.

Genre has been a persistent issue in film theory since the end of World War II and it was the battleground on which formalists had to defend their theory of the sanctity of the individual work. Northrop Frye's watershed *Anatomy of Criticism* (1957) formed enemies and alliances amongst critics in all the arts, for his book demanded a systematic view of literature as a whole rather than a focus on the single text.[3] Film critics and theorists naturally gravitated toward such systematic views since they felt more comfortable exploring their general interest in films than in studying one or another fleeting product of the industry (with the exception of a handful of "art" films invariably directed by Fellini, Antonioni, or Bergman). In addition, the massive popularity of the art form dictated a more sociological approach than that accorded to lyric poems, the favored mode of formalist critics.

The issue of genre brings to individual artworks at least two kinds of context to help account for the form and the appeal of each work.

Whereas formalist critics could point to nothing other than technical ingenuity or perfection to account for the strength of a poem or film, the issue of genre lets us lodge the value of the work within the culture itself or within the tradition of films from which it comes. Genre thus corrects the myopia of new criticism by suggesting not only how films function but why they function so crucially. The genre critic for example can call upon psychology in discussing the horror film, or sociology in analyzing the gangster. In this way is explained a film's power as well as its meaning. The genre critic can likewise see a range of related works as variations on a theme or problem, be it cultural or formal. The differing point-of-view strategies in detective films, for instance, are at once exercises in spectator psychology and successive answers to a basic issue in film form.

While genre theorists have always felt able to account for value as well as form, until the 1970's they have done so in a way hardly different from the formalists they had thought to supplant. Placing the individual artwork in a large and significant context, they nevertheless dealt with this context as a closed universe (the "world" of the Western). Northrop Frye's influence led scholars to work under the supposition that a genre ought to be a static construct, full of themes, symbols, standard plot devices, and the interrelation of all these. Critics operating from such a position are likely to find the Western itself to be beautiful or significant, whereas *She Wore a Yellow Ribbon* or any single Western is interesting only because it exposes certain facets of the genre. Individual films, like the motifs and traits of a poem as analyzed formally, become sensible and interpretable, not to say worthy, only in their interaction within the genre. As in Jungianism, what concerns such critics are the patterns and symbols hovering above every filmmaking situation just waiting to make their entry in one guise or another. Genres are thought to address questions of human existence (generally eternal ones like the individual in society, but occasionally local ones like the Japanese sci-fi cycle responding to the 1950's nuclear hysteria). In this they have much the same status as "eternal works of art" prized by humanists through the ages.

GENRE AND THE SYSTEM

The anti-humanist orientation of the contemporary period obviously signaled the demise of this sort of "essentialist" genre theory. The

age demanded a material and a dynamic view, this age which was con-
densed into a single month, May 1968. That year saw assaults carried
out on many important cultural pillars; more important, these assaults
were essentially directed against the very notion of the cultural pillar
itself.[4] Process, revolution, situation, change, and openness sought to
replace every established way of thinking.

Although the first structuralism, through its dependence on Lévi-
Strauss, had been sensitive to social and psychological contexts, it had
organized these beneath a theory that seemed at once closed and abstract. The fall from grace of Lévi-Strauss had enormous impact in all
fields, among which was film study. No longer would it do to enu-
merate elements of a genre or even to construct the logical and morphological rules of their interrelation.

Put succinctly, genres are now to be thought of not as changeless
structures ordained by some natural or psychological law and destined
to repeat themselves to every society; nor are they merely the taxon-
omic constructs of analysts. They serve a precise function in the overall economy of cinema, an economy involving an industry, a social
need for production of messages, a vast number of human subjects, a
technology, and a set of signifying practices. Genre is a rare category
in that it overtly involves every aspect of this economy; these aspects
are always at play whenever the cinema is concerned but their interrelation is generally very difficult to perceive. Genres give us synoptic
insight because they are, as Stephen Heath said in 1976, "instances of
equilibrium, characteristic relatings . . . of subject and machine in film
as particular closures of desire, forms of pleasure."[5]

Heath has aimed at the most distinctive aspect of genre, its patent
importance to the culture as testified to by history. But instead of seeing
genres as treasure chests of cultural values or as rituals exorcising cultural demons, he emphasizes their regulative role in the complex exchange system which makes up the cinema.

Genres are specific networks of formulas which deliver a certified
product to the waiting customer. They ensure the production of meaning by regulating the viewer's relation to the images and narratives
constructed for him or her. In fact, genres construct the proper spectator for their own consumption. They build the desire and then represent the satisfaction of what they have triggered. As a specific production practice in the industry ("let's make nine gangster films this
year" says Warner Bros. in 1933) and as a site of spectatorial pleasure

("I'm dying to see a musical tonight"), genres equilibrate spectators and that vast technical, signifying, and ideological machine of the cinema.

The consistency with which films appeal to us has made recent theorists question even the distinctiveness of genres themselves. After all the theater owner has no qualms substituting a musical for a gangster film; doubtlessly he has played them together on double bills. For those schooled in the ambience of Lévi-Strauss, it is only a minor leap from observations about the sameness of genre films to the claim that all genres effectively constitute a single sameness we call the "movies." In seeing beyond the superficial differences separating film from film and genre from genre, recent theory has had to abstract itself from the discussion of icons, plots, themes, and characters to a level of generality capable of characterizing all films. Movies are described as operating by means of phasure/disphasure, closings and repetitions, glances and vectorized desires, identification, suture, regulated loss, displacement, condensation, and so on. A typical passage from Stephen Heath's celebrated essay "Narrative Space" resumes a host of such terms.

> Narrativization is then the term of a film's entertaining; process and process contained, the subject bound in that process and its directions of meaning. The ideological operation lies in the balance, in the capture and regulation of energy; film circulates—rhythms, spaces, surfaces, moments, multiple intensities of signification—and narrativization entertains the subject—on screen in frame—in exact turnings of difference and repetition, semiotic and suture, negativity and negation.[6]

With such a rarefied vocabulary followers of Heath have felt able to include in this system even the non-narrative modes of the documentary, the animated film, the trailer, and the TV spot.[7] The Hollywood system has conquered. The movies draw us, have learned to draw us; in Heath's view they have taught us how to be drawn. This is the economy of sameness that will never be escaped so long as a production system makes and distributes films for a waiting populace which pays with its money, time, and concentration—which pays, in short, with its desire. This is the "sameness" of the movies incarnated in genres.

We could not be further here from the film scholarship of twenty-five years ago. The humanists of that era valued individual films, valued their particularity and the artistic uniqueness by which each was most perfectly and authentically itself. They listened to each text for the sound of its voice (for some, the voice of the author; for others, the voice of art or even the transcendent voice of nature). In sum, the film harbored an original power released to every sensitive spectator, a power the critic hoped to harness to his or her own meditation on the film.

The post-structuralism represented by Heath interests itself in quite the opposite aspect of the cinema, in the standardization beneath the apparent but insignificant differences among texts. The voice heard by today's theorists is the monotone of ideology, a voice to be isolated but certainly not to be amplified by the critic. It is ideology that fashions the ultimate sameness of all films. When we line up at the box office, lured there by the name on a marquee, a picture in a newspaper ad, a TV spot, or the title of the film, it is ideology calling to us through the genre. We seal a contract as we put down our money, certain to be given a known pleasure if we behave as proper spectators. The other party in this contract, the party which rewards our passivity, is a system with an impersonal voice. Genre is a specific guise of ideology, the visible edge of a vast subterranean implacement determining the various institutions and practices of culture, clandestinely working on the unconscious of spectators.

Many early theorists recognized cinema to be a magnificent machine of ideology, conveying the norms and values of the status quo. They observed films in their blatant or subtle insistence on certain clusters of ideas, of beliefs, and of symbols. Since 1968, however, a far more complicated view of ideology has led theorists to treat it as they treat genre, as a dynamic system of working relations in culture rather than as a storehouse of items and issues constantly reproduced.[8]

In all cases ideology refers to the representing of reality which goes on in specific historical settings for each culture. Classically thought to be dependent on the actual relations of production in society, ideology is the necessary force that turns human subjects into creatures fit to fulfill the functions demanded by such production. Obviously the notion of the world and of one's place in it was not the same for a medieval serf, a Renaissance scholar, or a nineteenth-century laborer. Each of these lived in a quite distinct reality, one attuned to the social and economic relations of the times. Ideology makes each of these subjects at home in his world by insisting first and foremost that his world is in fact *the* world, the natural order of things preordained by God and physical laws to be just the way it is.

In our culture the mass media are primary technologies of ideology, with the cinema standing in the forefront of these because of its remarkable illusionistic guise and because of the prestige and honor accorded it by the populace. Its technology has stressed the attainment of an ever-sharper realism through which to present the objects and stories which carry the messages of the day.

Nor is it a simple matter of communicating "reality" via the cinema. Ideology does not descend on the populace from some demonic mountain top of politics. It is a virtually impersonal system which produces reality for every subject of a culture. And it does this not so much by filling everyone's minds with the objects and values which make up the culture as by shaping the very forms of organization by which each subject constructs reality for him/herself. Ideology, to take a pertinent example, begins by building "himselves" and "herselves," by building sexual differences in language. Obviously culture represents each sex in a particular way, but, more primordially, sex distinctions are a function of the representational mechanism itself. The fact that language is gendered, together with other facts (for instance that narratives involve searches and pursuits), shapes all linguistic and narrative knowledge around a given structure of sexuality. Other differences and values are similarly built into the very modes of perceiving and processing information which seem to come to us so *naturally*.

Under the cover of such a far-reaching view we can begin to see the specifically ideological functioning of standard cinema. Audiences are, in the first place, assigned their roles as spectators beneath the narrating authority of the film. Straining to totalize the world they inhabit, straining to achieve a sense of personal unity, they submit willingly, even passionately to the experience of cohesion which the film delivers to them in the beautiful compositions of its images and in the exhilarating logic of its tales. Inside the movie theater there unrolls a spectacle in which man is the center of attention, a narrative in which knowledge finally graces the enigmas of the plot, and in which an ending, whether comic or tragic, is always attained. Just as important, the viewers feel themselves to be the totalizing agents of whatever appears before their eyes.

Thus it is that the machinery of cinema, a machinery composed like all machines of fragments and parts (and in this case one that relies literally on intermittent motion and on the operations of laboratories and chemicals) comes to take on the function of producing reality for its spectators, a seamless, coherent reality both in image and story. This gives to each spectator the belief that life itself, no matter how fragmented it may appear, is finally coherent and that his/her own position in it is fully accounted for.

Such are the primary needs and pleasures fulfilled by the cinema in Stephen Heath's formulation.[9] Genres then are specific equilibria balancing the desires of subjects and the machinery of the motion picture apparatus. For between bare human subjects and the existing industry of the cinema must come that other mechanism, this time a mental one, genre, which permits the transformation of sights and sounds into pictures and stories matching the desires those subjects have come to depend on.

A good example of the ideological workings of genre is that group of stories Todorov has so thoroughly delimited as "the Fantastic."[10] Whether in literature or film, the audience experiences stories such as "The Turn of the Screw," and "The Fall of the House of Usher" in a spirit of hesitation, believing and doubting the reality of what is told or shown them. Primarily a nineteenth-century literary phenomenon, this genre has readily been transplanted into the cinema as the mass audience for such stories deserted literature for movies. Furthermore, the technology of the medium could not be better suited to the structure of belief/doubt which defines the genre, for the cinema is at once exact in its reproduction of the minutiae of everyday life (belief) yet eager to startle its audience with tricks in optics, chemistry, and mise en scène (doubt).

What makes the Fantastic function so perfectly in the cinema is the coincidence of these technological propensities and the nearly religious need for ambiguity present in our culture. The Fantastic makes us at home with the idea that our lives are crossed by possibilities we seldom attend to. It makes us at once anxious and grateful; more important, it tells us to consider our lives as smaller than the mysterious powers that surround us, so that we may survive such powers or participate in their ultimate ascendancy. To see the world as shimmering with the vaguely supernatural is at once satisfying and debilitating, for it enervates any impulse we might have to shape our destiny. After all, the Fantastic shows us that the world we live in is already a destined universe, one we can enjoy but one we must fear.

The conserving function of such a genre is only too plain; so is its fertility for cinematic style. The film system, at the urgings of ideology, will continually develop new techniques to startle us with the real and the more than real. It will put into pictures still newer stories exercising our need to believe in appearances and our more uncertain hope that appearances hide powerful forces (ghosts, monsters, the spirit of love, a divine plan, and the like). As a genre the Fantastic is thus the crossing point of a technology, an industry, a way of making films, an audience desire, a societal need. Ideology makes these quite distinct structures and forces cohere, and that coherence is genre.

NARRATION: THE VOICE IN THE SYSTEM

In asserting a total view of the cinematic complex (from the dark caverns of spectator psychology to a global network of socio-economics) modern theory has forsaken the enterprise of criticism. How can the study of an individual film be important to anyone who senses the single voice of ideology emanating from every film? Criticism in this context could only be redundant.

Let us mark here the distance we have come from the humanism of the 1950's where the individual voice triumphed over a lugubrious system. The most extreme critical position of that earlier era was held by the Geneva critics of consciousness whose object of study was not an isolated text but the creative germ behind all the texts signed by a single author. Georges Poulet and his followers eagerly surrendered themselves to the governing structure of consciousness deep within the writings of Mallarmé, Mérimée, Balzac, and so on.[11] We can note here a source for the auteur criticism developing concurrently in French journals, a criticism ready to uphold the failures and aborted projects of certain directors as more valuable than the greatest successes of mere *metteurs-en-scène*.

Criticism of consciousness dives deeper into authorship than biographical criticism. The historical Honoré de Balzac is of only peripheral interest to Poulet. Instead Balzac is the name for a structure of inner experience made available to the critic (and to all serious readers) in the fabric of the writing he produced. A single germ, an obsessive way of permitting ideas to form, animates even the minor texts signed ''Balzac.''

In reality few auteur theorists went so far as Poulet. Fascinated by the actual circumstances of production, the journalists at *Cahiers du cinéma* prized interviews and biography. Nicholas Ray was certainly a director whose every image they felt emanated from a profound and consistent orientation toward life, but at the same time he was a man who had stood up to the Hollywood system and, against all odds, had won. It is here that the issue of genre first entered the modern debate over authority and authenticity in cinema.

For Poulet genre can be only an irrelevant critical category. Intuitions of states of consciousness may arise in Balzac's short stories as much as they do in his great novels. Even in his minor attempts at poetry or criticism one should look for and be able to find a singular, definite, and valuable mode of organizing experience. Since reading is above all a mode of merging with another consciousness, genre is something to traverse, not rest upon.

But for the auteur theorists in France, England, and America, genre became an important issue. First of all the cinematographic values of genres worked to counteract the prestige of self-important films of ideas. In this endeavor genre and auteur criticism cooperated, for both lodged real values in style, in the uniquely cinematic manner in which ideas become formed via images.

At the same time genre acts as a foil for the auteur approach. The import of any directorial vision is seldom directly visible in a collaborative and industrial art like the movies. No filmmaker spins the structures of consciousness spontaneously onto celluloid the way we imagine writers to ooze words onto a page in lonely evenings under lamplight. In order to retain the values insisted on by critics of consciousness, the film theorist must account for the exigencies of production in both quantity and quality. Genre is a shorthand for "convention," for the industrial prototype every director is given by the producer.

It is commonplace now to suggest that the values internal to any film result from the particular ratio it exhibits between convention and invention,[12] between the requirements of genre and the ingenuity and world view of an auteur working with that genre. Since the laws of genre are apparently open to inspection, it appears that they can be factored out of any film under question leaving the contribution of the auteur available for study and delectation. This at least has been the common sensical position adopted by film theory, a position between the Cartesian idealism of the critics of consciousness and the materialist determinism of today's post-structuralists.

As interest in film study shifted in the 1960's from the auteur and his revered text to the more general problems of film language, so the locus of perceived cinematic agency shifted. No longer was a single human agent, an auteur, to receive homage as the force muscularly inflecting the rigid rules of genre; now genre itself was described as a dynamic system with change built into it by definition.

What humanists of the past termed "creativity" materialist theorists now insist on seeing as simply one more ingredient in the general recipe, with that ingredient (the catalyst) necessary to ensure a modicum of change within the overall structure of repetition. After all, unlike most consumer items, the value of each film depends largely on its perceived distinctiveness. Invention, creativity, auteur—these terms locate the apparent dynamism without which the genre would be nothing more than a corpus, or, what is the same thing, a corpse. So much do genres thrive on changes and challenges that some critics feel they can best be understood only when they are up against the edge of what is conventional, reaching out to take on new subjects, forging into new realms of experience. In this view there can be no dead-center genre film for genre is always characterized by a journey from the center to the edge, by tension within convention. The thrill of such journeys carries with it immense ideological weight because the system is shown to function not just within the known confines of its home terrain, but in the darkness outside its boundaries. In this way cultural forms declare themselves to be at one with the natural order. Doubtlessly it consoles us to realize that a single human being is directing this voyage, even if he is acting under orders and moves in a "direction" set out in advance.

The most recent materialist theory completely obliterates "the personal" in accounting for the way films address their audience. Instead of conceiving it as a structure put to particular effect by an auteur eager to say something through film, the appearance of a new film is now most often seen as a formal permutation in the system of the genre itself. Even Todorov, representing a quite early structuralism, thought to bypass the personal aspect of narrative by instituting the category of "uttering" as distinct both from the "utterance" and from the shape or "system" of the work produced.[13] Consolidating the gains of this linguistic approach, Seymour Chatman's book, instructively titled *Story and Discourse,* maps out the logical subcategories at play involving a narrational presence in the act of uttering.[14] These include the relation of the narrator to character, the time of the telling with respect to the time of the event, the arrangement of discourses within the narrative (in film, the syntactic relations of story line to memories, dreams, speeches, off-screen narration, and music), and so forth.

In keeping with the Althuserian notion of ideology this narrative theory makes the category of the narrator a mere position or slot to be filled in with differential values. Such authorial attitudes as cynicism, irony, sympathy or the like, attitudes we customarily attribute to the humanity of the narrator, are calculated now as being inscribed in the text as effects of an impersonal scheme of representation.

Here as elsewhere structuralism appears to have gone too far. In striving to bring everything, including change, under the sway of convention, it has effectively eliminated that force of play from what is always, even by its own claims, an artistic *process.* More disturbing is the tendency this theory has to seal films off from history, accounting for change with reference to a virtually timeless "ideology" and a purely logical notion of formal permutation.

Ideology must lose its connotation of massive univocity. There are in fact many ideologies and it is important to distinguish the specific ideological project of a tale in its telling. This does not mean that we need give special credence or honor to the voice of invention, only that we treat it like a voice, respond to it as we would to any directed discourse that catches our attention. Nothing prevents us from discussing the ideological implications of the voice as it speaks its tale to us out of a particular historical moment. In fact, we ought to see genres themselves as self-vindicating systems which, far from striving to repeat, in some cleverly new way, a message common to all films, announce their distinctive value in every film. Genres struggle for supremacy and battle over the appropriateness of their own modes of discourse.[15] The hard-boiled detective novel (or the *film noir*) was not merely a new cultural expression, it was one that announced itself as particularly attuned to its era and as providing its audience with an entry to a facet of life never properly represented before.

Surely we need to criticize such claims of genres, just as we must be suspicious of the "inspiration" of individual artists as they feel called upon to express themselves through the system. Nevertheless it is exactly the work of film theory to be sensitive to the distinctions that films seem to make amongst themselves, and to follow out the consequences of those distinctions. We ought to see the film system in its living behavior with the films that history (the struggle of views and of agents) brings on as a certain productive disturbance. What we say about such disturbance is another matter, but theorists and historians of the medium must take account of real events in a field of cultural discourse and not assume their work is done once they have identified each new film as part of the system.

HIERARCHIES: INSIDE AND OUTSIDE THE SYSTEM

In our century, a major strain of aesthetics has refused to evaluate artworks, instead prizing description and explanation. Assuming that evaluation is a matter of mere taste, contemporary theorists have assiduously avoided entering the marketplace where artistic capital rises and falls in value. They have on the contrary sought to analyze that economy and sketch out the network of that marketplace.

But since, as we have seen, the products consumed in this economy are valued for their distinctiveness, and since the system, when fully described, must include not just the network but the events disturbing that network, and since, finally, the voice of ideology is really a chorus, even a babble, of competing voices and projects, discriminations in fact must be made if only to sort out the historical mutations of "the movies." In fact all periods and types of film theory have implicitly or explicitly evaluated the films they treat just by choosing to treat them and to treat them in such and such a manner.

The range of views we have already surveyed regarding the voice or authority of a film may be replicated in a survey of assessments of films themselves. In the first years of film scholarship, priority was predictably accorded those rare films deemed capable of standing alongside important works of literature or music, films most often signed by Murnau, Antonioni, Bergman, Fellini, or Dreyer. The second generation of scholars, the auteurists, were really humanists of the same sort, only brought up on the movies rather than on high culture. Thus they did not feel compelled to extol the great works of the art cinema but rather to reveal the unappreciated films of lesser known directors who, in workmanlike fashion, displayed notable styles, and, through style, consistent world views.

The chosen auteurs were treated with the seriousness accorded art directors even if they primarily worked in trivial genres or with insignificant scripts and ideas. For the auteurists the only worthwhile ideas were ideas of the cinema, but the cinema conceived in such a way that ideas of the cinema were equally and essentially ideas about the world. This is their humanism and it is against this that the materialists reacted.

Film theory since 1968 has been suspicious of all these hierarchies of films and filmmakers. Belief in the power of the system (together with the voice of ideology behind that system) has led materialists to amalgamate the varieties of films and genres into the standardization of "the movies." This single category does have the strength of industrial practice behind it, for it is "movies" that are customarily advertised, bought, and sold, not "unique artworks" made in celluloid, nor "visions of the world."

How can modern theory operate without a hierarchy of film values? How can it treat every film as just another instance of the same system? In fact it cannot. Standard cinema has been homogenized by these theorists for polemical reasons; it has been raised as a rigged backdrop against which they hope to stage their own dramatic event and insert their own values, the revolutionizing of film culture and film spectators.

As we shall see, this drama, when displayed in it baldest outline, pits the standard cinema against the radical avant-garde, a type of film that speaks from outside ideology, immune to it. The standard cinema and the avant-garde, then, are two imaginary poles between which all other films (the real films of film history) are laid out. In practice, modern theory has carefully considered the varying potential for ideological reinforcement or disruption in the whole range of films, creating a virtual hierarchy based on political rather than aesthetic criteria. In occasional systematic essays such as the 1970 *Cahiers du cinéma* piece "Cinema/Ideology/Criticism"[16] and in the practical criticism of journals like *Cahiers, Cinéthique,* and *Screen,* a clear schema of films emerges, each type separated from its neighbor on the basis of the source and power of its voice in relation to the general discourse of ideology. However catalogued, this scheme is a certain index to the values at the heart of modern film theory.

Instead of crowning this hierarchy, the art cinema of the great directors has been snubbed by modern theorists. Film history books may

advertise the great films of Welles, Antonioni, Fellini, Bergman, Buñuel, and other masters as standing outside genre, but it is only by means
of the self-deception of the intellectual classes that these movies can
claim the status of unique artworks. For in reality such films participate in a well-defined genre with its own distribution and exhibition
system, from the art houses of the metropolis to the 16mm. university
circuit. Under proclamations like "original genius," and "cinematic
art" audiences are encouraged to submit to an elevated meaning just
beyond their grasp. They feel cleansed by participating in a sacrament
of viewing in the chapel of the art theater. How different is this from
the catharsis by violence which motivates the audiences of adventure
films, or the lure of unattainable sexual gratifications for devotees of
pornography? The "higher sentiments" of art films may cater to a highly
schooled audience, but that audience nonetheless consumes these films
in a quite conventional manner. They admire or disparage what they
take to be an authoritative cinematic representation. If the film con-
fuses them, they accuse it of obscurity (that is, of failing to be a suitable representation) or accuse themselves of insufficiency (that is, of
failing to be adequate to a representation that seems to lie beyond them).
Such responses are different in degree but not in kind from those accorded the mass-audience film where millions of viewers either child-
ishly eat with relish or spit out the images set before them on a tray.

Undeniably so-called masterpieces do test the limits of the system,
but the institution of cinema actually profits from such experimentation
and is rarely threatened by it. The art cinema troubles the system from
within; and, like the capitalist order which spawned it, the movies thrive
on adversity, struggle, and disturbance; they thrive on disenchanted and
rebellious artists. The shocks and tremors art creates are easily folded
back into its invigorated, always dominant, body.[17]

In deflating the pretenses of the art cinema, materialist critics do not
seek to uplift standard genre cinema on some sort of aesthetic teeter-
totter. Certainly the mechanisms of standard movies have been much
studied of late, but studied so as to warn us of their insidious snares
and of the deadly ideological message they repeat week after week.
The standard genre film can be equated with the "readerly text" ex-
coriated by Barthes in *S/Z*.[18] Such a text permits little audience mo-
bility as we are assigned our place in observing a spectacle unroll uni-
vocally before us. The audience is merely a relay in a process that finds
the text essentially reading itself. Our collusion is demanded as we put

together the logic of the narrative, identify with the proper characters, invest the text with conventional values, and appreciate the clever twists and turns it makes en route to a satisfying conclusion in which all questions are carefully put to rest.

No matter what the subject matter, this scenario of viewing is thought to have pernicious consequences for the spectator who passively laps up whatever comes down from on high. Even popular leftist films like those by Costa-Gavras *(Z, State of Siege, Missing)* are thought to be politically debilitating. Indeed, the leftist film really is just one more genre in the system, and a genre not far removed from the standard problem, or police film. Viewers are led to identify with spectacular heroes incarnated by noted actors such as Yves Montand. Seeking to reach the largest possible audience, Costa-Gavras necessarily subjects the spectator to that state of childish wonder always fostered by the readerly text. The assurance of the form contradicts the message of alarm and outrage that these films presumably want to transmit. There is no democracy in a system where the spectator pays $4.00 and sits in fascinated silence before a spectacle designed to entice him by its mise-en-scène, designed to route him through its narrative by a network of opposed characters, camera angles, glances, and master shots. Although he pays for it, the viewer is the plaything of the movies. Every maker of horror films knows that.

Instead of popular leftist films, the modern theorist far prefers the more complicated films of conservative filmmakers because they confront the limits of classical cinema.[19] For this reason the notorious *Cahiers du cinéma* essay on John Ford's *Young Mr. Lincoln* takes such an ambivalent stance toward this reactionary film. Like Georg Lukács before them,[20] they find more merit in the honest but serious work of the old guard than in the simple and self-righteous alternatives posed by leftists who adopt the traditional forms. Ford, and all important filmmakers in the tradition (the whole hagiography of the early *Cahiers* comes to mind here: Preminger, Hitchcock, Nicholas Ray, Douglas Sirk, Minelli, and so on), struggle to make the classic film system express ostensibly commonplace values, but in their best work they do so with such complexity and honesty that everything is put in jeopardy. In these films the genre (the Western, the family melodrama, even the musical) are made to bear more weight than they are capable of carrying. Genres, the traditional seat of solid values, develop cracks so that the savvy spectator returns home only partly reassured by the spectacle. A remainder in excess of the narrative gnaws at the genre and demands an "awful" interpretation, one that has potentially revolutionary consequences, for it throws the spectator into a radically liberated relation to the system which had previously engulfed him or her utterly.

Despite the preference shown for "difficult" films within the system, recent theorists refuse to follow the path of their progenitors at *Cahiers* in raising such films to an artistic plateau. No matter how complex and honest these films appear to be, they nevertheless can be only symptoms of the culture whose contradictions they inadvertently express. The most austere of these critics have always urged the total rejection of the pleasures of the classic cinema in any of its guises. Readings like those of *Young Mr. Lincoln* may set out to expose the contradictions inherent in the film, in the genre, and in the culture which both descend from, but they readily promote the pleasures of their own discoveries, contributing to a sense of the richness of the film, the genre, and the culture. No one can read, much less write, fifty pages on *Young Mr. Lincoln* or one hundred on *Touch of Evil* without thereby paying tribute to the auteurs who have mastered such a powerful system and spoken so densely through it.[21]

How can an avowedly political hierarchy be ruled by such clearly aesthetic concepts as density, complexity, and excess? Whereas some critics like Peter Wollen openly confess that aesthetic preference is an indispensable point of departure even for Marxist analysis,[22] most others solve this paradox by referring back to Barthes. The excessive film demands to be taken more seriously than the leftist narrative on the basis of the plurality of readings it opens up. The spectator (or at least the critic) is afforded an opportunity to multiply meanings, to compare and rework them. If these films receive undue attention it is only to help release their potential power, a power which is doubly subversive since it is lodged in the very seat of the genre system unable to contain them.

In Roland Barthes's breakdown,[23] the films of Ford, Sirk, Minelli, and company are "plural texts," seemingly coherent narratives which nevertheless invite and reward many, even contradictory interpretations. Much of the best theoretical work of the 1970's went into determining, not the range or relative importance of such interpretations, but the structure of a text that could support and guide them all. This at least was the avowed purpose of the *Cahiers* piece on *Young Mr. Lincoln* and Heath's essay on *Touch of Evil.*

But Barthes did not stop with the readerly and the plural text. His ultimate category was of course the writerly, that text which thumbs its nose at coherence, which obstreperously and boisterously subverts the very project of authoritative meaning. In the cinema the most rigorous and sustained efforts in this direction belong naturally to the experimental film, not to that wing of the avant-garde which grows out of American romanticism (the "visionary" tradition that P. Adams Sitney has surveyed)[24] but the structural-materialist film which has developed self-consciously alongside modern theory since the mid-1960's.

At the base of the structural-materialist movement of cinema is a belief that humans think with, or simply think, the symbol systems they are given rather than adapting those systems to their airy thoughts. The materiality of the sign system, then, is worthy of becoming the focus for a rigorous filmmaking practice eager to test the limits of film, to express its physical characteristics, and to allow those characteristics to shape our responses, our subjectivity. This at least has been the reason for the popularity of such difficult films as Snow's *Wavelength* and Murphy's *Print Generation;* the first film is based on the structural principles of the zoom shot, the second on the optical and chemical properties of film grain. Both films permit their obsessions to develop dramatically (Snow's ever-tightening zoom, Murphy's progression toward and away from complete representation), but it is as though the filmmaking process has expressed itself rather than the thoughts and feelings of a creator.

Now, in essays and films, the British have theorized precisely this notion of filmmaking to arrive at a more politicized view.[25] The crisis of representation and intelligibility into which such films throw the spectator is meant to lead him or her to a productive, rather than passive, relation with the film. In the first place this appears as a crisis of subjectivity for the spectator, who is no longer comfortably catered to by a film carefully groomed to that spectator's sense of logic, coherence, and vision.

In fact, Stephen Heath tells us, there are always three different types of subjectivity at work in a film, though we are conscious only of the unified ego served by the classic cinema.[26] Even before a film begins, the subject exists as "preconstructed" by the film's genre and by all the cultural notions that the film will knowingly invoke. The viewer can be expected to inhabit the film in just a certain way because of the fact of preconstructed subjectivity. "Construction" refers to the specific place eventually assigned to the viewer in any given filmed narrative. This is the ego function that finds itself comfortably placed in the classic cinema and angry or befuddled by the avant-garde. A final mode of subjectivity, and the one of most concern to modern theory, is that which Heath labels "passage." Every film, just because it exists in a temporal flow, shapes the spectatorial activity through variations of desire, anxiety, knowledge, contradiction, meditation, and so forth. From the perspective of much recent psychoanalysis, the passage of the subject through the event of the film is a far more comprehensive aspect of subjectivity than the stable ego constructed as a final resting place for the spectator. "Passage" indicates not just process, but hiddenness, tension, even contradiction. The ego feels unified and the classic film flatters this feeling by its own coherence, but the spectator arrives at such a feeling only after an intricate itinerary which the term "passage" is meant to define.

The structural-materialist film, Heath claims, is one which is concerned only with process. Preconstruction is neutralized in such films by their reduction of the number of recognizable objects and ideas (Gidal argues for a fully non-representational cinema, where perception must start from scratch).[27] In this way the spectator relies on few generic or cultural predispositions. The constructed subject (ego) is neutralized as well through the squelching of narrative and character identification. After all, in these films there is no "situation" about which one must take a "point of view." Thus "passage" alone remains, the subject acting consciously and unconsciously in relation to a flow of images and sounds, circulating in the symbolic chain without ever being pinned down. Such primal assaults on the very function of film viewing are thought to have the widest possible consequences in that they help produce an open, "playful" spectator, one ready to relinquish the stable world of received values and to construct new values, new meanings, even a new society, in a perpetual process of overturnings.

In the Oedipal drama of academic film scholarship it is fitting that the discourse surrounding such films should be arrogant and self-serving, especially when set off against the finely critical tone attached to the discussion of art or genre films. The far-reaching claims of this movement are tied to the belief that the films of the radical avant-garde are essentially "different" from that "sameness" we have been calling the system of the cinema. True, these films have irrevocably broken with standard signifying practice. As objects they are put together under different principles (for example, serialization and spatial sequencing, instead of cause/effect). But from the perspective of the whole economy of cinema do these films not replicate in miniature that which they hope to supplant? After all, they are representations produced for spectators, and like all such representations they may be (and have been) classed by genre. Arts magazines give them capsule reviews as they do to any type of film; they are advertised in newspapers (underground presses perhaps, but newspapers all the same); they are exhibited with other examples of the same genre in art theaters or on campuses to audiences who know what to expect. In short, spectators are aware of the work that will be required of them in these films just as they know what detective thrillers demand of them. Audiences for radical films may prefer process and multiplicity of meaning over narrative closure, but how radical is this difference in taste? Cinema in the largest sense of the term has always looked for new tastes to cater to. And since novelty has been central to the institution of genre, radical films perform an age-old function, renewing the language of cinema for a renewed audience.

In the struggle of ideas in film studies, the radical film appears feeble indeed. Modern theory may cheer for David over Goliath, but the structural-materialist mode seems destined to remain a closet hobby, satisfyingly abstract but ultimately disengaged from the problems of film history in our day.

Far more serious attention, however, has been accorded another branch of the avant-garde, a branch we may think of in terms of the narrative avant-garde or as the cinema of *écriture*. Doubtlessly modern theory is partial to the films of Straub/Huillet, Mulvey/Wollen, Oshima, and Duras because these filmmakers are serious and progressive critics themselves; but more to the point is the fact that the films they produce work with and on codes without utterly turning their backs on the history of cinema. Their films receive highest acclaim from Stephen Heath for the theoretical address they make to such basic issues as representation, identification, the function of the look of the camera, and the spectator. In a celebrated essay, Heath finds Oshima's *In the Realm of the Senses* to be a radical re-working of the best Hollywood examples of voyeurism.[28] Not only does Oshima put into question the conventional Hollywood movie, represented for Heath by the ironic overuse of Hollywood techniques in Ophuls's *Letter from an Unknown Woman,* Oshima also undercuts the so-called liberated use of the technique in Robbe-Grillet's films. Where Robbe-Grillet pushes cinema's voyeuristic tendencies toward explicit sadism (not changing, by the way, the basic representation of viewing and sexuality), Oshima has provided us with a new form of sexual representation altogether, one inspired no doubt by the feminist movement of the 1970's. The result is a complete reappraisal of viewing and of sexuality, amounting to a serious political stance.

Taking their cue from such cultural critics as Julia Kristeva (*Desire in Language*) and from the whole *Tel Quel* focus on *écriture* (the materiality of the sign and of all signifying practices), these films have brought into question the traditional separation of theory and practice.[29] It should not be surprising that feminist thought has fueled this mode of filmmaking, for at least one strain of feminism has been most concerned with altering not the explicit content of representations of the sexes, but the very forms of representation. Like the other films in this group, those of Chantal Ackerman, and of Yvonne Rainer, not to mention titles like *Dora* and *Thriller,* enter a theoretical debate at the same time that they stand up against other genres. Notable here is the essentially historical and dialectical nature of the projects of these films, as they respond to, by rewriting, conventional ways of portraying and commenting on males, females, and their social and psychological positions.

The texts of cinematic *écriture* are made to the measure of a new, or renewed spectator, one obsessed both with the history of cinematic and cultural codes while eager to play productively with them. This characterizes as well the best efforts of contemporary film theory.

FILM THEORY AS AN INSTITUTION

Whether it be the struggle of the avant-garde against Hollywood, or of an auteur against a genre, events in the field of film occur as an interplay of novelty and stability. The complexity of this interplay has a name: history. Not a sequence of events, history is rather the revaluation by which events are singled out and understood in successive eras.

When formalized, the concepts of stability and novelty can be defined as institution and change. Institutions are the sites of history because only within or against institutions does the process of revaluation run its course. While change may take place on the underside of culture, in the transmutation of species and the evolution of the earth, we dare not term these changes "events of history" without falling into some version of animism. On the other side of culture we may want to recognize moments of great personal alteration in religious, aesthetic, or affective life, but these in fact constitute the domain of madness or mysticism and are, by definition, outside history and beyond all scales of values.

Unquestionably the "events of 1968" mark a key moment in cultural history because they were directed at institutions. In film culture, as we have seen, contemporary criticism ordained a new canon of acceptable works; furthermore, it settled on a protocol by which to treat the various films it deems important enough to reckon with. Altogether these discriminations amongst objects and amongst responses to those objects constitute a revaluation of the field of film. Not only has this revaluation given us a new history of film, the event of modern theory is itself an important step in the development of the institution of film studies.

For the most part this development occurred self-consciously as young theorists expressly attacked the status quo, personified by Jean Mitry in theory, and by Mitry and Georges Sadoul in history. It is only when such attacks ignored the historical dimension of their discourse or directed that discourse at an inappropriate institution that their revolutionary fervor has appeared bombastic.

Heroic interventions in the discourse of any institution often assert themselves as standing beyond history, unconditioned and immutable. The rhetoric of fanatics is a full reminder of this. Yet it is surprising to discover a movement like contemporary film theory that is avowedly based on historical materialism loudly proclaiming its *essential* superiority over other theories, as though its arrival marked a final event in the development of the institution.

At its least responsible, contemporary theory sees itself as putting an end to the chorus of voices bickering over the value of this or that film, this or that view of film. Its own voice, we are asked to believe, has the final say not just because of its position at the end of a chain of views, but because it stands above that chain, looking down and placing views from its own privileged vantage point. This explains the presumptuous assertions of the editors of *Cahiers du cinéma* that theirs is not another interpretation of *Young Mr. Lincoln* but a reading of the film that will bring out the conditions under which any interpretation is possible.[30] *Cahiers*, as the forum of Marxism and modernism, does not replace older theories, it theorizes them from a position above them. Others are the playthings of history and ideology, but *Cahiers* speaks from an essential position, from knowledge.

While recognizing the rhetorical need of every movement to justify itself, indeed to assert its superiority to alternatives, we must be most suspicious of such claims. Contemporary theory has effectively reoriented the institution of film scholarship by redescribing the workings of film and art (focusing, as we have seen, on its ideological dimension). But the success of this endeavor should not blind us to the standard cultural function at work here. For every cultural movement reshapes the institution of which it is a part through redescription. This was as true of the formalists as it is of today's post-structuralists. Doubtlessly we have witnessed a crucial change in film theory over the past fifteen years; nevertheless, this change has taken place within, and as part of, an institution that outlasts the change. Film theory, in other words, like film genre, involves a perpetual interplay of fixity and alteration. When modernist theory sees itself as pure change, or as change authorized from outside the institution, it is a victim of the very sort of romantic myopia which it attacks in the formalists.

More often than not recent theory is content to understand its discourse as praxis rather than as pure philosophy. It has sought to level all films under genre and all genre under ideology in order to clear the terrain for a film practice which might protect itself and its viewers from the ideological. It has deconstructed the representational film so that the non-representational film may take its place. It has questioned the function of pleasure in cinema to make room for a cinema uncontaminated by the sexist consciousness of our culture. It has hoped to shatter spectacle to permit a productive play with signs as a first step toward a productive re-working of culture itself.

The rhetoric of Marxism and post-structuralism has clearly sought to be effective, to make changes. Its conquest of humanism and formalism within the institutions of the university and serious film journals is not, however, the conquest of criticism by theory or of soft values by hard knowledge. It is, like every cultural renovation or revolution, a shift from one set of values to another.

The modesty brought on by an historical rather than essential view of the project of film theory ought to comfort those radicals who feel betrayed that theory has not utterly revamped the entire film complex. Post-structural thought has completely dominated the institution of theory but has had little impact on the institution of filmmaking. The theoretical ground it has cleared swallows up the few non-representational and modernist films that have come to settle there. The partial autonomy of institutions explains the asymmetry of the double-pronged modernist attack on film culture: a powerful criticism literally rewriting the field of film theory and a pathetically minuscule film practice sitting like a bad conscience on the shoulders of the institutions of production.

Though we ought to expect some influence amongst institutions, it is misguided to expect a fallout from theory capable of revitalizing in a parallel way the other institutions of cinema. From the historical point of view this would not only be a utopian but a dangerous conception of theory which we have tried to describe not as a controlling institution but as one discourse amongst other parallel discourses.

Most theorists have fully understood this, realizing that theirs is a labor on the activities of reading, not of production. Whereas they may take responsibility for developing a theory of reading adequate to the modernist film, such a theory must extend beyond this one type of film to literature as a whole. Barthes's terms "readerly," "writerly," and "plural" effectively distinguish not texts but interpretations. Even though Barthes was a lifelong proponent of radical fiction from Robbe-Grillet to Sollers and beyond, his own critical activity happily stretched along a broad range of literature, literature which he neither denigrated nor paternalistically organized into a scheme. Literature was for him an opportunity for reading, for that special reading he called rewriting.[31]

Actually Barthes's categories effectively disentangle the types of criticism that have fought for supremacy in film studies. Critical discourse literally parallels the films it deals with when we think of standard film criticism as "readerly" promoting a journalistic appreciation that is complicit with the industry it hopes to foster. Academic criticism, then, would offer "plural" interpretations like the art films it most often treats, claiming thereby to avoid the meretriciousness of journalism by attending to the most lasting qualities of the most significant films. The final category, the "writerly," applies to *Cahiers* and all radical criticism after 1968. True to the model, radical film criticism promises to remain fully outside, on the margins of the institution.

At its most productive, modern film theory has gone far beyond its moralistic pigeonholing of works into complicit texts (standard or artistic) on the one hand and radical texts on the other. It has generated reading practices that have recovered for us a great number of films from even the weakest categories. Examine Thierry Kuntzel's deconstructive essay on a 1932 adventure film, *The Most Dangerous Game*.[32] In attitude this reading is fully consistent with the radical video experiments he was producing at the same moment. Kuntzel exemplifies the writerly attitude Barthes wanted to foster. In his essays and in his video production, Kuntzel's is always a work on codes, never a submission to or dismissal of them.

And Kuntzel is representative of the strongest direction in contemporary discourse about film. While one strain of such discourse has tiresomely characterized all but radical production as bourgeois or phallocentric or the like, most writing about even classic films has shown, and increasingly shows, attention to the subtleties of their historical context, discursive ambitions, and psychological undersides. With this attitude critics neither deride nor honor films; instead they work with (on) the codes which the films have intricately intertwined.

The function of the institution of film criticism is to attend to the discriminations within and among films. When criticism expands to a trans-historical, fully analytic vantage point it exposes its own anxiety in the face of films. Such pretentiously grand systems seek to net all films so that we might not be netted by them in turn; but this returns us, despite claims of dynamism, to a static structural model. A truly historical view of culture and of meaning must consider even this model to be just one more net thrown out to sea.

The institution of theory is always hermeneutic, always bound to context and to the texts of the past rewritten for the present. Having insisted on the process rather than the structure of texts, modern theory ought to treat itself in a similar manner. Not a governing discourse outside history and films, theory is exactly the process of rewriting our historical moment through films. Like genre, like the institution of the movies itself, film theory is a stable site crossed by continual re-evaluation. In its own way and in its own time film theory re-evaluates (revalues) the life of textuality, the power and function of texts. But this work of rewriting, because it is a writing, becomes at the same time part of the institution it changes and permits us in our turn to interpret it.

8

Identification

WHY PSYCHOANALYSIS?

Our earliest film theorist, Hugo Münsterberg, an eminent Harvard professor of psychology, declared that "the story of the subconscious mind could be told in three words: there is none."[1] A proponent of neo-Kantian rationalism, Münsterberg represents all those for whom the intelligibility of human action and motivation is a genuine project. To Münsterberg, and to most twentieth-century thinkers, intelligibility is by no means synonymous with logic or reason. But an activity might nevertheless be investigated and understood even though it lies outside what we think of as the rational. His *Photoplay: A Psychological Study* makes Münsterberg the first phenomenologist of the film experience.

Where a phenomenology strives to unveil the reason in human activity by attending in a special way to its surface manifestations, its arch-rival, structuralism, translates the surface features of a phenomenon into abstract terms which are then shown to bear a hidden logical relation. This relation in turn is capable of explaining the activity.

These two antagonistic approaches to the study of human life join forces in their interest in the underside of rationality (addressing topics such as ritual, sexual customs, and art) and in their confidence that this underside is comprehensible. Although they could not differ more on their criteria for understanding human life, neither approach sees any block standing in the path of intelligibility.

My own investigations of the cinema in this book have up to this point been in accord with these beliefs and goals, employing now one and now the other method. Filmic representation, for example, was described primarily in a phenomenological manner; narrative was treated structurally. Taken in isolation, films and the filmic system seem perfectly explicable, but, as the last chapter began to stress, films cannot be taken in isolation. Intentional objects, they involve the murky domains of ideology and psychology. In short, they involve "desire."

"Desire" is a term for which neither structuralism nor phenomenology has any use. Its entry into the field around 1970 indicates a need to invoke a new method, psychoanalysis, to help account for whatever is important about cinema. Always on the fringe of film theory, in this year psychoanalysis comes center stage to invite a complete redescription of the field.

Charles F. Altman chronicled this event by pointing to a shift in metaphors which theorists were compelled to fashion in their writing.[2] Most telling is a revitalized conception of the screen itself. Recall that in classical film theory two metaphors of the screen had vied for supremacy.[3] André Bazin and the realists championed the notion that the screen was a "window" on the world, implying abundant space and innumerable objects just outside its border. But to Eisenstein, Arnheim, and the formalists, the screen was a frame whose boundaries shaped the images appearing on it. The frame constructed meaning and effects; the window displayed them. As I have pointed out before, Jean Mitry holds that cinema's particular advantage and appeal lies in maintaining the implications of both these metaphors.[4] The cinema is at once a window and a frame.

Classical film theory could go no further. Only by shifting the discourse to another plane and invoking another system could modern theory develop. A new metaphor was advanced: the screen was termed a *mirror*. On the force of this coinage, new relations suddenly came to light and were for the first time open to systematic inquiry. Questions about the connections cinema maintains with reality and with art (window and frame, respectively) were subsumed under the consideration of cinema's rapport with the spectator. A new faculty, the unconscious, instantly became a necessary part of any overarching film theory, and a new discourse, psychoanalysis, was called upon to explain what before had been of little consequence, the fact and the force of desire. While earlier film theory could hardly have been blind to so conspicuous a concept as desire, and while, under auspices other than psychoanalysis, questions had been posed relating to viewer identification, plot lures, the dreamlike flow of images, and the function of pornography, only our more self-conscious age felt compelled to collect these haphazard ruminations into a set of categories involving a system larger than that of film, involving precisely the relation of two systems, that of the psyche and that of the cinema.

We can catalogue approaches to this expanded field of inquiry by adapting Christian Metz's famous breakdown from the first pages of his *Imaginary Signifier*,[5] focusing successively, and with increasing generality, on (a) the unconscious lives of filmmakers and spectators, (b) the persistence of fantasies within films, (c) the form of films as fantastic *per se*, (d) identification as the precondition for any fantasy whatsoever, and (e) general reflections on psychoanalysis and culture.

THE SECRETS OF CREATION AND RECEPTION

Although it is not a practice much in vogue today, the decipherment of the psychic complexes of directors through their films has been encouraged by such personalities as Bergman, Fellini, and Herzog. Indeed the entire auteur policy in film criticism follows this, the most venerable method descending to us from Freud, because it treats images and entire films as symptoms of the artist who signs his name to them.

Freud's essay "Creative Writers and Daydreaming" provides the justification for this method, and his lengthy study of Leonardo da Vinci is a model of its application.[6] The first of an enormous genre of critical writing, usually called "psycho-biography," Freud's "Leonardo" traces the art as psychic overflow back to its source in the structure and history of the mind creating it. It is apparent that to Freud the formal aspects of art make up only a kind of ornamentation or filigree around the central fantasies represented by the work as a whole. Indeed, he likens our interest in form to sexual foreplay which prepares us for the truly dislocating, orgasmic encounter with the fantasy. "I am of the opinion that all the aesthetic pleasure we gain from the works of imaginative writers is of the same type as this 'forepleasure,' and that the true enjoyment of literature proceeds from the release of tensions in our minds."[7]

Freud seemed unusually concerned with the place of such fantasies in the lives of those geniuses who gave them powerful though covert expression. What experiences in childhood and later life could have activated the fantasies? From what properties of the mind do they arise? Freud's obsession with exceptional men (Shakespeare, Michelangelo, Dostoievsky, and so on), probably tells us more about his personality than about his theories. Certainly we can only be tantalized by the image of the great man coming to grips with the most terrifying anxieties which beset the race, and we are equally fascinated to see the ordinary fears and foibles of this same great man exposed for all to see, almost in the fashion of the gossip column. In both cases we are brought closer to the gods of our culture.

In his better moments Freud avoided this vain competition with the famous men of history. His general psychoanalytic mission in fact goes in quite the opposite direction, demystifying the cult of the individual. Recent film theory, as a "critical theory," has been inspired more by Freud's distrust of institutions than by his obsession with the monuments of culture. Intrigued by, but skeptical of, religion, which he claimed arose as part of a struggle for social supremacy, Freud was likewise ambivalent about art and artists. He claims to want "to lessen the distance between their kind and ordinary human beings" by looking "in the child for the first traces of imaginative activity. . . . Now the writer does the same thing as the child at play; he creates a world of fantasy which he takes very seriously."[8] Art, he goes on to suggest, is a socially acceptable substitution for neurotic disclosures gilded in a form that masks this fact. While he had a clear respect for the "secrets of a creation" which give the poet access to the uncanny aspects of psychic life and make these aspects socially valuable, his is always a leveling theory. Just as he undermined the position of God the Father by returning authority to the psyche in the form of the superego, so in art his followers have debunked the parallel mystification of the artist "as a free conscious subject, the father of his works as God is of creation."[9]

When in Freud's era the philosopher George Santayana proclaimed that "God created the world so that Beethoven could compose the choral symphony," he meant, "God is dead; long live the greatness of man." But Freud went further than this, for his theories cast doubt not only on divinity but on man and his self-possession. Beethoven may have possessed extraordinary talent and courage; still these only mask and mediate the most ordinary human anxieties (fears of loss, infantile desires of fusion, and so forth). Man himself, without exception, is a bundle of conflicting needs and instincts. Even the greatest art represents this more than the mastery of humanity over itself and its conditions.[10]

Although he never pursued it himself, Freud's view leads directly to the social psychology of art. If genius is reduced to the level of the merely human, psychoanalysis ought now to specify the conditions governing artists and audiences in culture. This project has been increasingly popular amongst films scholars, for as a collaborative art form, and one so subject to cultural fads, the cinema would seem to demand studies focusing on the recipients rather than the creators of fantasies. Why are certain fantasies preferred in some cultures or subcultures? Why do particular individuals react so passionately for or against a given film?

The Freudian approach to aesthetic reception has been most ambitiously undertaken by Norman Holland, a scholar whose interest in cinema as well as literature makes him especially intriguing. Holland has, in fact, limited his recent investigations to mass art genres, particularly soft-core pornography, in an attempt to determine the vagaries of taste.[11] His argument is simple. Aesthetic value is measured as a relation between the core fantasy represented in a film and the particular psychic type of the spectator. Relying on the single hypothesis that "like attracts like," Holland matches up viewers and films.[12] Those viewers whose psycho-biographies indicate obsessions with oral fantasies, for example, will invariably prefer Fellini to Bergman. Holland uses viewer diaries to collect his data, supplementing these with reports of his own reactions and with film analysis.

The minimal attention that this approach pays to artistic labor (to the surface of the "work"), not to mention its crude determinism, has left most critics appalled by Holland's brand of Freudianism. Similar objections greet Jungian theories as well, though here personal psycho-biography is discounted in favor of the psycho-cultural study of those certain fantasies and images which are identified as intrinsically valuable. To Jung's followers, those films that richly incorporate such images are of unquestionable interest.[13]

In semiotic terms, both the Jungian approach and Freudian psycho-biography suffer from a fixation on a "transcendental signified." The very words "core fantasy" or "archetype" imply an imbalance wherein signifiers (the sensory surface of films) are touched upon only insofar as they deliver a particular timeless signified. Such a conception of art amounts to a profane theology in which film style plays a servile role. Few film scholars, even those with psychoanalytic proclivities, are attracted to such a model.

And so Freud's ideas seem to support two extreme and opposed traditions, neither of which is deemed satisfactory anymore: the sacred study of individual auteurs and the profane study of cultural obsessions. Both versions neglect the distancing and mediating power of art. Both hope to go quickly through art to something solid behind it in the individual or in culture. If Freud was more silent on art than he ought to have been, it was because he respected its complexity. While it is "related" to daydreaming, art employs "secrets" too deep for easy analysis. Those secrets lie not in the psyche of the artist nor in the collective obsessions of the masses but in the language of art itself. Anyone wishing to deal with the cinema psychoanalytically must, then, study not auteurs, nor audiences, but the cinema itself.

DESIRE IN THE TEXT

Those film scholars intrigued by psychoanalysis yet unwilling to pass so quickly through their treasured films to reach the mind of the filmmaker or viewer have another obvious object of study open to them, the stories told in films. Even a passing familiarity with Freud's techniques reveals the extent to which he was above all fascinated by stories and their exegeses. Indeed the psychoanalyst works exclusively on narratives of dreams rather than on dreams *per se*.

Earlier I described narrative and its study in a fully structuralist manner. Relying on Todorov's clearcut definition I observed that every narrative involves a storyteller who relates the changing status of characters and actions as the tale moves from an actual or implied moment of equilibrium to a different, terminal equilibrium.[14] Plot is triggered by an action or perception that opens a gap, a "lack" in the initial state, causing it to fall away from its balance and devolve into a sequence of remedial actions, detours, and shifting character relations on the path to a re-established steady state.[15]

Although structural methods create simulacra of these various aspects of narrative, they offer no motive for the existence of stories in general or of any particular story. The key term in their definition, the "lack" that propels the tale, bears an unmistakable relation to another system of discourse, that of psychoanalysis. Psychoanalysis proposes to explain tales, not just to describe them. It proposes to account for their power, for the value we place on them over and above their mere logic or intelligibility.

With the subheading "Desire *in* the Text" I mean to discuss that impulse in psychoanalysis that discovers and identifies the charged values scripted into movies. The following section, "Desire *of* the Text," treats film not as a place where fantasies are played out but as a fantastic discourse through and through. Whereas certain psychoanalysts address what is represented *in* discourse; others, relying on theorists like Lacan, address the unconscious *of* the discourse itself in its act of representing anything. This we shall encounter shortly.

The major precedent for the former type of study comes once again from Freud, only from a subtler side of Freud than the one obsessed with treating the artwork as a symptom of something within the artist which we can identify. To Freud the contents of the unconscious are truly inaccessible. Dreams and images themselves are only representations of the real forces giving rise to them, forces which are constitutionally repressed. In telling one's dream one constructs a representation of a representation. This is all the psychoanalyst has to work on, and this is precisely what makes his work similar to that of the critic. Dreams, dream reports, and artworks never succeed in presenting what is by definition repressed. Instead they create a substitute for it, a representation, which can be managed because it comes in the form of a discourse and is therefore open to inspection and to integration into the rest of the life of the subject.

Because their structures are similar Freud and many of his followers felt at ease in considering fictional tales alongside reports of dreams. One need only recall that the name for the most typical and profound dream report is borrowed from literature: the Oedipal drama. This exchange between literature and psychology goes both ways. Critics of novels and films trace the plots and characters of the fictions they study with the aid of psychoanalytic templates. Raymond Bellour's exhaustive treatment of *North by Northwest* exemplifies this method at its most compelling, while revealing, through its excesses, certain unavoidable limitations.[16] Entitled "Le Blocage symbolique," this essay paints Cary Grant as a modern Oedipus obsessed by a mother whose excessive attentions keep him from forming normal attachments to other women. This initial equilibrium is broken quite by accident when he is mistaken for another man and drawn into a tale of murder and espionage. This tale quite overtly involves his quest to find the proper father (the UN delegate who is killed early on, Van Dam, the suave but vicious ego ideal, and the wise and clever professor as the ideal ego).

Bellour ingeniously searches this script for clues in the form of props (the miniature shaving razor), witticisms, and strong figural images (the father Alfred Hitchcock climbing aboard a bus, the founding fathers of our country on whose stoney faces is played out the final conflict). In this way the internal logic of this film, a film audiences intuitively find compelling, is shown to be one with the logic of the Oedipus story, of its innumerable avatars, and of the psychological complex which would seem to motivate all of them.

Bellour's is a highly elaborate version of a common project in criticism in that it seeks the psychological complexes underlying and motivating the arrangement of events and the behavior of characters in fictions. As immediately satisfying as such studies are, joining two prime but veiled dimensions of our humanity (art and the unconscious), Freud himself cautioned against their proliferation.

In his only major foray into the realm of literary criticism proper, "Dream and Delusion," he chose to work on a minor tale largely because in it the character himself reports his dream life.[17] This particular story is in fact a direct representation of the psychoanalytic situation, complete with transference and cure. It was obviously open to Freud's customary methods.

But what of other types of stories? Here the master was less sanguine. Most characters cannot be readily analyzed. Insofar as their motives can be said to exist at all, they reside in the aesthetic of an author who is not available to discuss them. It is misguided for critics to treat a clearly "secondary" discourse (that of a tale designed according to rules of logic, genre, and style) as though it were a dream or a primary datum of the unconscious.

Paul Ricoeur has gone much further in his critique of this impulse. Even though he accepts the fact that artworks (novels, operas, and films) share with dream reports and with dreams themselves the function of representing human wishes and fears, he refuses to believe in their interchangeability. An essential asymmetry exists between art and fantasy such that "one can go from the work to the fantasy; one cannot find the work in the fantasy.''[18] Thus, while artworks may well signal the return of the repressed, just as do dreams and fantasies, art manages this situation in a peculiar way that the culture values beyond other ways. In short, all Oedipal dreams are at a certain level interchangeable. You dream your version; I dream mine. But neither of our dreams can be satisfactorily substituted for the version Sophocles succeeded in dramatizing in the fourth century before Christ.

Perhaps now we can understand our misgivings about criticism such as Raymond Bellour's. The epigraph preceding his analysis of *North by Northwest,* an epigraph ascribed to Barthes, insists that all novels are ultimately the story of Oedipus.[19] For Bellour to conclude after pages of close analysis that the Hitchcock film is indeed a re-working of *Oedipus Rex* is not only self-fulfilling, it is patently reductive. Although he has ingeniously demonstrated certain strategies of detour and thrust peculiar to the cinema's re-working of this standard psychological complex, he provides no means to distinguish the value of Hitchcock's version over against *Hamlet* or *Parsifal* or any of the countless other narratives that bear this fantasy. Not only are the differences amongst artworks thereby flattened, all versions are explicitly grouped under a transcendental drama (the true psychic complex) which Bellour evidently believes motivates all its avatars.

Tzvetan Todorov aptly points to the hidden theological project which this sort of criticism exhibits.[20] No real difference, he suggests, separates medieval exegesis from this branch of psychoanalytic reading. In the Middle Ages stories of all sorts were interpreted via the fourfold hermeneutic (literal, symbolic, analogic, and anagogic) until each spoke the same fundamental themes. We might go so far as to say that in the Middle Ages all stories were one story, that of the fall of man and his rescue through the sacrifice of Christ on the cross.

Today the theology has changed, but the hermeneutic enterprise remains intact. Today all stories seem to speak one fundamental condition: a tale of infancy, of successive preoccupation with the parts of the body, and then with the primitive social relations (the mother and the family) which every human subject discovers and constructs. The subsequent history of each subject is determined by this template and the shape of all representations of that history, that is, of all stories, must be congruent with it as well.

Todorov is no apostate; nor is Ricoeur. Doubtless both subscribe to the Freudian faith in the importance of childhood and its traumas. Yet both profess reservations about a purely psychoanalytic criticism of narratives. To Todorov the complex surface differences of artworks get lost as soon as psychoanalysis is brought in to explain them. To Ricoeur there is no logical reason for according one version of life and behavior primacy over all other versions. Psychoanalysis, he points out, is nothing other than an abstract representation drawn from dream reports. Criticism like that of Bellour's succeeds in demonstrating the relation of one kind of representation (a film) to another (*Oedipus Rex,* or the Oedipal Complex detailed by Freud). But such criticism goes wrong when it insinuates, or works from the assumption, that today's artworks are truly based on an original formula tied to real conditions.

Neither Sophocles nor Freud discovered, or claimed to have discovered, the thing itself against which we must measure all other shadowy narratives, because psychoanalysis itself consists solely of stories and interpretations. In this respect it is on a par with literature, not prior to it. Furthermore, as will be argued later, artistic stories are oriented not to our infancy, as is psychoanalysis, but to our future. This has been Ricoeur's message: art stands before us shaped into a fully constituted structure which bears not only a relation to the eternally repressed, but to a history of meaning, a history which is not as yet complete. Art is a public discourse, and it is one that consists not just in dissimulation (masking the repressed) but in transforming representations in culture. Through interpretation we all participate in this project.[21]

Such an attitude amounts to a substantial advance over that crasser Freudian view, initiated by Freud himself it must be granted, holding artistic form to be mere forepleasure preparing the way for the unspeakable impact of unconscious wishes. To Freud and his first followers, and to most popular psychoanalytic critics today, artistic form is essentially a disguise.

One analogy makes art a ritual of smuggling. The artwork conceals inside its lovely but deceptive form the unconscious wishes which constitute its true value. Like pornography, drugs, or diamonds, it must slip past the customs agents both in its native country (the author's censoring faculty) and in the country of its destination (the defenses of the audience). Disguised as art, these wishes invade the psyche of the audience which is unaware of its true desires. When asked for their feelings about a film, spectators praise or damn its form ("I did not care for the editing"; "the character relations were intricate and real").

But all this is merely displaced discourse hovering around, but unable to mention, that which is paramount in the experience. Film analysts exemplify this situation at its limit when they spend weeks pouring over every detail of a treasured film without being able to utter, or even recognize, what motivates their interest.

Ricoeur's is only one of many voices to be outraged by this view which makes art nothing other than a bearer of fantasies. If we truly value the *work* performed in an artwork, we must make room for style and tradition without discarding Freud's central belief that art mediates the unconscious in a special way.

DESIRE OF THE TEXT

The reductionism we have scorned in so much psychoanalytic criticism can nevertheless render a synoptic view of narrative leading to a profitable psychoanalysis of style. The temptation to conflate all stories under a limited number of myths (Oedipus has been our example) arises only because the very act of telling a story involves certain essential psychic features which we can describe stylistically.

All stories proceed by a flow that aims to fill a lack. The storytelling ritual is a universal phenomenon because of the constitutional emptiness in experience, what before psychoanalysis was called "the human condition." Stories satisfy our need to sense the filling of a lack and the achievement of stasis. How that lack is identified (as a maiden, a father, a treasure, an integrated view of the past, or whatever) is of less moment here than how it is managed in narrative. For stories, while seeking a timeless goal ("happily ever after"), are in fact defined by the opposite of stasis, by flow, change, and interaction. In this context we might add incidentally that the flow of film in its basic perceptual mode necessarily prepares the way for its narrative dimension, explaining perhaps the primacy of narrative over other forms of film.

Film narrative, indeed narrative in general, is fueled by and satisfies to varying degrees the unconscious drives of its audience. This fact is prior to the incidental one that certain plots and characters represent or replicate basic psychoanalytic situations. To put it formulaically, desire represented *in* the text is but a specialized subset of a more pervasive thrust, the desire *of* the text.

To treat films as mechanisms of desire is to involve directly their formal aspects and hence the category of style. Instead of enumerating and interpreting motifs, as do the psychoanalysts of plot, we can explore the way any film (and every film) creates dams and detours, and sustains viewer identification and psychic valences. The film experience resembles a fun house attraction, a wild ride, the itinerary of which has been calculated in advance but is unknown to the spectator. By spurts and stops, twists and roller coaster plunges, we are taken through a dark passage, alert and anxious, yet confident we shall return satisfied and unharmed.

As might be expected, the study of this process has depended almost entirely on the Hollywood cinema, even on the lower echelon genre cinema. Where else are we more clearly authorized to explore the general lure of the movies? Thierry Kuntzel's ingenious analysis of *The Most Dangerous Game* exemplifies this critical stance at its best.[22] A thoughtless and hurried production, this film nonetheless partakes of certain universal patterns which cannot but involve the spectator. What its authors designed it to mean or do is inconsequential, for if the unconscious is structured like a language, then even a banal use of cinematic language will exemplify the thrust, repression, and detour of meaning. Kuntzel's prime insight concerns the opening of this, and by extension, every film. In its credits and expository sequence *The Most Dangerous Game* assaults the spectator with the force of the primary processes. As yet undisciplined by the logic of narrative or argument, the opening minutes expose the film's unconscious in a particularly direct way.

Not only does the iconography of the credits (an ornate door knocker featuring a wounded centaur holding a woman) assault us baldly, but the primitive action represented in the credits (a hand grabbing the knocker and rapping thrice) is a direct exemplification of the narrative drive itself. Even before it has been identified as belonging to the hero, we cannot help but identify with this hand calling at the door. As Kuntzel brilliantly demonstrates, the film is nothing other than a series of doors knocked upon and entered. The drive to enter into the unknown and the forbidden constitutes its true and final meaning, rather than any particular discovery behind the door or in the text.

The precise mechanism of entry into this film involves a series of reversals based on the initial expository scene. The security of the experts aboard a ship, their gentlemanly conversation concerning the superiority of man over beast, and even the stable horizontal compositions are fractured in an instant when the ship founders on a reef. Suddenly confidence turns to panic, the stuffed fish in the stateroom are replaced by man-eating sharks, and the horizontal normalcy of the narration splinters into fragments each of which represents the falling away of stability. Vertical movement in virtually every shot drills a gaping hole in the equilibrium of the narrative, representing precisely the return of the repressed (the figure of a man as beast, of beast as prey, and finally of woman, not fish or game, as trophy).

The succeeding tale is merely an elaboration of the values and anxieties laid out and fissured in this first sequence. Kuntzel is at pains to demonstrate not only the relationship of the plot to the iconography of the film's first moments, but the essential universality of the film's obsessions. Although the episodes of hiding and hunting make up fully 80 percent of the film, they represent, in a logically elaborated format, the selfsame complexes articulated in the single image of the wounded centaur bearing off the virgin, especially as this image is dramatized by the hand that enters it to knock at the door.

Kuntzel's conclusion follows that of the film. The final portal, the underwater gate, leads the hero and heroine away from the terrifying island and back in their rowboat to the universal sea of life. This film, like all standard films, results in a re-establishment of its initial conditions. Above all, it represents the desire to open doors, to go through films, to go on to the next film.

In achieving a vision of the overall mechanism of the movies at the end of his study, Kuntzel justifies the title of his essay, "The Film Work." *The Most Dangerous Game* is meaningful not in itself but as an example of a process which recurs ritualistically. In 1932 the spectator came out of it anxious to see another film the next week; in 1984 the analyst moves on from this film to study further examples: *M, Touch of Evil, Young Mr. Lincoln, Morocco.*[23]

Of course the film scholar differs from the spectator in seeking a representation of the film experience in general. Like psychoanalysis itself this mode of criticism thrives on the interplay between close readings and broad conjectures. Without his having chronicled so many dreams and case studies, Freud's theories would not only be less seductive, they would be empty, impossible. So Kuntzel, Heath, and other theorists find that the way to the heart of the film system leads through the labyrinths of its products.

If the workings of films (the "film work" as Kuntzel calls it, "the desire of the text'' in our language) seem known in such a flimsy and speculative way when compared even to what psychoanalysts know of the workings of the mind, we must blame the paucity of close readings of films especially when compared to the rich materials collected and analyzed by Freud and his followers. Still the impulse to uncover as quickly as possible the psychic underside of narrative cinema is understandable. In this arena Stephen Heath's publications have been seminal. Not only has Heath contributed intricate studies of individual films (most significantly his immense essay on *Touch of Evil*), but his knowledge of recent trends in art history, literary theory, and psychoanalysis gives him the background needed to erect with some authority a full account of the hidden functions and functioning of films. The titles of his two broadest essays, ''Narrative Space'' and ''On Screen, in Frame,'' aim to address the very basis of cinematic organization.[24] Why do films unroll the way they do? What kind of space expands and contracts before the viewer? Furthermore, what kind of viewer craves to dream within such space?

Heath's inquiry takes him deep into the prehistory of cinema as he searches for the prime ideological functions latching onto the new invention of the movies. Delving as far back as the Renaissance and the appearance of easel painting, Heath sees cinema as the last in a series of inventions designed to provide the spectator with a centered and continuous view of a scene or an action. Pierre Francastel and John Berger pointed out the implications of such a spectatorial position long before Heath when they associated visual ''mastery'' with private property and indicated that perspectives, if not actual paintings, might be possessed.[25]

This secularization of the function of art was propelled by the camera obscura and seemed to culminate in the still camera. The camera eye represents the eye of each spectator at the center of an organized world. In this context cinema at first might appear a disrupting invention, for it bears with it mobile framing and a temporal dimension, both of which can trouble the omniscient eye of the spectator. It is here that narrative arrives to humanize time and space and to recover in this new medium the age-old mimetic function of art.

Heath's essay invites us to rethink the potentials of cinema from scratch. To start with, our conception of framing depends entirely on the spectator's position vis-à-vis the narrative demands of the text. The permanence of screen size (except for a few notable exceptions together with the now forgotten tradition of "masking") bends all images into a consistent pattern of lines of force measured out by the narrative. The story maps the way any field can be viewed, making objects and characters a dramatic tableau. Whereas early films were constructed largely as a series of tableaux, a higher unity than that of scenic space began to break these tableaux into scenes and angles. In this way the demands of narrative, of storytelling and comprehension, overcame the initial impulse to fix the spectator before the event photographed.

Now with the fragmentation of scenic space came the danger of visual anarchy. To maintain order, the 180-degree rule contrived to keep the mobile camera (and with it, the spectator) on the proper side of the screen, hiding the mechanism of photography in the process. Other cutting rules, such as the 30-degree minimum shift, eyeline matching, field/reverse field patterns, and so forth, rapidly developed to create a spiderweb of relations capable of allowing the viewer to maintain mastery over the constantly unrolling fragments. As Heath points out, even off-screen space was contained with point-of-view shots and with the subordinate role assumed by the soundtrack. One can add to this the effects of independent camera movement, of subjective or authorial excesses (spinning cameras, cocked angles, slow motion, freeze frames, and even shifting film stock). All such tricks are organized for the spectator under the rubric of narrative. In short, the properties of perspective keep the viewer at the center of every image, while the resources of visual tricks and editing permit the spectator, rather than the space on the screen, to become the figure of continuity holding the entire film together across time.

The psychoanalytic context behind Heath's discussion of narrative film comes to the foreground in his essay "Sexual Difference." [26] But it is surely Laura Mulvey's "Visual Pleasure and the Cinema" that has most explicitly and influentially joined the domains of psychoanalysis and film stylistics. [27] The traditional narrative cinema, she states, invokes and satisfies the scopophilic drive through the obvious voyeurism of the theater situation. At the same time it appeals to the ego drive of narcissism via the enlarged figures with whom we identify on the screen. These correlated impulses come together in the standard film where a passive female star, who is fetishistically costumed and highlighted, serves as the object of both the gaze and the action of a male hero. We identify with this hero and through him take our pleasure at the movies.

Mulvey convincingly argues that all the elements of the mise-en-scène are deployed to light up the field of action like a pinball machine, ringing up values and bonuses which differentiate the characters, objects, and events depicted. The narrative cinema is designed precisely to exploit the characteristics of our psychic life, most prominently the valences of sexual difference which obsess us. All the resources of the cinema function to promote the pleasures associated with such obsessions and the still greater pleasure of our security that these obsessions are natural, that the fictions of cinema mirror the facts of life.

Although Mulvey's thesis has met with strong opposition, and although she and others have reformulated many of her assertions,[28] few theorists object to the direction of her thinking. She and Heath, after all, are merely generalizing from the results of close textual analysis. Recall that Kuntzel could properly conclude the study of a single film with a meditation on the desire to see and know. The hand that knocks thrice on the door of *The Most Dangerous Game* is first and foremost our hand, even though it may later be identified as that of the hero. It is we who seek entry into the closed world behind which the Other is master. Forever blocked, or rather held off, from this primal scene, we enter the door only to find another in our way. Desiring to possess the film, we are confined merely to viewing it. Consequently, the successful film can never ultimately satisfy us; rather, it rewards our passion to see by offering us still more to see until we are thrown beyond the bounds of its narrative space and out into the queue waiting for the next film to light up on the screen, to light up in the cavern of our psyches.

THE MACHINERY AND MECHANISM OF IDENTIFICATION

We have pursued the psychoanalytic dimension of cinema from its most obvious but local appearance as embodied in plots and characters to its more general existence in the ritual of storytelling itself. Beyond this we have seen that psychoanalysis offers us a privileged way of accounting for the extraordinary lure, the pleasure, of standard films by redescribing cinematic technique as "the film work." This is Hollywood's software which programs spectators while it programs films.

Yet even here we have not reached the end. Not only can the shape and techniques of film be understood psychoanalytically, but so also can the very technology of the medium together with its function in culture. This step, the ultimate one, was taken first by Jean-Louis Baudry[29] and then followed with far more care by Metz in the title essay of *The Imaginary Signifier.*

Both these theorists agree with Heath that the moving pictures as a technology and an institution achieve their goals through the centering of the spectator. It is the spectator's eye, or rather the deficiency of that eye, that creates the illusion of movement across the twenty-four breaks per second constituting the basis of film. It is this same spectator who organizes the fragments of each film into a narrative unity. In short, for Heath, Baudry, and Metz, identification with characters and stories is based on an identification with the process of viewing itself and ultimately with the camera which views.

Here arises the analogy of the screen as mirror which has propelled the advances of recent theory. Our fascination with films is now thought to be not a fascination with particular characters and intrigues so much as a fascination with the image itself, based on a primal "mirror stage" in our psychic growth. Just as we were, when infants, confronted with the gloriously complete view of ourselves in the mirror, so now we identify with the gloriously complete presentation of a spectacle on the screen. What that spectacle concerns is second to the power we exercise over its presence as a centered and continuous set of images. Metz puts it most forcefully:

> As he identifies with himself as look, the spectator can do no other than identify with the camera too which has looked before him at what he is now looking at and whose stationing (= framing) determines the vanishing point. During the projection this camera is absent, but it has a representative consisting of another apparatus called precisely a "projector." An apparatus the spectator has behind him, *at the back of his head,* that is, precisely where fantasy locates the "focus" of all vision.[30]

From this it follows that in the cinema perception and representation must become confused, occasioning a regression to "an hallucination" where all wishes are satisfied. The primary wish, Metz and Baudry argue, is to be master of what is before one, to see and thereby possess it all.[31]

Just as he seems prepared to make the most outrageous claims for the psychic basis of cinema, Metz characteristically steps back to question himself. The mirror analogy breaks down at one crucial point: in the cinema one is able to see everything except onself, whereas a mirror exists precisely for self-reflection. Equally troubling, Metz must note that the mirror stage belongs properly to the psyche's pre-symbolic era, a moment when it is locked into primary relations with itself (narcissism) and its immediate other (the mother, later the image in the mirror). Cinema, as cultural institution, is by definition a symbolic system, mediating the spectator and the world in countless exchangeable ways.

But Metz refuses to let these problems puncture his central observation: the pleasure derived from viewing films is related to that primitive pleasure the subject attained when sight first gave to it a sense of mastery over itself and its environment. For convenience psychoanalysts have located the essence of this narcissistic moment in the recognition of the self in the mirror. Viewing cinema, then, is a special type of symbolic behavior distinguished by its essentially regressive character. Thus is the film image bifurcated: it is an "imaginary signifier." In relation to the spectator it links two distinct realms of the psyche. In relation to the world it figures the presence of an absent object.

Metz lodges the specificity of cinema right here in the peculiarity of its image. He supports this designation of the image in numerous ways. In the chapter entitled "The Fiction Film and Its Spectator: a Metapsychological Study," he reserves for cinema a special place in the psychic life of man.[32] Enumerating the preconditions of the film experience (the solitude in darkened room, the common ingestion of food, the erotic milieu of the theater itself), Metz tests the analogy between film and dream. Ultimately he links film with daydream or fantasy in which a certain narrative logic makes believable the desires and fears we represent to ourselves. Through weakened motor activity, our imaginations are heightened and prepared to engage in the work that the machinery of the imaginary signifier was invented to perform.

Psychoanalytic theory can go no further than this, for the "basic cinematic apparatus" as well as the social institution of "going to the movies" are here put at the mercy of unconscious and preconscious factors.

PSYCHOANALYSIS AND THE PROBLEM OF MEANING

What kind of film experience has Metz attempted to describe? Although he hopes to have encompassed the full range of possibilities inherent in the fictional mode, it is clear that his analysis departs from and returns to a single type of fiction: namely, the all-engrossing experience characteristic of our childhood days at the movies. Metz barely masks his obsession with this lost experience, frequently criticizing his work as nostalgic and festishistic. With childhood film experiences taken as the paradigm of all fictional cinema, it is no wonder that a concept like that of "the imaginary signifier" should come to dominate his theory, and that this theory should stress the hallucinatory lure of the movies.

The regression to childhood which Metz feels every fiction film promises explains his interest in the mechanics of "spectator positioning." At the movies the adult viewer is treated like a child, ordered to sit passively before the screen and to function as a relay for the images appearing there. The film is a world made present to this spectator who is locked into a primary relation with the recording camera. Evidently Metz's ideal movie, the one he pines for though distrusts, is the speakerless dream which arises of its own accord. Such a film is more "world" than "text," engendering more primary effects (sensory and psychological) than meaning.

But how typical are such oceanic experiences at the movies? Without discarding its evident illusionism, let us focus for a moment on the cinema as text, that is, on the cinema as a constructed representation whose discursive properties address an audience in a highly mediated way. Whenever this discourse overruns what it represents, the spectator must give up the delicious childish daydream and become actively involved in building the meaning of the film. Irony is the most potent way of shocking viewers to life, since it results from a break between the "saying" and the "said." In the cinema we sense this break between a story and its presentation every time gaps appear in the events or reversals crop up in the standard conventions of the genre. Other figures bring the viewer out of the passive ingestion of images in other ways. The excesses of mannerism, for instance, or the laconic side-by-side portrayal of opposites force the presence of the narrator to be felt. Everything, in short, which calls attention to the work of style retards the unmediated flow of illusion and lifts the film experience from the obsessions of the imaginary to the realm of symbolic exchange.

To focus on the symbolic dimension of the film experience, on the film as a text exchanged and worked on, utterly alters the conception we have developed about the situation of the viewer. No longer silent voyeurs, peeping at a spectacle which is oblivious to our gaze, we as spectators of the ironic film find ourselves directly addressed. Explicitly exhibitionist, a film such as *Singin' in the Rain* drapes itself in a style meant for our eyes and dependent on our response. Whereas Metz's fictional film involved the spectator only as a hollow at the center of a fully enclosed world, satisfactory in itself, the text which features narration, the "dialogic text," requires spectator participation in the form of laughter, recognition, and so on.[33] Nearly all film comedy is based precisely on this model, as are musicals and most modernist cinema. The stories of such films may certainly engage our fancies, but they are mediated in a narrational exchange or transaction.

The psychoanalytic aspects of such transactions are by no means trivial. Indeed their very complication casts suspicion on Metz's blanket metapsychology which has the tendency to erase distinctions between cinematic texts and stylistic strategies. As the next chapter is designed to show, the psychic dimension of cinematic meaning is paramount but only as regulated and shaped in cinematic discourse. Such discourse includes at the very least the language of the medium, the context in which the film is made and seen, and the particular psychic drives of the filmmakers and viewers. No over-arching theory could ever be adequate to the essentially historical complexities of this phenomenon. Metz's essays rid cinema of these complexities by returning to a primal situation, the childish infatuation with the perfect illusion of a charged world before its eyes. But history and discourse, factored out of this situation, have a way of returning to question the general applicability of Metz's thesis.

Nevertheless his theory is attractive for all that, perhaps because of its too simple opposition between story and narration. Thought of one way, as stories, films seem only to haunt the imaginary; thought of another way, as discourse, they address the symbolic. We might say that all films operate in some ratio of force to meaning, where force emanates from the cauldron of the unconscious and meaning persists in the conscious constructs of culture.

The relationship of force to meaning is in fact the primary problem for psychoanalysis; and it shows itself with special clarity in the realm of art, for representations are precisely the point of juncture where force pushes toward meaning. In this vocabulary Metz obviously accords to force a primary reality of which meaning is only a deflected and blurred refraction. Films chart the production of a battered sense churned in the seas of the instincts. Hence his self-limiting attitude in describing the work of film analysis as a deviation (a fetish) which circles back to recover the primitive (more real) experience of being engulfed by the movies.

In treating the force of illusion in the cinema as more essential than the exchange of a tale between a narrator and a spectator, Metz follows the lead of Freud himself. Whenever he was confronted by a practice or an institution bearing an alliance between the private and the public (and art is perhaps the prime example of this), Freud inevitably threw his weight on the private. The public or cultural manifestation of religious, artistic, or social phenomena he inevitably saw as a symptom of something prior and more basic.

What is often forgotten is that the endeavor of psychoanalysis itself is as subject to the private/public ratio as are other, less self-conscious institutions. In his daily work Freud rewrote the life of the instincts in a progressive, enlightened, scientific discourse. This discourse could be nothing other than a displacement of the more direct trajectory of the unconscious forces it dealt with; yet Freud, and an immense medical establishment born after him, profess faith in the therapeutic value of this cultural displacement. Institutions, then, at least as exemplified by those of art and psychoanalysis, organize and interrelate the chaos of the unconscious by rerouting the drive of the instincts onto the road toward conscious goals (the goal of the perfectly formed work in art and that of scientific knowledge in psychoanalysis).

In taking the part of the unconscious, Metz follows Freud's metapsychology and its proto-structuralist orientation. For the contents of dreams, the behavior of patients, and the history of culture (like the content of films and the stuff of their history) matter to these thinkers only as exemplifications of a system of instincts and energy which Freud termed "the indestructible."[34] It is not surprising, therefore, to find that Metz and structuralists like him inevitably work back to a single system no matter what facets of the cinema or its history arise in discourse. The bare system is seen to generate all human behavior and might be thought of as the transcendental signified of every instance of human meaning.

But Freud's own practice offers an alternative to his voracious metapsychology. While never fully tethering his urge to concoct abstract theories of the psychic system, Freud did proceed with equal seriousness on what can only be called a hermeneutic path. The interpreter of dreams, of art, of behavior, Freud taught us to question our most deeply held theories in the face of texts that cry out for discussion.

At his best Freud was suspicious of every metapsychological framework he constructed, returning again and again to the surface behavior he felt it his job to engage. This surface (words, images, institutional practices) is exactly what makes up culture and the sphere of the public. The relation of these to the drives of the unconscious is by no means resolved by a metapyschology which is, after all, just one more representation.

The hermeneutic endeavor is no less psychoanalytic than a structural metapsychology, but it is less final. Every interpretation is based on displacement, since the interpreter redirects the original object by inserting it into a new frame of reference. We may see art as a displacement of certain fundamental energies of the psyche, or a particular film as a remolding of a psychic complex within the tradition and language of cinema. Film theory and criticism are further displacements, for they work not on original fantasies or psychic structures but on textual displacements of fantasies, on films and on the cinema.

Insofar as psychoanalysis supports hermeneutics, it does so by insisting on an "interminable analysis."[35] A text, be it a film, a religious ritual, or the report of a dream, makes sense not in itself but only to someone and from a certain perspective. Other people may focus on different textual elements from an altered perspective and construct a different sense from the same text. A person may even change perspectives; in fact this is precisely what Freud sought in his therapy. The patient represents a dream or a state for the analyst who, through the interjection of an interpretation, re-establishes the same representation in a new context, permitting a transference of discourses. In this way the patterns of the unconscious modify themselves in relation to the dialogue between patient and analyst. Thus the knotty private condensations of the psyche are socialized through a work of representation and interpretation.

As a philosophy of suspicion, psychoanalysis is often suspicious of itself and its own constructs. Certainly Freud relied heavily on his variously stated beliefs in the workings of the psyche (id/ego/superego, unconscious/preconscious/conscious, pleasure/unpleasure/reality, and so forth), but as his replacement of one construct by another indicates, he was not fully satisfied with any of them. Especially as his theories drew near to cultural issues he seemed beset by gnawing hesitations. Paul Ricoeur condenses these problems in Freud's inability to deal with sublimation.[36] How is it that an artist may respond to certain obvious psychic complexes by creating something in the discipline of art? Unable to consider art either part of the repressive machinery of culture or a deviation such as fetishism, Freud despaired of answering the riddle of creativity.

From the hermeneutic point of view we might say that sublimation offers an exit from the reductive psychoanalysis that has been unwilling to deal with history and culture. Culture, as the repository of civilization's values and lessons, is not only at the mercy of psychoanalysis; it is in dialogue with that "science." Freud needed a cultural product, *Oedipus Rex,* to understand and represent aspects of the unconscious. On the other side, culture, as the public life we share together, has profited from the definition given it by psychoanalysis which treats it, on the whole, as a displacement of the psyche.

Here the relations become inextricably entangled. For psychoanalysis questions the status of culture and of meaning in its search to discover the dynamics of experience. But how can this drive toward meaning (a drive represented as a psychic displacement) be accounted for by the discourse of psychoanalysis which is itself meaningful and cultured?

From the standpoint of hermeneutics we are as condemned to meaning as we are to instinct. Culture is a necessity, not just a deviant outgrowth of some deeper reality. Art stands in a peculiar position within this conundrum. Ricoeur reminds us that, as the product of culture and desire, art actually becomes a new reality consisting of body (its physical form and energy) and spirit (its call for interpretation and its promise of a different sort of knowledge and wisdom).[37]

In the framework of hermeneutics there can be no talk of a reality at the base of everything; there can be only forms and our views of them, configurations and interpretations. Another era would indeed have called this "body and soul." In our era art, more than any other activity, and cinema, more than any other art, brings us to this realization. For cinema exists as a haunted body, a physical force that pushes toward meaningful representation, demanding from us both experience and interpretation. As the art most deeply obsessed with the psychoanalytic, cinema reminds us that art and psychoanalysis are not so much spheres of knowledge as activities. In the cinema they join together in a particularly fascinating way.

9

Figuration

FIGURES AS EVENTS OF DESTRUCTURATION

In pointing toward a hermeneutics of film, psychoanalysis seconds the project already indicated at the end of our discussion of semiotics.[1] There we discovered connotation to be the congenital condition, if not of language in general, at least of artistic language and assuredly of imagistic discourse like the cinema. Psychoanalysis makes the primacy of interpretation over structural analysis even more obvious, because its notion of the sign is truly radical. Although connotation seriously complicates the originally pristine Saussurian description of the sign as an invariable relation of a signifier to its signified, Roland Barthes and other critics nevertheless were optimistic in their belief that, if cleverly employed, the circuitous techniques of etymology, rhetorical analysis, and so on could ultimately restore to intelligence the thrust of every sign, no matter how involuted. Psychoanalysis dashes this hope by severing forever the relation of signifier and signified. Certainly signs do indeed involve unconscious signifieds, but this involvement proceeds by a logic unavailable to standard analysis. It takes precisely a "psychoanalysis" to tease out, if not the meaning, at least the force of any charged discourse like that of art.

Unfortunately psychoanalysts differ profoundly in their conception of this relation. Jacques Lacan, undoubtedly the most influential source of such ideas, posits that the unconscious is structured like a language and that an intensive analysis can account for the eruption of the primary processes in the secondary flow of discourse.[2] His most persistent critic, Jean-François Lyotard, is less sanguine.[3] For him, all conscious acts of signification have as their first object the suppression of unconscious desires. There is no easy access to the primary flow of images and dreams.

Both approaches, however, insist on the indicative nature of "figures," those twists and complications in discourse that mark out a difficulty in the path of meaning. As its name implies, a figure is a direct representation of meaning, nearly a visual representation, as opposed to the sequential logic of grammatical language. Figures (metaphors, parallelisms, disjunctions, and so forth) transgress or manipulate grammar and, by doing so, insist on the importance of their peculiar mode of presentation. Figures, thus, have a special tie to fantasies and are, for the psychoanalyst, the focus of any investigation that hopes to get at the force (that is, the deep significance) of discourse.

From every perspective, figuration assumes the first rank in an overall theory of film. From the point of view of signification, it takes over where semiotics was forced to leave off. From the psychoanalytic standpoint figures mark the terrain of analysis. From the position of genre and of the history of the cinema, figures make up on the one hand the only true dictionary we have (dissolves figure a change in time or location, black hats signify that their wearers are evil, at least in Westerns up to 1950, and so forth), while on the other hand they provide the energy that alters the system. In all these cases, the term "figure" implies either a conscious or unconscious work against the ordinary language of filmic discourse in the service of something that presses to be expressed. It is, in short, an indication of the presence of narration, of a narrator employing film in addressing spectators.

The category of figural discourse marks a return to certain earlier assumptions in film theory. It implies a hierarchy of texts based on the density of their signification, for instance. Studies of cinematic figures have generally been conducted on the works of filmmakers like Buñuel where narration clearly sets itself in opposition to standard narrative grammar and where the primary processes seem hardly suppressed at all.[4] In the era of Lévi-Straussian structuralism, all texts were treated as equal versions of a central myth whose importance lay in its structure. But figures are exactly those textual elements that complicate and derail structure. For the same reason, where Lévi-Strauss and his followers disregarded narration and the event of creation, discussion of figures wants to flow back to the moment in which a particular meaning was shaped. It flows back to the act of narration or to that of reception and is, consequently, bound to historical and psychological contexts. In sum, the category of figuration is paramount because it involves structure and process simultaneously, and because by its very nature it insists on the primacy of interpretation. In this it helps right the topsy-turvy world of film studies by restoring to the texts themselves an integrity worthy of discussion, and by fostering an interplay of theory and interpretation rather than a dominance of the former.

The opposition I have implied between the study of structure and the interpretation of figures or texts is historical, not logical. Christian Metz is a perfect example of a scholar whose original focus on structure (the laws of film syntax, most obviously) has shifted to that of cinematic figures. The parallax this shift produces is designed to account for the effect on the viewer, something his early semiotics neglected and his later psychoanalysis took up.

Metz sees no discontinuity in these changing projects of film study because, for him, a single model of the mind rules every phase of the work. In brief, Metz is committed to Jakobson's position that the mind (and all its processes) works by selection and ordering.[5]

In linguistics and semiotics this is easy to see. The dictionary (the paradigmatic law) contains our possibilities of selection whereas the grammar book (the syntagmatic law) governs the ordering of whatever is selected. Lacanian psychoanalysis (followed by Metz and most film theorists) explicitly echoes this same model. The unconscious is structured like a language because it too operates via principles of selection and ordering, only this time the results are difficult to catalogue in dictionaries and grammars. But our terms for the major work of the psyche match the model very well, "condensation" operating by means of a radical selection and "displacement" by means of circuitous ordering. Freud's third concept for the dream work, "secondary revision," is actually only a coefficient regulating the degree of condensation or displacement functioning in a dream, a work of art, a habit, and so on. Metz has made great use of this, labeling as "highly secondarized" common conventions (like a slow motion run of two lovers, cut as a parallel syntagma).[6] Shockingly new cinematic effects (the freeze frame conclusion of *The 400 Blows*) are barely subject to revision. These would seem to have arisen as nearly direct expressions of the psyche instead of being carefully selected from the already established codes of cinema.

Bringing the psychoanalytic concept of secondary revision into the realm of codes makes these same principles of selection and ordering available to rhetoric also. This is hardly surprising since psychoanalysis from the first adopted a rhetorical vocabulary (terms like antithesis, negation, and metalepsis are common to both fields). In the 1950's we find the psychoanalyst Lacan seconding the linguist Jakobson in attaching metaphor to the pole of selection, and metonymy which operates by means of contiguity to the pole of ordering.

Altogether, the master concepts of selection and ordering (similarity and sequence) permit the structuralist scholar to move from semiotics to rhetorical analyses and even to psychoanalysis. This holds true when the subject is a single film like *Young Mr. Lincoln* or a general problem in the cinema. Metz, as usual interested in general problems, takes great pains to discriminate among the related but not fully synonymous vocabularies of semiotics, rhetoric, and psychoanalysis. Yet his discriminations serve not to promote some new approach to the cinema but to refine its structural description. The obtuse presence of figures in cinematic discourse forced such a refinement in structuralism. In my estimation they force much more than this, as the remainder of this chapter hopes to demonstrate.

BETWEEN THE PSYCHE AND THE SYSTEM

Structuralism and semiotics of film have been enormously attractive enterprises because they promise to supply procedures capable of dealing systematically with a phenomenon that staunchly resisted systematizing for its first seventy years. The smooth visual surface of the movies could rebuff the advances of all but "global" scholars ready to fawn over or rebuke their charms. Until the mid-1960's, scholars of the art were scarcely distinguishable from popular reviewers. Many performed both functions.

Cinema was adored or feared but in all cases it was deemed inaccessible to scientific or even scientistic labor, this despite such pretentious organizations as the "Institut de filmologie" in Paris and America's poor copy of it, "The Society of Cinematologists."[7] Such groups floundered about in phenomenology, behavioral study, and psychosociology searching for keys to enter the inner workings of the mystic screen. Structuralism and semiotics at last opened the door.

The greatest immediate breakthrough in these infant disciplines came in relation to genre films, especially those of the so-called classic American period (1935–55). Here the rewards seemed highest. If ever a cinema consistently guised itself as reality, it was in this era. If ever cinema brooked no challengers, it was then. The goal of structuralism and semiotics, therefore, was to "crack" this hermetic system, expose its workings, and provide social critics with the evidence they needed to perform a symptomatic reading of American culture through a study of the elements and rules structuring its movie reality.

At the same time, the hopes for success in this enterprise could hardly be higher, for the classic American genre film displayed a consistency that could be only the result of regularization achieved by some hidden application of rules. The sheer accumulation of 450 films a year for twenty years all coming from Hollywood under essentially a single production system foretold an aesthetic system mediating the production situation and the final product. Semiotics promised to track down the units of representation in that aesthetic system; structuralism promised to account for the specific narrative shape of the values represented. Both derived from structural linguistics, a master discipline which, in 1960, seemed on its way to the complete delineation of the communicative powers of language from its smallest elements to their ordered and "meaningful" combinations.

If structuralism has run up against resistance in the past few years, it is in part because cultural studies have felt the need to pass from the logical clarity of linguistics to the murkier discipline of rhetoric. Henceforth the study of *figures,* not codes, must be paramount in an examination of cultural artifacts. This is an especially appropriate attitude to adopt in relation to film which even in the case of the classic American genres has always seemed more a collection of strategies than a well-ordered system. Recent interest in the study of Third World films, art films, experimental pieces, and documentaries has confirmed this priority.

In practice this shift to rhetoric has meant supplementing categories of semiotics (codes) and of discourse theory (syntagms, paradigms, aspects of narration) by introducing the terminology of rhetoric (tropes of metaphor, metonymy, irony, and so forth) and of psychoanalysis (condensation, displacement, representability, secondary elaboration, and so forth). As we have noted, all these disciplines share a method of organizing a text according to the selection and placement of elements. It was this vision of the structure of cinema which at first provided such impetus to treat it as a legitimately linguistic system since selection and ordering make up the very processes of language (dictionary and grammar).

And it is only an enlarged concern for selection and ordering that has forced a semiotician like Christian Metz to shift his categories from those of discourse theory to those of rhetorical and especially psychoanalytic theory. The cynic may find this shift perfectly congruent with the changing intellectual fads in France. The more serious student will see in this shift the recognition by film scholars themselves that film is ordered not as a natural language but at best as a set of practices and strategies that are in some way "ready-to-hand" but hardly form a system in any strong sense of the term.[8] This aspect of *bricolage* at the heart of the medium suggests that meaning in film comes largely by way of conventions which began as figures. A dissolve denotes the passage of time today only because for years it figured that passage palpably through the physical intertwining of adjacent but distinct scenes.

While we may be accustomed to thinking of figures as abnormal, disordering embellishments in well-ordered rational discourse, Metz suggests that they are, especially in cinema, the normal marks of an irrational discourse which becomes progressively ordered. He sees film operating at three levels: semiotically (through grammar and syntax and an invariant relation of signifier to signified), rhetorically (where figures extend or replace the domain of the signified thus developing an unstable relation between it and its signifier), and psychoanalytically (where a free play of signifiers responds to dynamic instinctual forces and organizes itself through the processes associated with the dream work).

In his most recent writings, Metz has reversed our conventional order in handling cinematic meaning. Instead of proceeding from the ordered discourse back through figures of discourse to the psychic wellsprings of discourse, Metz has suggested that the true source and referent of all discourse is the "indestructible" (the drives and processes of the unconscious). The progressive displacement of meaning operating in relation to a censoring process turns a desire into a pattern of flight and detour that surfaces as a discoursive form. This form is composed of the figurative movements of the medium which are ultimately constrained into a semiotic matrix that can be rationally exchanged in a communicative act.

Film has freed us, Metz feels, from dealing with figures as instances of disordered speech, classifiable by logic or philology. From Aristotle to our own day, figures have been treated as obscure units replacing conventional units. Taxonomies have enumerated them.[9] But the movement of meaning in film suggests that grammar, order, and semiotic consistency are a last order consideration and that discourse proceeds by way of figures and, through figures, by way of the unconscious. Thus he finds it more appropriate to speak of "figuration" rather than "figure," of great processes in which signifiers seek for, attain, extend, and often lose their signifieds.

For Metz, metonymy is the key and most usual figure, the figure of association by which we pass from one aspect or image to a related one in search of a satisfying final picture. When this process becomes fully "secondarized," that is, elaborated in logical (namely, semiotic) patterns, we have before us a filmed narrative. Only the close inspection of the remaining figures that protrude from the otherwise clean path of narrative provides an inkling of the complex detours which were taken in the production of an acceptable story. Thus metonymy does double duty, marking the displacement of psychic energy in its shifting trajectory refracted through censorship, and entering into the sheer contiguity of narrative successivity in which everything is, "in the end," well placed. Metonymies are midpoints between force and signification.

Metz's dynamic conception of textuality as a flow, a filtering, and successive detours observable in the struggle between volatile figures and a ruled narrative does not, however, free him from a limited structural stance in the analysis of texts. He calls for the classification of figures in film along four separate axes: degree of secondarization, dominance of metonymy or metaphor, suggestion of condensation or displacement, and the type of incorporation in the text (syntagmatic or paradigmatic).[10] Here once again a closed structuralism dominates its object of research, even though that object is avowedly free and open. In genre study, to return to our clearest instance, the analyst may classify the figurative markers in the texts as they respond over the years to a timeless unconscious source (Lévi-Strauss's "inherent contradiction") in varying historical contexts.

If our interest is not to interpret what lies beyond the text but rather to classify methods of textual disfiguration, then Metz may help us construct a history of rhetorical strategies. The tropology of classical rhetorical theory has its counterpart in Metz's four-axis classification method. The result of both schemas (despite their opposing theories of texts) is a list of genres, practices, and specific tropes by which art carries in its own (artistic) way the force of unconscious drives or the direction toward reasonable signification.

Let us take as an example the horror film. From their beginnings to our own day such films have fulfilled a set of constant functions. They have even told a limited number of tales. To chronicle the horror film is to examine the changing styles by which the unspeakable is represented. Hollywood in the classical era of the 1930's and 1940's relied primarily on makeup and model work to depict monsters incarnating whatever horror the film could express. But the European cinema of the 1920's often employed other elements, figuring horror through convoluted and irrational set designs (*Caligari*), through rhythms and mise-en-scène (Nosferatu's implacable trip to Bremen and to the bedroom of Mina), or through camera movement and optical effects (Dreyer's *Vampyr*). In the modern era, special effects have developed to such an extent that the audience is challenged to "figure" out the magic employed. *Poltergeist,* for example, carefully arranges its key scenes to occur in broad daylight, instead of the never-ending night of classical films.

Naturally this sort of inquiry could continue across hundreds of films and hundreds of pages. An astute and fastidious structural critic could, presumably, calculate a shifting dictionary of figures of horror, treating their interrelationships in a single film and across films as part of a history of representation.

Whereas this is most assuredly a necessary and valuable enterprise, it is nevertheless insufficient as a final research strategy. For all Metz makes of the unconscious origins of textuality, his is essentially a theory of narration wherein filtering and detour (selection and association) operate to shape a logical and closed story. Classical rhetorical theories of texts comprise the inverse of Metz's psychoanalytic view. The text for these stands in relation to a direct prose sense whereas for Metz it stands in relation to an unconscious non-sense. To take our example again from a horror film, *Vampyr,* classical rhetoric might begin by explaining that a figure like the superimposition of David Gray's ghost over his body substitutes for more prosaic ways of signifying his mental life (using an intertitle, or a close-up of his eyes closing in thought). The trope of the superimposition is thus straightened out, permitting us to understand the direct sense of the film and to appreciate the ingenuity of Carl Dreyer in presenting that sense to us in such a striking way.

Now Metz's interest in aspects of the horror film would be quite different. The particular manner by which supernatural or horrific elements are represented becomes the basis for an inquiry into the deep forces responsible for our interest in the tale at all. The visual splitting of David Gray, via superimposition, links up with other moments of splitting scattered throughout *Vampyr.* Indeed the entire film is fractured so deeply that it is useless if not impossible to try to reconstruct some linear sense. It is a schizophrenic tale, rising up out of the unconscious. The figure of the doubled hero is from this point of view not a finishing rhetorical touch added to the story to give it weight; it is first and foremost the palpable expression of schizophrenia, outside all narrative context and before it is integrated into the logic of the rest of the film.

Despite their quite different levels of interest, classical rhetorical analysis and the contemporary sort descending from psychoanalysis hold in common a transitive conception of figures. In both cases figures operate as detours from, and substitutions for, a more direct formulation that the author cannot or will not provide. Thus in both cases the figural nature of a text is a transitional stage through which, as critics, we may try to pass on our way to the recovery of total sense (meaning) or total energy (the drives).

From neither point of view (rationalist or psychoanalytic) is the specific figural movement of a given text worth pursuing in and for itself. Structural analysis studies artistic speech without listening to it. It either translates such speech into the "real" discourse (of the unconscious or of reason) or it treats such speech as a cultural object, a datum for classification.

THE CENTRALITY OF INTERPRETATION IN FILM THEORY

If figural discourse has anything to say to us by means of its unique form only a hermeneutic, not a structural, orientation will prepare us to deal with it. It is hardly coincidental that the leading authority on hermeneutics, Paul Ricoeur, has recently published a lengthy treatise on metaphor.[11]

Ever the arbiter, Ricoeur threads his way between a theory of figural substitution for proper meaning coming from Aristotle (conscious, grammatical, ordered, and secondary) and a theory of sheer figural process coming from Freud (unconscious, disordered, disordering, and primary). Retaining both substitution and process, Ricoeur emphasizes the *event* of discourse rather than its structure. From this perspective a figure is reducible neither to its proper sense nor to some timeless process it exemplifies, for it has the ability to change the rules of the discursive game in which it participates. Its meaning is not purely substitutionary, nor is it irrecoverable in the indestructible unconscious, for while it depends on rules, sense, and grammar, and while it undoubtedly rests on psychological preconditions, a figural event in discourse expands the space of meaning and invites us to fill in that space through interpretation. Figures alter, but do not dispense with, the dictionary.

Now film historians and genre theorists may very well be content to trace the development of film art in terms of the figural markers that serve each generation. To return a final time to the horror film, in 1920 a superimposition was the appropriate marker to denote the presence of spirits (*Phantom Chariot*) and to connote "art." In 1961 the same denotation was carried by an electronic sound accompanying an overexposed long shot of a man (*The Innocents*). The history of the cinema and of any of its genres is not so much a compilation of the tales it has told as a development in the figures it employs to denote such tales and to signal to its audience that this tale is presented "artistically."

Without denying the utility of this sort of scholarship, Ricoeur implies that it is unable to attend to the specific world of meaning opened up in a genre film by means of figural operations. More important, neither can it accurately account for the general *process* by which films make artistic meaning. Metz's four categories of figure analysis, for instance, do not provide a dynamic model of the work of figures even though he asserts that figures are dynamic. His is an analysis of the various levels at which a figure may be thought of as working, levels which Metz is at pains to keep separate (the unconscious, the rhetorical, the grammatical, and the diachronic, corresponding to his examination of displacement, metonymy, syntagmatics, and degree of secondarization).

Ricoeur opposes this method of "analysis through separation" by treating the figural process dialectically. It is not a matter, he claims, of a metaphor being drawn from the lexicon and responding to a certain psychic pressure; the metaphor is an event within which the psyche and the linguistic system adjust to one another. No analysis of this event can afford to neglect this interaction. Perhaps we can see now why Ricoeur privileges metaphor above all figures whereas Metz demotes it to an occasional and special form of association seldom if ever appearing in pure state. Every metaphor, Ricoeur claims, alters the discourse (artwork) while changing our sense of (name for) the referent.

Metz's view is an essentially narrative one in which a progressive filtering directs the successive signifying elements, ruling out unrelated connotations from the objects and events we recognize in the images. Metonymy has always been the privileged figure of narrative. Ricoeur, for his part, is eager to lift poetry, and its prime figure, metaphor, to the summit of artistic activity and by doing so to give metaphor a special function in the life of language.[12]

If metonymy proceeds by redirecting and filtering meanings, we may say that metaphor completely reorients meaning with respect to the situation in which it is used. It is the redescription of a semantic field (let us say, for example, the field of musical sounds) via a statement employing a term transferred from a foreign signifying domain (labels used to cover colors). We not only can speak in a given instance of a "bright or saturated tone" but the entire system of musical distinctions suddenly becomes vulnerable to a "chromatic" redescription. This is much more than the redirection of meaning. It is indeed the very birth of meaning as both language and its object are altered in adjusting to one another. It is not a special manner of traversing a semantic field but a way of permanently restructuring it through an "impertinent attribution" which demands interpretation in order to restore pertinence at some higher point.

Once metaphor is conceived of not as a verbal substitution but as a process resulting in the redescription of a semantic field, it becomes useful to film theory. For we may say that metaphor can occur as the calculated introduction of dissonance into any stage of the film process. That process we have broken into perception, representation, signification, structure, adaptation, and genre. When operating smoothly, as in a conventional educational film, we should expect the images to be clear, to mark out (represent) a recognizable field of interest, to transmit a stream of unambiguous messages through standard relations of images and sounds, and to organize those images and sounds into a progressive outline or argument.

There is very little need to discuss such a zero degree film. But curiously, very few films seem unworthy of discussion. Most films, particularly most fictional ones, disrupt the smooth flow toward intelligibility and encourage, if not demand, our active interpretation. Such disruptions can block our trajectory through the film momentarily or vigorously and they may do so at any stage of this progressive process. We might liken these stages to successive thresholds across which we pass: from recognizing light and shadows as objects and actions, to understanding their signification, to seeing the overall pattern they develop, and to understanding this pattern in relation to the filmic system (genre) and filmic discourse (narration).

Cinematic representation (the image itself) is normally an unquestioned mapping of the visible field. Despite its limitations and because of its photochemical origins, we accept the image as a threshold to the properly narrative and rhetorical levels of discourse. Our sense of the perceptual field can, however, be questioned by a work on the elements of the sign (grain, focus, color, depth, camera stability, and so forth). Patterns and games played with these elements, once brought to a level of pertinence for the spectator, might then form a model adequate in itself and suggestive of new relations in the field, relations formerly unmapped and therefore insignificant or nonsignifying. Avantgarde cinema has proven this.

A figure functions only when it is observed to function, only when it stands in the way of an automatic movement across signs. If, as is usual, nothing halts us at the level of perception, the next potential figural work occurs at the level of narrative. Here, more than at the first level, we recognize the norm as a residue of figural strategies coming down to us through the years as a trial-and-error process in the attempt adequately to map the field of interlacing actions. But here, more easily than at the first level, we can see at work the concept of the model, the heuristic fiction, which, built in such a way that it is consistent to itself, may give us the terms to redescribe our life-world of objects, actions, and their interrelations.

The conventions of genre and the rules of verisimiltude make up the norms of narrative. The construction of an inconsistent world or one whose maniacal logic does not fit our experience (as in the *nouveau roman*) forces us to imagine the world by wrestling with this problem which poses as a model of the world. Similarly the introduction of elements totally foreign to a genre breaks the code of likeness, thereby figuring a new relation of artwork to life.

Figuration can even occur globally at the level of adaptation. Jean-Marie Straub has made an entire reputation by representing classic texts from what can only be called a figural perspective. His *Othon,* for example, features Corneillean dialogue spoken by actors all of whom carry heavy foreign accents. And this is only the most obvious way he has shaped the play. The camera moves in and out of the action with insistence but without relation to the dramatic flow of the original. Finally, the set is a "stage" in ancient Rome behind which one catches glimpses of modern traffic patterns. The Corneille play comes to us, to be sure, but it does so figuratively.

Finally, the narrational stage involves the codes of discourse and of personal style by which a text foregrounds certain of its aspects. In a film like Robert Bresson's *Pickpocket* we have no trouble construing either the images or the story set before us; but Bresson's importation of baroque music and a literary voice-over, not to mention his formal camera movement and obsessive close-ups, halt our easy access to this film. We find ourselves seeking the appropriate level of discourse, that is, interpreting the film at the level its incongruities and obsessions seem to point to. This jump in levels is precisely a metaphoric one, since no literal reading of these marks of discourse is adequate to the work of the film. The film, then, becomes for us a model of a moral stance applicable to the world at large.

Although in practice these stages in the process of signification in the cinema occur simultaneously, metaphor always localizes itself at a particular stage as it strives to disrupt the system of signification in order to signify something "other." What guides the propriety of a metaphorical shift and what guides our subsequent effort to interpret it? I would have to say here that a metaphor only points to a potentially fruitful rapport with the semantic field, a rapport which it is up to the spectator to work out. The metaphor demands close description since by definition no rule or convention can determine or locate its utility and scope. As it is elaborated in detail it becomes a model for the redescription of reality as such.

Only the manifold of experience can determine the extent of a metaphor's power. Hence the metaphor demands an interrogation between experience and system, between the field and the map, which is largely self-regulating. The point should be clear. A semiotics of film hoped to specify the meaning of its elements. A rhetoric of film hopes to point to its figural moments and to initiate an interpretative process which may go on for as long as it is fruitful.

It should be evident now why structuralism can only provide a partial explanation for the workings of film and no real comprehension of the achievement of any given film. For structuralism will not recognize the event of cinematic discourse. It will always and only provide a description of the system which is put into use in the event. If, as I claim with Ricoeur, the system is altered by the event, if (to make a stronger claim) the system was born and exists only as a residue of such events of figuration, then we need a broader vision of the creation of meaning in films.

Semiotics and structuralism taught us to study the system through which signs are recognized as images and stories. We need to focus now on those instances when a sign is not assimilated by the narrative and where therefore a misrecognition occurs. For Metz such misrecognition arises from the unconscious and points back to it even while a radical filtering reorients the context as the film moves toward its proper closure. All figuration for him is merely displaced narration.

Ricoeur's view is stronger. For him misrecognition forces us to put into play all the possibilities of the sign and then leap to a new possibility, the one that will change the context itself and make us see it through the "improper and impertinent" sign. This is what produces a seismic shift of the contextual field. In politics we call such condensation "revolution," in psychoanalysis "transference," and in artistic and religious experience "insight." Figures are thus more than shortcuts by way of association and substitution; they have the power to disrupt the relation of context to sign and reorient not only the discursive event but the system itself which will never be the same afterwards.

The institution of film proceeds by a tension between rules and a force of discourse trying to say something. This force overdetermines a sign within a conventional context so that the sign overflows both recognition and narrative placement, disturbing the system through misrecognition until, in the tension, we recognize what was meant. Such misrecognition can occur in the presentation of the elementary cinematic sign, in its placement in a scene, in the scene's placement in the narrative, and in the film's relation to a cultural context. Though we may be fascinated by the rules of genre, for example, we ought to be still more fascinated by the play of misrecognition which makes a particular genre film interesting to us and which makes it a useful and not merely a redundant way to view culture. The great film puts the genre and the culture into question, permanently altering both by means of its defiance of meaning and its simultaneous search for a true meaning. This can occur only in a process that incorporates structure as one of its constitutive elements, but that could never be exhausted by a study of structure.

10

Interpretation

FILM THEORY IN THE TRADITION OF HERMENEUTICS

Cinematic figures openly require the work of interpretation to complete them. Interpretation is integral to the specific structure of discourse they constitute, a structure that is by definition complex in that it involves both signification and significance, both semiotic mechanism and referential thrust.

Figural or poetic discourse may crown our view of cinema (as it certainly crowns Mitry's view), but it does so as an apotheosis rather than as an imposition. Figures do not rescue film theory from an otherwise sterile semiotic concern with the mechanics of signification. Instead, they make up the densest instances of a process that is operative at every stage of cinematic comprehension. From basic perception of images through the labyrinths of psychological engagement, from the representation of a recognizable scene to the fully elaborated functioning of genres and figures, interpretation plays an irreplaceable role.

Interpretation invokes the context for meaning and establishes whatever is pertinent about such meaning. History is one of its most common guises as it brings the "otherness" of texts into the life of individuals and cultures. Even those who hold a trenchantly materialist view of life can no longer afford to neglect history, be it the private chronicle of the psyche or the public archive of ideology. I have argued that any adaptation and every genre, for example, must be considered in relation to cultural and film history not just as an extra scholarly task but as an integral part of comprehending the phenomenon in the first instance.

Interpretation, then, has been my thrust; and not mine alone. For ours is an age obsessed with its theory and practice. Indeed, it is the crowning concept in contemporary textual theory even though, throughout most of the history of civilization, it has been a mere, though necessary, technique.[1] What is meant by interpretation in our day, what ambitions have accrued to it so that it now reigns over such a broad cultural terrain—these are the subjects of this final chapter. We need to glimpse its history; we need in short to interpret interpretation.

Let us remind ourselves of the stakes at play. The widespread popularity of the new hermeneutics has brought interpretation to the center of higher realms of cultural philosophy and we will have to confront it there; but hermeneutics is more than another critical fad, for it rests on a modernist concern about the relativity of judgment that affects all disciplines, particularly humanistic ones such as aesthetics. Indeed, as soon as we go beyond sheerly biological processes like sensation, modern theorists feel the need to invoke interpretation. Basic perceptual theory, for instance, now rests on the founding notion of contextual alignment wherein the organism selects the stimuli it needs to attend to in any given instance. Such previous perception theories as nativism and empiricism here are corrected by a theory that is sensitive to the situations within which perception occurs. There is no longer a single notion of seeing; rather there are "modes of seeing," and every mode depends on the project the organism finds itself engaged in.[2]

At a higher level representations of all sorts, as E. H. Gombrich has so incontrovertibly shown, result from complexes of interpretation which might be called "seeing as" to oppose it to the mere perceptual "seeing."[3] All instances of "seeing as" must be based on initial interpretations, a fact brought out every time we are forced to convince another viewer of the rightness of our view of the representation standing before both of us. We see an array of lines as a duck or as a rabbit. We take Marcello Mastroianni in *8½* as a filmmaker and certain of the film's images as his direct inner thoughts or visions.

When we go beyond these activities that form the base of artworks we begin to encounter head on such intertextual issues as style, genre, and allusion—all of which are by definition historically determined and subject in the first instance to complex processes of interpretation. Here the artworks themselves not only call for specific acts of interpretation, but they also function as interpreters of tradition themselves. These and other aspects of artworks, such as identification, require more or less automatic acts of interpretation from the reader or spectator in the normal functioning of the experience. A much more concentrated locus of interpretation is occasioned by those parts of artworks we designate as figures. It is here that the issue of interpretation was originally seen as an issue at all, for figures are portions of artworks which, by definition, defy common sense and immediate understanding. They are meant to be difficult and to engender a specific type of work on the part of the reader/spectator, even if, as seems to be the case in classical aesthetics, they ultimately must be resolved into a standard meaning.

Figures are the highest instances of interpretive operations which go on all through the experience of artworks. The fact that they point to this effort, however, allows us to use them in considering the value art places on itself in different epochs. We can say schematically that figures in classical art from the Greeks to the Romantics were meant to arouse active interest, to embellish and underline ideas, and to certify the work as indeed artistic. Interpretation in such an aesthetic was called upon to rectify the confusing, appreciate the subtle, and multiply the thought of the text as it developed itself in a measured way.

Since the Romantics, figures have enjoyed a more primary value in our conception of the work of art, and interpretation has consequently taken on a more central status. Figures can now be thought of as original and irreducible ways of expressing whatever works of art are thought to express. Interpretation then becomes the special way we have of talking about the irreducible. If we value artistic expression, and privilege it as a kind of discourse from which we gain something unavailable to other modes of discourse, then interpretation may become an essential way of dealing with the essential. Far from merely rectifying the confusions of art with the clarity of logical or moral discourse, interpretation in the Post-Romantic Age is valuable in itself as it romps within the areas marked out by the figures it is tied to.

Interpretation is a highly regarded concept today because it negotiates the space between mind and body that modern culture wants so badly to traverse. Supported by Greek philosophy, our Christian, particularly Protestant, heritage polarized man and his activities, generally according priority to purely rational thought. This rationality might appreciate and analogize the physical side of life but seldom wanted to take its cue from the body or even from the body of physical situations we call history. Kant's *Critique of Judgment* was instrumental in raising "taste" and our perpetual concern for the physically beautiful to a level of key philosophic importance, where it might sanction the operation of pure and moral reason, crippled by its own inability to justify itself.

Since Kant and the Age of Romanticism, philosophy has been primarily the story of various integrations of mind and body, until philosophy allowed itself to be undermined by the more body-sensitive disciplines of anthropology and psychoanalysis. Rationality today is seldom conceived of in pure terms; rather it is determined by culture, by need, by power, and by the physical limits of language. This orientation shapes the thought of thinkers with quite varied attitudes toward life. Michel Foucault inherits a European pessimism from Nietzsche and discovers all thought to be self-interested, with philosophy existing as merely another index of a culture's peculiar way of promoting certain voices and repressing others. Instead of interpreting an age for us, philosophy conspires with the age to be its justification. This blind determinism has little in common with the American pragmatism of someone like John Dewey, but Richard Rorty finds the two men engaged in quite the same project:[4] that of lodging reason inside the needs of the body and of history. Dewey simply wants to make the best use of the situation, to the point of glorying in the muscular operations of the mind. Even a conservative and essentially religious thinker like Michael Polanyi, eager as he is to maintain against Foucault such notions as freedom and faith, feels the need to open his book *Meaning* with a solid attack on the alleged faculties of scientific rationality and to close it with a plea for attention to and belief in the symbols we are drawn to.[5] For him humans carry within them structures of "tacit knowledge" which direct their conscious projects and dictate value.

And so, from the profoundly skeptical Foucault right up to the religious Polanyi, reason is seen as a governed as much as a governing power. Its most elegant and transcendent flights start from what Yeats called "the foul rag and bone shop of the heart."[6] The flesh of reason gives Polanyi hope that truth is embedded in the skin of things, whereas Foucault finds in this same flesh only the seethings of an irrational struggle for survival and power.

Central to prevalent attitudes toward mind and body has been the movement of phenomenology, especially in its French, existentialist emanation, and it is in this climate that the most current hermeneutics grew. When Merleau-Ponty determined to seek and describe the "body's reasons," he paved the way for studies as diverse as those on religion, sexuality, social demographics, and so on. But most lasting has been the theory of language and texts that phenomenology ushered in; under the pressure of a rising interest in structural linguistics, it was to the "skin of language" that Merleau-Ponty felt most drawn in order to bring forth his final meditations.[7]

Interest in hermeneutics stems directly from an interest in the confrontation of the human subject with texts that at first are foreign or befuddling. Against the computer-age structural methodologies which eliminate the reader while foregrounding the mechanism of meaning in the text, hermeneutics has tried to remind us that reading is an activity whereby the mind is incarnated in the pulp of a book and behaves in describable ways. Instead of putting the analyst in a position of power over the text as structuralism has often explicitly sought to do, hermeneutics is a theory that entertains the relationship between a text worthy of respect and a consequential, historically grounded reading of that text. We might think of structuralism as bearing a most cerebral attitude toward meaning, even though it finds all meaning to depend on mere mechanism. Hermeneutics, on the other hand, proceeds from history, desire, and value. It seeks in the body of the text the significance that only that body has for it.

The hermeneutic tradition which comes to us from the Romantic Age arose as a desperate response to the experience of spatial and temporal viscosity in the pursuit of meaning.[8] Up to 1800, readers were capable, or so it seems, of digesting unproblematically whatever texts were presented them (assuming they were familiar with the language of the writing). But Schleiermacher, and later Dilthey, found it necessary to overcome obstacles of cultural and historical distance thrown in the way above all by theological skeptics. Hermeneutics developed first as a concern, then as a method, and finally as a theory about the behavior of mind in confrontation with the austerity of texts, especially those from which it is physically (historically, culturally, and linguistically) estranged.

As it grew toward the ambitious philosophical proportions it was to assume under Heidegger and Gadamer, hermeneutics had first to establish itself as an enterprise distinct from the disciplines of linguistics and philology which, especially in the nineteenth century, had set about conquering the foreignness of languages and texts.

This development was aided in the first place by the decisive shift linguistics underwent in our century under the banner of Saussurean structuralism. Systematically repudiating the importance of history in the study of language, Saussure and his followers have attempted the description of the logic of syntax ("langue") according little value to actual speech events ("parole"). And so hermeneutics, far more intrigued by the historicity of actual discursive events than by some invariable linguistic capability, found a field in which to grow that had become rich through years of fallowness. Naturally it has employed the astounding gains of structural linguistics, but it has in no way set itself up as a rival discipline. Its object is quite different. More recently, structural linguistics has given way to generative grammar, discourse analysis, and even speech act theory, all tending to blur the distinction between langue and parole and to bring hermeneutics potentially into the mainstream of language study. In its formative years, however, hermeneutics upheld as its own the study of the behavior of "significance" as opposed to the logic of "meaning."[9]

A second venerable tradition from which hermeneutics has disengaged itself has been philology. Even older than linguistics, philology is the discipline associated with distant texts, primarily classical ones. Its methods are historical in the extreme, and its goal is the correct understanding of the text as it was written. Philology relies on the history of languages, on etymology, dialect study, the vicissitudes of syntax and vocabulary, but it adds to this the fruits of cultural erudition. The philologist feels in a position to pass down distant texts to us because he has read so widely that every text takes its proper place in his mind and every word settles into its most likely acceptation. Biography and history round out the philologist's undertaking to provide the densest possible situation out of which the words of the text usher. The philologist really feels himself a part of the original audience of the text; all his schooling permits him this outrageous presumption.

The decline of philology in our day is due in large part to the decline of classical education. Who now has mastered the innumerable languages and cultures that Leo Spitzer or Erich Auerbach felt right at home in?[10] Who has read the bodies of literature that permit easy access to any given text? In our theoretically sophisticated era we have as a group lost contact with literature. Certainly experts exist for every period, but few are left who command sufficient knowledge of languages, stylistics, metrics, and comparative grammar and who can put these skills at the service of a sweeping view of texts in an array of cultures.

Perhaps a more telling reason for the debasement of philology is an internal crisis of its own making. Nietzsche's case is paradigmatic, for as the leading philologist of his day he only intermittently felt comfortable plying his trade.[11] Far more of his energy went into a critique of interpretation, so radical that it altogether paralyzed the conservative and self-satisfied philological tradition. With Nietzsche begins a metaphysical interest wherein the issues of interpretation become so problematized that they are raised to key concerns in philosophy. Heidegger and Gadamer have extended this questioning, but the ideal of a clear and regulated philology is so attractive that it still has its proponents today. E. D. Hirsch has been central to the popularization of hermeneutics precisely because of the eloquent and staunchly conservative philological position that he has held for two decades. Hirsch's position is really quite simple.[12] Given innumerable ways to read a text, we ought, he claims, to give preeminence to that reading which captures the meaning lodged in the text at the moment of its composition. Once accepted, this position devolves into a panoply of techniques capable of determining the meaning closest to that which the author intended.

Hirsch's view has always been the norm in debates over interpretation, but attacks on this tradition have grown stronger since Heidegger. Hirsch himself summarized the opposition by placing meaning over and against significance, claiming that interpretation must strive to recover meaning, while mere criticism may assert the significance of a text for such and such an individual or age. Even his subtlest opponents are prepared to accept Hirsch's distinction, though they either deny the existence of primal meaning or maintain that it is no more consequential than other significant readings of the text. Stemming as it does from phenomenological roots, hermeneutics must clearly oppose any objectivist notion of truth or of the text. The point of departure for phenomenologists is not the text but rather the act of reading or interpreting. Indeed they would surely assert that the text exists only as read and that Hirsch's program to discover the meaning of the pristine text, as it exists unread and eternal, is altogether phantasmic. As was the case with linguistics, hermeneutics relies upon the techniques of philology but plans a very different program of textual study. In past decades that program has outstripped the projects of philology to become one of the crucial means by which modern intellectual culture assesses its life.

The point of departure for hermeneutics could not be more evident: What do we have to do when we do not understand what we read? This problem arises with force only when the need for understanding is great; and it is thus natural that the term and the first methods of hermeneutics developed in relation to the Bible. The Bible and other religious texts, but the Bible in particular, make an extraordinary demand on every reader. Indeed, we might characterize the Bible *in toto* as a demand or at least an invitation. The stakes of understanding have never been higher, for lives are shaped in response to this demand and entire cultures develop around the reading of this text. The fact that the Bible is written in obscure language, that it is recalcitrant and often contradictory, makes interpretation necessary even to the point of institutionalizing hermeneutics. For the Bible needs to readdress itself to each generation and, it is claimed, to each individual; and if salvation comes via a proper way of living in relation to the word of God, then that way must be achieved and ensured through interpretation. All religions founded on a sacred text regulate the reading of the text through institutionalized interpretation.

To turn to another sphere, hermeneutics has come into play in the application of legal precedents, particularly when a founding document supports the culture. As in the case of religious life, the civic organization of society depends on the continued interrelation between the principles of the past and the events of the present. Those principles may be lodged exclusively in a charter, or code, especially when this is given the force of a religious text (for example, the Koran); or the principle may be thought to evolve in history wherein interpretation builds on the precedent of earlier interpretation, all based on a very few principles thought to be inviolable. This latter would seem to be the system operating in the United States, and it is one that clarifies the project of hermeneutics in a remarkable way. Examine any legal case and you immediately find two quite different sorts of discourse: that which invokes legal precedent (cases heard by appeals courts, most often) or first principle (the Constitution or Bill of Rights) and that which lays out in intricate and often loving detail the historical circumstances of the case at hand. The fusion of the present and the past, of history and earlier interpretations of justice, is a complex human activity that can be reduced neither to pure description nor to logic. This interpenetration of horizons (the present and the past) requires acts of judgment, requires acts of reading which are exemplary for all reading. Of course we promote and institutionalize this effort because the stakes again are high, far higher in our legalistic culture than the interpretation of religious texts. We feel the specific weight of legal writing in civic life, which exists as a web of interpretations so intricate it could inspire a Borges or a Calvino.

The texts of literature are really very similar to those of religion and law. Poetic, narrative, or dramatic formulations of values that the culture cannot or does not want to let go readdress every generation required to read them. This requirement may have the force of law behind it, as when *Paradise Lost* was in the course schedule of all college students; but it may also emerge as a strong invitation to a select number of readers, an invitation through the name of the author, other books of the period or genre, and various other signposts by which the mechanism of cultural dissemination goes about its work. However felt, the urge to read a literary text ushers in a hermeneutic situation comparable to that operating in religion and law, for the reader is confronted in the present with a valued discourse written in the past. In what way can the text be approached or assimilated? This problem is exacerbated by the deeply figurative language characterizing literary texts and by our sense that in such language lie harbored the values a culture continually returns to or questions.

As in the areas of law and religion, it is evident that an institution had to grow up to regulate the interpretation of these cultural treasures we call literature, both to guard the national values and to ensure the proper education of each literate citizen. Whenever the citizen is called for whatever reason to read a text, he or she is forced to flesh out the meaning offered by that text. The institution by which the individual and the culture deal with literature can be termed criticism; its theory is hermeneutics.

TWO HERMENEUTIC PATHS: ROLAND BARTHES AND PAUL RICOEUR

The recent surge of interest in hermeneutics comes from at least two quite different wellsprings, that of reflective philosophy and that of avant-garde literary practice. These two sources are readily represented in the careers of Paul Ricoeur and Roland Barthes.

Ricoeur's turn toward hermeneutics derives from a perfectly consistent, life-long body of work which began with his studies of Husserl.[13] His immense study of the problem of will culminated in a renunciation of direct reflection. The way to understand man's discontinuity with himself was barred, he felt, by the limitations of reflection itself, by the disjunction between reason and that which it hoped to understand. A detour was needed through the quasi-rational expressions of history and of bodily life, expressions we call symbols. In *The Symbolism of Evil* we find Ricoeur's first interpretive gesture. Although as a philosopher he had been reading the rational thought of his predecessors for years, he now confronted another type of thinking: the physical, deeply coded, and value-laden expressions that individuals and cultures build up over and over to heal the breaks in life.

As provocative and stimulating as *The Symbolism of Evil* is, it only initiated what has become a labyrinth of detours, for Ricoeur was uncomfortable with the success he so quickly attained. In the face of structuralism, psychoanalysis, and ideological critiques, how could he maintain the right to interpret the expressions of the past in such an unproblematic way? His debates with Lévi-Strauss, his monumental study of Freud, his essays on linguistics and on metaphor, all led him to formulate a hermeneutics in which the goals, problems, and claims of interpretation could be precisely marked out.[14]

His system is deceptively simple, breaking our experience with any major text into a traditional triad of moments.[15] "Understanding" accounts for our initial acceptance of the work, our recognition of its importance in our lives, and, in short, our capitulation to its textual force. Without understanding we would pass over a text as we do over perceptual life; it would be a moment of recognition hardly persisting into our future. But understanding thrusts the text into our life of meaning and exposes it thereby to the critiques which Ricoeur labels "explanation." Nearly the whole of academic life in the humanities concerns itself with explaining the assertions of texts. Primarily a regressive mode of interpretation, explanation aims to dissolve the text in its origins, to find the reasons for its claim on us. The text is situated in its various contexts (biographical, generic, historical) and is subjected to linguistic study, psychoanalysis, and ideological critique until the particularity of its appeal is explained as an effect of these generating forces. This important step in our relation with a given text removes us somewhat from its aura and forces us to recognize that language does not permit truths to be uttered directly or at all, that the forces of the unconscious derail and reroute our purported drive toward truth and that, in any case, truth is conditioned by the historical situation, since texts never arise in limbo, but always derive from the struggle of discourses, a struggle we must never separate from the social struggle that is the life of history.

Understanding and explanation account for the work of the academic profession in relation to texts and to students, for we teach, generally in succession, the appreciation of major texts and then the methods of analysis that turn appreciation into suspicion if not explanation. In short, to use Ricoeur's terms, we allow the text to master us only to return with the mastering disciplines of analysis.

If Ricoeur is critical of the life of interpretation in academia, it is not because he resents the analytical moment of explanation. Without it we would be caught in a narcissistic union with the text and be blind to its cultural interconnections. But explanation is not our last moment with a text, or rather, it is not for many readers at many times. Despite our analytical distance, we are still able to return to those texts that appeal to us and derive value from renewed contact with them. This third moment he names "comprehension," signaling thereby the expansion of the reader to the size of the text and to its specific shape. Comprehension is synthetic in that it listens to the wholeness of the text rather than breaking it into parts; further, it responds to the cues that it finds in the work, initiating a project of meaning that is never complete. To think with and through the work is the final step of Ricoeur's hermeneutics even while this final step is interminable (at least in the cases of those texts on which we depend personally or culturally). The work lives in the web of its interpretations, in their history, and in the projected meanings to which they point. It lives even in their conflict.

This sketch of Ricoeur's attitudes points up the priority of discourse over meaning, of interpretation over structure. Analysis would try to fix the position of a text, whereas interpretation presumes that the work of meaning is ongoing. As he has often pointed out, every speech involves both an event in which it occurs and a meaning that persists beyond the event. Hermeneutics tries to be adequate to the whole complex of discourse by keeping both poles of speech (meaning and event) in constant interplay. One can analyze the meaning of the text as a relation of signifiers and signifieds, but the *significance* of the moment of speech (that is, of the reading) involves context and reference. The text is about something and therefore calls for our continued appraisal. Ricoeur here butts up against one of the great philosophical issues of our century: the relation of meaning, sense, and reference. As a philosopher, it is only right that his heremeneutics arises in such a reflection, or rather, as a response to the inability of pure reflection to solve the disjunction between these terms.

Roland Barthes has come to a different type of heremeneutics from a totally different path. A reader rather than a philosopher, his development has not the consistent growth from a central node that one can see so clearly in Ricoeur. Barthes is perhaps the greatest critic of our epoch because of his responsiveness to texts, to culture, and to the movement of his own mind and body. That movement has been one of perpetual oscillation between a passion for system and a concern for the particularity of texts. Barthes began his career responding in *Writing Degree Zero* to the postwar polemics of Sartre's *Que' est-ce que la littérature?*, yet he circled back in his final book *Camera lucida* to the prewar, phenomenological Sartre, the Sartre of *L'Imaginaire*. Even if he ultimately eludes classification, Barthes consciously wrote within the structuralism/phenomenology debate which spanned the past thirty years and his theory and practice of interpretation must be studied in relation to that debate.[16]

Specifically, the phenomenological method of his 1954 study of Michelet was followed a decade later by the trenchantly structuralist *Elements of Semiology* and "Introduction to the Structural Analysis of Narratives." Then came the codes of *S/Z* which in turn gave way to the anarchic *Pleasure of the Text* and the quasi-autobiographical essays published at the time of his death in 1980.

More than any other figure of our era Barthes embodies the opposition of mind and body posed at the outset of this chapter. His early defense of the new novel and his notorious critical modernity promote the domination of texts by the play of reason in all its computeristic potentiality. Yet the recent Barthes focuses on the unanalyzable particularity of texts, on what he, above all critics, was apt to call their bodies. Criticism became for him an erotics, a sensory exploration of words, discourse and mind, just as his friend Susan Sontag had demanded in her like-minded *Against Interpretation*.[17]

Barthes's special brand of interpretation stems from a neo-hedon-

ism, from the call of pleasure, the claims of the instant, and the obsessions of the reader that resist system. This was clear as early as his
1970 film essay, "The Third Meaning," where he struggled to name
the unnamable, to signify the kind of significance that, in certain images, cannot be explained by reference to story, rhetoric, or even style.
Certain images simply call to us from the epidermis of their presence.[18]

Unconcerned about the logic or argument of the texts he prefers,
Barthes finally abandoned the study of sequence and consequence.
Several of his own late writings are organized alphabetically by topic
so that he might remain faithful to the immediacy of the kind of significance he sought to represent. In addition he attempted to rid his last
essays of all metalanguage, writing instead entirely out of what he termed
"primary language."

These aspects make his hermeneutical project the opposite of the
carefully composed philosophical discourse of Ricoeur. Yet like Ricoeur he is interested in pursuing not the text so much as that which
the text insists upon. For Barthes, this referential aspect is essentially
emotional. Texts in their most hieratic moments point to the inner states
recognized by the reader as anxiety, waiting, jealousy, and so on. The
text embodies these states carnally, and Barthes's direct, lengthy, unsystematic attention to them is meant to leave them open to an ongoing
(re)reading.

Hermeneutics has given back to the study of literature and film its
pretense to referentiality. No text is exhausted by a study of its logic
and system, for certain of its nodes are directly related to, and express,
aspects of lived life. Barthes limited these aspects to personal, inti-
mate, psychological memories, but he left the door open for claims to
larger domains of reference. Although he died without having to confront those post-structuralists bent on eliminating reference from texts,
his whole career might be seen as a type of answer to them: literary
discourse was for him an oscillation between logic and figure, between
an imposed mediated system and unmediated sensation produced by
the text. Criticism must oscillate as well, never abandoning its investigation of the mechanism of meaning even while it isolates and ca-
resses those privileged points of significance that strike with the force
of the purely physical.

One of Barthes's earliest meditations on this issue arose in connection with the problem of connotation as discussed in the final essay of

Mythologies.[19] There he maintained the difference of denotation (logic) from connotation (body) and the dependence of the latter on the former. Repeating Hjelmslev's classic formulation, he demonstrated the hidden logic of all connotation, indicating thereby that all meaning is systematic and connects in no special way to nature or history. Though ideology will always marshal certain connotations of meaning to insist on their natural or historical priority, in fact this is only the deception of a mechanism that the analyst can and must uncover.

With this essay Barthes led the way for a full-scale attack on the rhetoric of figures, tropes, and special meanings of all sorts. With structural linguistics being unchallenged in Europe in the 1960's, such witch-hunts proceeded confidently under a belief in synchrony, in system, and in the power of the almighty "langue" over any of its emanations, including sacred texts or newly forged figures.

While there has been no relaxation in this nearly scientific drive to describe the workings of poetic language (witness the work of the Liège group),[20] a clear shift in the intellectual climate has occurred, evidenced above all in Barthes's reformulation of his initial proposition. As early as *Système de la mode,* begun in the 1950s, Barthes reversed Hjelmslev's hierarchy. Denotation, far from being the irreducible origin of all other, more extended meanings, now must be understood to exist only as the final sum of connotation, as its settling down to the proper pertinency of meaning in such and such a situation. This shift supports Ricoeur's monumental study of metaphor in which he upholds the growing suspicion that all standard meanings arose figuratively and that the dictionary is merely a record of previous meaning events rather than a rule book of an ideal semantic universe.[21] True, the events of language have largely been forgotten in the dictionary except in the exemplary sentences drawn most often from literary sources, but the meanings remain as testimony to the linguistic struggles to say something in situations. We who use the dictionary do so in our own history as we seek to bend the system of language to our needed purpose. The event in which we replicate earlier uses of the system, or force it to meet our own requirements under the pressure of a figure that we develop, is the standard event of language, not some aberration or perverse use of a logical machine. Thus connotation makes us attend to the sentence as much as to the word as we construe or construct a pertinent implication with the force of new usage.

In redescribing the dictionary as a pulsing, historically sensitive re-

cord of human exchange, Ricoeur justifies the detour through hermeneutics that the mind must take in its quest for certainty, a detour involving the body of language and the flesh of history. In clearing ground
for his own measured hermeneutics, Ricoeur has also opened up a field
of play for the figural acrobatics of Roland Barthes. "Figure," a word
that connotes both abstract patterning and the physicality of a face, thus
holds together the philosophical projects of Ricoeur and the nearly narcissistic ramblings of Barthes. More precisely, figure is the pertinent
unit of study for all those pursuing mind through body and the body
in the mind. Sentences and meanings may be exchangeable, but the
figure is what it is as it is. Its appeal to us is as carnal and as irreplaceable as a face we love. Our response to it is also carnal—a caress, a
savoring, an exploration and extension of the sense we feel in it for
our lives.[22]

The anthropomorphism of the figure in the text has a long tradition.
Ricoeur appeals to this tradition when he argues that certain texts call
to the reader as a person calls. Doubtlessly thinking foremost of the
Bible, his point spreads across the whole of literature and becomes the
catchword of hermeneutics. The call of the text is the responsibility of
us readers, who must interpret by "fleshing out" what stands before
us toward our future. Barthes has taken this view in his inimitable and
personal way: a figure is any textual unit exerting its own force on us
as we read, making us halt and contemplate if only to feel more deli-
ciously the thrust of its formulation. Barthes was always interested in
reading as a process of rewriting small figures embedded in the relent-
less structure of huge texts, figures that fascinate and address him, figures that cannot be dissolved in an overriding understanding of the text
as a whole. This is the Barthes who sought out the "third meaning"
in certain images from Eisenstein, a personal and nearly mystical
meaning. In these places Barthes listens to the possibilities of a voice
"about to speak," the "grain of the voice" as a site of future meaning, or more precisely, as the site of meaning in action. A gymnastic
figural meaning is that which is caught in a *pose* and not contemplated
in *repose*. From here Barthes can go on to his "anti-criticism" labeled
in the "Discourse of the Lover" as that which reaches out toward figures in a bodily gesture of desire.

Barthes shamelessly discards all pretense toward generalizable
meaning and lapses into a kind of private hedonism. Figures are like
arias in an opera, he says, nodes that persist totally estranged from the

argument or narrative that ostensibly gave rise to them. They are places of departure, turns of phrases, deviant images, anything in a text which is physically alluring. And the *signifiance* they embody has a very limited plurality, usually associated, as pointed out before, with psychic states recognized or remembered by the reader. Instead of the infinitude of readings he formerly wished on every writerly text,[23] Barthes now champions those portions of texts that control us, master us, force us to attend to something undeniable in the shape of their formulation.

In his Protestant way, Ricoeur likewise asserts the directed sense presided over by the figure; but for him a figure is more likely to include much larger units. Even an entire poem or novel may be said to comprise a figure insofar as the physicality of its formulation admits no substitution and forces us to reimagine our semantic universe from the perspective of the pose it takes. The extended metaphor is not simply a clever rearranging of signifiers; it is an assertion that calls on our imagination to complete it and that rewards us by the fruitfulness of the redescription it permits. Like Barthes, Ricoeur here insists on the role of the imagination and of new interpretation, but this role is played out under the control of the figure, whose posture demands that we think with it in *just this* way, no matter how extensive our thoughts may be as they spread across our past (Barthes) or future (Ricoeur). Ricoeur would consolidate the gains in thought permitted by a figure through his "approach/retreat" dialectical hermeneutics that moves from understanding to analysis and on to a more comprehensive synthesis. Barthes doubtless would find this another snare by which the system tries to amalgamate the unique, by which mind tries to level the delicious differences which the body is able to touch.

THE ENDLESS CLAIM OF INTERPRETATION

The question of figuration in art may allow us to reintroduce some older concepts in aesthetics that have had a troubled history in our century and that film theory desperately needs to employ properly: representation and expression. To say that a text or artifact represents a person or idea or state of affairs suggests that there exists a determinate, public referent which the signifiers aim to call up. The job of the audience or reader is to fill in the cues in order to complete the representation. But artistic artifacts and texts reserve for themselves the additional term "expression" to which no mechanical filling in is adequate. An expression, in Nelson Goodman's terms, exemplifies that which it represents.[24] It is an embodiment of itself. We cannot simply go from it to the concept of interest, for it *is* that concept just as a sample of red terry cloth is red terry cloth.

What is the work of the reader in front of the expression of a figure or a whole artistic text? Barthes suggests that we abandon metalanguage and extend the body of the figure across our minds, writing out of the figure. Ricoeur would agree, though, to keep ourselves honest and to avoid solipsism, he would insist on distancing ourselves from the figure even as we determine to let it guide our thinking and our writing. In both cases, whatever such a text or fragment represents is merely a first step to our real interest, which is in the posture it adopts while representing. If structural methodologies taught us how to determine representation, hermeneutics is the science of reading expressive language, fleshing out the indeterminate array of concepts and feelings introduced and regulated by the work.

After two decades of structuralism had virtually elided the particular in favor of the mechanisms of language, the psyche, and ideology, one can sense now (in camps as different as those of Ricoeur and Barthes) a renewed fascination with the incarnate symbol and with a theory of reading demanded by it. The impact of particular texts in the particularity of our own history and in that of our culture calls for the close scrutiny of the details of the case at hand, even while we must seek to understand that case with all the grand theories at our disposal.

The dialectic implicit in interpretation between comprehension and explanation, between living history and logical system, makes onerous demands on the theorist who might otherwise have been content to languish in the particular or escape to the abstract. As a new activity, film study, one can imagine, has not often been driven to play out this dialectic. All too early, by 1965 in our estimation, it was forced to put away its youthful dreams of complete self-possession (the goal of every classical theory to start from scratch and deduce the principles of the art). Now it must discard its adolescent visions of being totally possessed (by structuralism or psychoanalysis or semiotics or any other strong and aggressive discipline).

The mature film study of which I speak is already with us whenever theory confronts films and their history. The highlight of recent film study, I believe, has been exactly a kind of close analysis, on the one hand, and historical research on the other, which, while theoretically sophisticated, proceeds by the progressive adjustment of theory to the particularly cinematic stuff of the field. Normally thought to lie at opposite ends of the discipline, close analysis and film history, when practiced responsibly, participate in the overall goal of enlarging texts and contexts with the perspectives derived from systematic analysis (from Lévi-Strauss, Lacan, Marx, Chomsky, and others).

The inclination to invoke philosophy, psychoanalysis, linguistics, logic, or ideological theory in undertaking film study suggests not so much that film is ruled by other disciplines as the fact that films are the site of myriad problematics, involving multiple aspects of culture. More important, close textual or historical analysis reveals that these aspects are more than mutually inflecting (as when ideological and psychoanalytic concepts are shown to interact in *Young Mr. Lincoln*); their appearance in films requires a textual reworking that must thwart any attempt to read films directly. The textual system is therefore privileged over any of the already elaborated systems entwined within it. As a consequence, film analysis and genuine film history have made serious contributions to cultural studies in general. This can clearly be seen in feminist theory and semiotics, both of which have profited from the textual analysis of complicated films. It can be seen as well in the writings of Marie-Claire Ropars and Pierre Sorlin whose studies of Russia or of Italian fascism are propelled by the discoveries they make *in* films (as opposed to *about* films).[25]

The most telling example of the power of the dialectic principle of interpretation is Jean-Pierre Schefer's *L'Homme ordinaire du cinéma*.[26] Unschooled in film history or criticism, Schefer poses anew the most purely theoretical questions associated with film study. What is it like to go to a movie? Why do we do it and what happens to us as a consequence of our participation? Setting himself up in explicit opposition to the overly systematic reflections Metz deduced in *The Imaginary Signifier*, Schefer lodges the dialectic at the very heart of this primary fact of film viewing: at the cinema we are both ourselves and the representation built for us. Our memories are fed by the images, yet what we see is absolutely present to us now. The very words "we" and "us" must be qualified, not according to some strict Lacanian model of subjectivity but according to a dialectic in which we are alternately ruled by the representation and rule it. To use his words, film viewing is both a doxical and paradoxical experience, both ruled and anarchic.

Schefer evocatively reminds us that film theory will only progress by interrogating concrete instances for their systematic ramifications, and that in turn these ramifications are of interest only insofar as they return us to those aspects of our experience which are particular and unsystematic. Whereas Ricoeur and Barthes suggested this very fact in relation to texts of all sorts, Schefer points to the privileged place the cinema occupies in our lives. For the cinema in a unique way merges public reality and private dreams. Codes and systematic theories float in and out of focus through the history of cinema, a fact every theoretician will have to be aware of, take advantage of.

Schefer is sensitive to the fascination of unforgettable images and in this way links up once more to Barthes. For both critics and for many others, the body of films and the flesh of their figures have intervened in the airy "sciences of man." Hermeneutics has gone out to meet that body. While we may still be interested in textuality as a type of behavior and still concern ourselves with the meanings of representations, these behavioral and philological tasks must no longer keep us from the more human one of answering the call expressed by the text in the aspirations and gutterals of its voice. To utter an expression is more than to designate a meaning; it is to respond to a situation with a certain cry. Figures are the cries we cannot dismiss. What we do with them (fuse with them, enjoy them, analyze them, extend them, and so forth) is as varied as the variety of interpreters and theories of interpretation. Yet doing anything with them whatsoever shows the interdependence of mind and body, of thought and voice, of meaning and expression. Certainly this is not an untroubled interdependence, but it is one that gives to viewing, reading, and writing a place in human life different from philosophy, analysis, or sheer behavior. This border zone of reading is the life of the imagination. It is worth as much as we imagine it to be.

Notes

CHAPTER 1

1. Representative of this sort of research are such unpublished Ph.D. dissertations as J. M. Foley, "The Bilateral Effect of Film Context" (University of Iowa, 1966); Stephen S. Ryan, "The Recognition of Film Techniques Related to Selected Characteristics of Film Sophistication: A Pilot Study" (Ohio State, 1975); Roger Penn, "An Experimental Study of the Meaning of Cutting-Rate Variables in Motion Pictures" (University of Iowa, 1967); and F. Dennis Lynch, "Clozentropy: A New Technique for Analyzing Audience Response to Film" (University of Iowa, 1974). The *AV Communication Review* has published many communication research articles dealing with film as has the *Journal of Applied Psychology*.

2. Peter L. Berger and Thomas Luckmann, *The Social Construction of Reality* (Garden City, N.Y.: Doubleday Anchor, 1966); Jurgen Habermas, *Legitimation Crisis*, trans. Thomas McCarthy (Boston: Beacon Press, 1975); Alfred Schutz, *The Phenomenology of the Social World*, trans. George Walsh and F. Lehnert (Evanston: Northwestern University Press, 1967); and Roland Barthes, *Image, Music, Text*, trans. Stephen Heath (Boston: Hill & Wang, 1978).

3. These generalities are already fast upon us. See, for example, Jerry Hendrix and James A. Wood, "The Rhetoric of Film: Toward a Critical Methodology," *Southern Speech Communication Journal*, no. 39 (Winter 1973): 105–22.

4. Slavko Vorkaptich, "Lecture Series," American Film Institute 1974; also Vorkapitch, "Toward a True Cinema," *Film Culture*, no. 19 (1959): 10–17.

5. Mojmir Drvota, "Theses on Film" (unpublished notes, Columbia University, 1968). Stefan Scharff, also of Columbia University, has pursued this sort of research as has Vlada Petric at Harvard University. See Petric, "For a Close Cinematic Analysis,"*Quarterly Review of Film Studies* 1, no. 4 (November 1976): 453–73.

6. J. M. Carroll and T. G. Berger, "Segmentation in Cinema Perception," *Science* 191 (March 12, 1976): 1053–55; J. M. Carroll, "A Linguistic Analysis of Deletion in Cinema," *Semiotica*, 1978; also Carroll, "A Program for Cinema Theory," *Journal of Aesthetics and Art Criticism* 35 (1977): 337–51.

7. Noel Burch, *Theory of Film Practice* (New York: Praeger, 1973); also Burch, *To the Distant Observer* (Berkeley: University of California Press, 1979).

8. William Arrowsmith, "Film as Educator," *Journal of Aesthetic Education* 3, no. 3 (July 1969): 75–83.

9. "Cumulative Index Volumes I–XXXV, 1941–1977," *Journal of Aesthetics and Art Criticism*.

10. Arthur Danto, "Moving Pictures," *Quarterly Review of Film Studies* 4, no. 1 (Winter 1979): 1–22; Stanley Cavell has published on film in journals such as *Critical Theory, The Georgia Review,* and *Quarterly Review of Film Studies.* His book on film, *The World Viewed,* has gone into an expanded edition (Boston: Beacon Press, 1979), and Harvard Press published his *Pursuits of Happiness* (1982).

11. Noel Carrol, "Film Theory and Film History: An Outline for an Institutional Theory of Film," *Film Reader,* no. 4 (1979): 81–98.

12. Jean Mitry, *Esthétique et psychologie du cinéma* (Paris: Editions Universitaires; 1963, (vol. I), and 1965 (vol. II); Christian Metz, "Le Cinéma: Langue ou langage?," *Communications,* no. 4 (1964): 52–90.

13. I had hoped to accomplish this task to some extent in both *The Major Film Theories* (New York: Oxford University Press, 1976) and *André Bazin* (New York: Oxford University Press, 1978). Recently, Brian Henderson has pursued the same goal in his *A Critique of Film Theory* (New York: Dutton, 1979).

14. Charles F. Altman, "Psychoanalysis and Cinema, the Imaginary Discourse," *Quarterly Review of Film Studies* 2, no. 3 (Summer 1977).

15. For more information about the historical aspects of film theory, see my article "The Neglected Tradition of Phenomenology in Film Theory," *Wide Angle* 2, no.2 (1978): 44–49.

16. Christian Metz, "Current Problems in Film Theory," trans. Diana Matias, *Screen* (Spring/Summer 1972): 40–82.

17. *Communications,* no. 15 (1975), is devoted totally to *le Vraisemblable.* For discussions of representation in the cinema, see, for example, Um-

berto Eco, "A Critique of Iconism," in *Theory of Semiotics* (Blooming-ton: Indiana University Press, 1976), pp. 172–90; Paul Willemen, "On Realism in the Cinema," *Screen Reader I* (London: Society for Education in Film and TV, 1977), pp. 47–56; Christian Metz, "Problems of De-notation in the Fiction Film" and "The *Saying* and the *Said*: Notes on the Decline of Plausiblity in the Cinema," in *Film Language* (New York: Oxford University Press, 1974), pp. 108–48 and 325–52.

18. James Spellerberg, "Technology and Ideology in the Cinema," *Quarterly Review of Film Studies* 2, no. 3 (August 1977): 288–301; *Film Reader*, no. 2 (1977): 125–225; Jean-Patrick Lebel, *Cinéma et idéologie* (Paris: Editions Sociales, 1971); *Cinétique*, "Texte Collectif," nos. 9–10, pp. 1–70. Jean-Louis Comolli's seminal work appears scattered through is-sues of *Cahiers du cinéma*, no. 229 (June 1971), no. 230 (July 1971), no. 231 (August–September 1971), no. 233 (November 1971), no. 234–35 (December 1971–January 1972), and no. 241 (September–October 1972).

19. Rick Altman, ed., "Cinema Sounds," *Yale French Studies*, no. 60 (Spring 1980), is the latest in a series of intensive studies devoted to the sound-track. A comprehensive bibliography is appended to this issue. Stephen Heath and Teresa de Lauretis, eds., *Technology and Ideology* (New York: Macmillan, 1980), reprints many of the papers delivered at the Milwau-kee conference on that subject held in March 1978.

20. For references to Comolli, see note 18; for critiques of his position in ad-dition to Lebel (note 18 also), see James Spellerberg, "Technology and the Film Industry: The Adoption of Cinemascope" (unpublished Ph.D. dissertation, University of Iowa, 1980); Douglas Gomery, "Problems in Film History: How Fox Innovated Sound," *Quarterly Review of Film Studies* 1, no. 3 (August 1976): 315–30; and Tom Anderson, "Cinema and its Discontents" (unpublished MS., Columbus, Ohio, 1978–79).

21. See especially Keith Cohen, *Film and Literature: The Dynamics of Ex-change* (New Haven: Yale University Press, 1979).

22. Most important in this area has been the work of Barry Salt, David Bord-well and Kristin Thompson, Edw. Branigan, and, of course, Noël Burch. For Burch, see note 7; Barry Salt, "Film Style and Technology in the Thirties," *Film Quarterly* 20, no. 1 (Fall 1977): 19–32; Salt, "Film Style and Technology in the Forties," *Film Quarterly* 31, no. 1 (Fall 1978): 45–57; David Bordwell and Kristin Thompson, "Space and Narrative in the Films of Ozu," *Screen* 17, no. 2 (Summer 1976): 41–73; and Edward Branigan, "Formal Permutations in the Point of View Shot," *Screen* 16, no. 3 (Autumn 1975): 54–64.

23. The work of Marie-Claire Ropars is exemplary here, especially in her book *Octobre* (Paris: Editions Albatros, 1976). See also Mary Ann Doane, "The Dialogic Text: Filmic Irony and the Spectator" (unpublished Ph.D. dis-

sertation, University of Iowa, 1979). The work of Stephen Heath, Raymond Bellour, Thierry Kuntzel, Charles F. Altman, and a host of others could be appended here to verify the strength of this critical turn in film theory toward an intense investigation of the workings of filmic systems.

CHAPTER 2

1. Andrew, *Film Theories*. 103–15.
2. Jean Mitry, *Esthétique*. See the end of vol. II, particularly p. 454.
3. *Ibid.*, chs. 5 and 11.
4. Interest in the soundtrack has produced many articles and one entire journal issue in recent years; see the bibliography in "Cinema Sounds," *Yale French Studies*, no. 60. Also, see Jean Chion, *La Voix au cinéma* (Paris: Cahiers du cinéma, 1983).
5. Umberto Eco, "Articulations of the Cinematic Code," in Bill Nichols, *Movies and Methods* (Berkeley: University of California Press, 1976), pp. 590–607.
6. Umberto Eco, *A Theory of Semiotics* (Bloomington: Indiana University Press, 1976), pp. 6–7.
7. Edgar Morin, *Le Cinéma ou l'homme imaginaire* (Paris: Editions Minuit, 1958), p. 15 and all of ch. 3.
8. André Bazin, "Ontology of the Photographic Image," in *What Is Cinema?*, trans. Hugh Gray (Berkelely: University of California Press, 1967), p. 16.
9. The two most important theorists working in this vein are Jean-Louis Baudry, whose essays are collected in *L'Effet cinéma* (Paris: Albatros, 1978) and Jean-Louis Comolli, whose "Cinema et idéologie" appeared serially in *Cahiers du cinéma* in 1971 (nos. 229, 230, 231, 233, 234–35, and 241).
10. Bazin, "Ontology," p. 13.
11. French film theorists have in the main relied heavily on the work of Pierre Francastel; his original insights were published in 1951 but two of his most important works appeared exactly in the period which concerns us: *La Réalité figurée* (Paris: Donoël/Gonthier, 1965) and *La Figure et le lieu* (Paris: Gallimard, 1967). In English the Marxist author and critic John Berger promoted similar ideas in his *Ways of Seeing* (London: Penguin, 1972).
12. Jean-Patrick Lebel argues, for instance, that technology is "neutral" and available as a tool for the use of classes to promote their own interests. This alternate Marxist position appears in his *Cinéma et idéologie*.
13. Christian Metz, "Au-delà de l'analogie," *Essais sur le signification au cinéma*, vol. II (Paris: Klincksieck, 1972), pp. 151–62.

14. See Nicholas Pastore, *Selective History of Theories of Visual Perception, 1650–1950* (New York: Oxford University Press, 1971). For a further account of the empirical school, see Julian Hochberg's contribution, "The Representation of Things and People," to E. H. Gombrich, Hochberg, and Max Black, *Art, Perception and Reality* (Baltimore: Johns Hopkins University Press, 1972), pp. 47–94.
15. Sully's 1884 observation appears in Pastore, *Selective History*, p. 186.
16. For a history of the origins of the Gestalt movement and an excellent critique of its position, see D. W. Hamlyn, *The Psychology of Perception* (London: Routledge & Kegan Paul, 1957).
17. Hochberg in Gombrich, Hochberg, and Black, *Art*, p. 52.
18. Hamlyn, *Perception*, ch. 6.
19. Danto, "Moving Pictures," pp. 1–22.
20. Nelson Goodman distinguishes various terms of this sort in chapter 1 of his *Languages of Art* (Indianapolis: Hackett, 1976).
21. The original experiment was performed by G. M. Stratton and reported in the *Psychological Review* in 1896. For an extended discussion of this and related experiments see Ivo Kohler, "The Formation and Transformation of the Perceptual World," *Psychological Issues* 3, no. 4 (Monograph 12, 1964). Current research in this area is being conducted by Richard Held, Charles Harris, and Irvin Rock.
22. Gombrich's views are laid out in chapter 9 of his classic *Art and Illusion* (Princeton: Princeton University Press, 1956) and have been reiterated in innumerable essays.
23. This argument is detailed in Samuel Y. Edgerton, *The Rediscovery of Perspective in the Renaissance* (New York: Basic Books, 1975).
24. Gombrich, Hochberg, and Black, *Art*, p. 55.
25. Pastore, *Selective Theories*, p. 270. This view has become a commonplace, as is clear from its appearance in *Scientific American* 219, no. 3 (1968): 214.
26. George A. Miller, *Language and Perception* (Cambridge, England; Cambridge University Press, 1976).
27. Maurice Merleau-Ponty, *The Primacy of Perception* (Evanston: Northwestern University Press, 1964), pp. 4, 5.
28. *Ibid.*, p. 17.
29. Pier-Paulo Pasolini, "The Cinema of Poetry" (1965), in Nichols, *Movies*, pp. 546–47.

CHAPTER 3

1. Hamlyn, *Perception*, pp. 110–15.
2. Nelson Goodman, *Languages*, pp. 27–31, Gombrich, *Art and Illusion*, pp.

4–9; Ludwig Wittgenstein, *The Philosophical Investigations* (New York: Macmillan, 1953) pp.194 ff.

3. Nelson Goodman, *Ways of Worldmaking* (Indianapolis: Hackett, 1978), pts. I and VI present the nominalist position.
4. *Ibid.*, p. 20.
5. Jean-Paul Sartre, *Psychology of the Imagination* (Secaucus, N.J.: Citadel Press, 1948); Schutz, *Social World;* and Mikel Dufrenne, *The Phenomenology of the Aesthetic Experience* (Evanston: Northwestern University Press, 1973).
6. Béla Belázs, *Theory of the Film* (New York: Dover, 1970) p. 126. Balázs explicitly conjurs up this electrical metaphor with its aspects of "spark" and "flow."
7. Christian Metz, *Film Language: A Semiotics of the Cinema,* trans. Michael Taylor (New York: Oxford University Press, 1974), ch. 1.
8. Sartre, *Imagination,* ch. 2.
9. Mitry, *Esthétique,* vol. I, ch. 31. See also my *Major Film Theories,* p. 191.
10. See Jean-Pierre Meunier, *Les Structures de l'expérience filmique* (Louvain: Vaner, 1969).
11. Barbet Shroeder's *General Idi Amin Dada,* first screened in New York in April 1975.
12. Hugo Münsterberg, *Film: A Psychological Study,* (N.Y.: Dover Press, 1971), p. 74.
13. See Stephen Heath's essay, "Narrative Space," in *Questions of Cinema* (Bloomington: Indiana University Press, 1981), ch. 2.
14. Christian Metz, "Story and Discourse," in Christian Metz, *The Imaginary Signifier* (Bloomington: Indiana University Press, 1981), pp. 89–98. Roland Barthes, *S/Z* (Boston: Hill & Wang, 1974), esp. pp. 1–16. Barthes has denigrated plot in favor of other signifying aspects or codes in many other essays as well.
15. Gombrich, *Art and Illusion,* ch. 9.
16. Sergei Eisenstein, *The Film Sense* (New York: Harcourt Brace, 1975), p. 17.
17. See David Bordwell, "Eisenstein's Epistemological Shift," *Screen* 15, no. 4 (Winter 1974, 1975): 59–70. See also my *Major Film Theories,* pp. 60 ff.
18. Andrew, *Major Film Theories,* pp. 159–70. Bazin's clearest distinction between classical realism and cinematic realism comes in his "Defense of Rossellini," *What is Cinema?,* vol. II, p. 98.
19. Roger Scrutton, "Photography and Representation," *Critical Inquiry* 7, no. 3 (Spring 1981): 577–604.
20. Among semioticians criticizing the notion of representation we can men-

tion Umberto Eco; among structuralists, Gerard Genette and Tzvetan To-dorov; and among post-structuralists, Barthes and Derrida. These names are meant to suggest that virtually all of continental thought in philosophy and criticism since 1960 has worked in one way or another to expose and deflate representation. Their writings subtend the film theories of the *Screen* school (Ben Brewster, Peter Wollen, Colin MacCabe, and Paul Wille-men), which have constantly attacked representation in cinema.

21. Eisenstein, *Film Sense*, pp. 10, 17, and 37–40.
22. Sigmund Freud, *The Interpretation of Dreams* (New York. Avon Books, 1965), sect. VI, pt. D.
23. Eisenstein, "Word and Image" in *Film Sense,* p. 7.

CHAPTER 4

1. Mitry, *Esthétique,* chs. 3 and 4; Albert Laffay, *Logique du cinéma* (Paris: Masson, 1964); and Dina Dreyfus "Cinema and Language," *Diogenes,* no. 35 (Fall, 1961): 23–33.
2. Metz's essays on punctuation and on trick effects appear as chapters 5 and 9 of *Essais sur le signification au cinéma,* vol. II (Paris: Klincksieck, 1972).
3. I. A. Richards and C. K. Ogden, *The Meaning of Meaning* (New York: Harcourt Brace, 1946, originally published in 1923).
4. Richards's essays collected in his *Principles of Literary Criticism* (New York: Harcourt Brace, 1925) amount to an ethics and a psychology of reading signs in culture.
5. For an explication of Saussure's basic position and of its influence see Jonathan Culler, *Ferdinand de Saussure* (London; Modern Masters Se-ries, Penguin Books, 1977).
6. Sol Worth, "Symbolic Strategies," *Journal of Communication* 24 (Au-tumn, 1974): 27–39. Also see his posthumous book, *Studying Visual Communication* (Philadelphia: University of Pennsylvania Press, 1981) where this essay is reprinted alongside other important essays in visual semiotics.
7. Umberto Eco, *Semiotics,* pp. 8–28.
8. André Bazin's writings reflect this impulse throughout, most forcefully in "Ontology," and "Cinema and Exploration" in *What is Cinema?,* vol. I.
9. The most thorough treatment of this topic is certainly Metz's *Language and Cinema* (The Hague: Mouton, 1975) translated from *Langage et ci-néma* (Paris: Larousse, 1971).
10. Eco, "Articulations," in Nichols, *Movies,* pp. 590–607.
11. Bazin's famous phrase appears in his *Jean Renoir* (Paris: Editions Champs

Libre, 1971), p. 84. The Simon & Schuster translation of this book (1973) uses the phrase "simple cloak of reality" (p. 91).

12. The entire issue of *Communications* 11 (1968) is devoted to the question of *le Vraisemblable*. It includes key essays by Gerard Genette, "Vraisemblance et motivation," 5–21; Barthes, "L'Effet du réel," 84–89; Metz, "Le Dire et le dit au cinema," 22–33; and two brief essays by Todorov.

13. Barthes, "L'Effet du réel," pp. 84, 85.

14. See especially Eisenstein's essays "A Course in Treatment," and "The Structure of the Film," both in *Film Form: Essays in Film Theory*, ed. and trans., Jay Leyda (New York: Harcourt Brace, 1949). Also see his "Problems of Soviet Historical Films" in *Film Criticism* 3, no. 1 (1979): 1–16.

15. Bazin's discussion of non-signifying details crops up primarily in his essays on neorealism. See *What is Cinema?*, vol. II, pp. 30–38.

16. Christian Metz, "To Study Films: Two Different Starting Points," *Language and Cinema*, pt. 5, sect. 1.

17. Christian Metz, *Language and Cinema*, pt. 10: "Specific/Non-Specific . . ."

18. Christian Metz, "Trucage et cinéma," *Essais*, vol. II, pp. 173–92.

19. Christian Metz, "The Cinema: Language or Language System," in *Film Language*, pp. 31–91.

20. Christian Metz, "Spécificité des codes et spécificité des langages," *Semiotica* 1 (1969): 379. See also Stephen Heath, "Cinema/Text/Cinetext," *Screen* 14, nos. 1–2 (Spring/Summer 1973): 118.

21. Prime examples here would be Metz's "Metaphor and Metonymy: the Imaginary Referent," in *The Imaginary Signifier*, which views semiotics as a sub-science assisting both rhetoric and psychoanalysis. *Camera Obscura* follows a policy of employing semiotics in the service of an overarching ideological view of cinema. In this it takes its cue from Stephen Heath and the *Screen* school who in turn rely on the early issues of *Cinétique*.

22. Metz, "The Cinema," esp. p. 58. Also see Metz, *Language and Cinema*, pt. 4.

23. Roland Barthes, *Mythologies* (Boston: Hill & Wang, 1972), originally published in French in 1957. See especially the concluding section, "Myth Today," and esp. p. 115.

24. I am indebted to Sister Mary Basehart and her essay "Christian Metz' Theory of Connotation," *Film Criticism* 4, no. 2 (1979): 21–37. Metz himself gives a chronology of his positions in "Le Connotation de nouveau," *Essais*, vol. II, 162–72, though he continued to develop his views after this, especially in "Metaphor and Metonymy," pp. 238 and 239.

25. Barthes, *S/Z*, p. 9.

26. Barthes, *Elements of Semiology* (Boston: Hill & Wang, 1968), p. 11.
27. See Metz, "Cinematographic Language and Filmic Writing," the concluding chapter of *Language and Cinema*.

CHAPTER 5

1. Jean Mitry, *Esthétique,* vol. II, p. 354.
2. Claude Lévi-Strauss, "The Structural Study of Myth," in his *Structural Anthropology* (Garden City, N.Y.: Doubleday, 1963), pp. 202–27.
3. Northrop Frye, "Polemical Introduction," *The Anatomy of Criticism* (Princeton: Princeton University Press, 1957).
4. Roland Barthes, "Introduction to the Structural Analysis of Narratives," in his *Image, Music, Text,* trans. Stephen Heath (New York: Hill & Wang, 1977), pp. 79–82.
5. *Ibid.,* p. 83.
6. *Ibid.,* p. 84.
7. Boris Eichenbaum, "O. Henry and the Theory of the Short Story," in *Readings in Russian Poetics,* ed. Ladislav Matejka and Krystyna Pomorska (Cambridge, Mass.: MIT Press 1971), pp. 231–38.
8. Tzvetan Todorov, *Grammaire du Décaméron* (The Hague: Mouton, 1970).
9. Roman Jakobson, *Shifters, Verbal Categories, and the Russian Verb,* in *Selected Writings,* vol. 2 (The Hague: Mouton, 1971), p. 134.
10. André Jolles, *Einfache Formen* (Tübingen: Max Niemeyer, 1930; 2nd ed. 1958), cited by Tzvetan Todorov in "Poétique," *Qu'est-ce que le structuralisme?* ed. Oswald Ducrot et al. (Paris; Editions du Seuil, 1969), p. 143.
11. This terminology comes from Boris Tomashevsky, "Thematics," in *Russian Formalist Criticism,* ed. Lee T. Lemon and Marion J. Reis (Lincoln: University of Nebraska Press, 1965), p. 68.
12. Barthes, "Structural Analysis of Narratives," p. 86.
13. Vladimir Propp, *The Morphology of the Folktale,* trans. L. Scott (Austin, Texas: University of Texas Press, 1968), p. 60.
14. *Ibid.,* pp. 17–24.
15. Claude Bremond, "La Message narratif," *Communications* 4 (1964): 4–32.
16. Todorov, "Poétique," pp. 123–32.
17. Claude Bremond, "La Logique des possibles narratifs," *Communications* 8 (1966): 62–64.
18. Tzvetan Todorov, "The Fantastic in Fiction," *Twentieth Century Studies* 3 (May 1970): 88.
19. Claude Bremond, "The Logic of Narrative Possibilities," *New Literary History* 11, no. 3 (Spring 1980): 387–412.

20. Tzvetan Todorov, in a seminar at the University of Iowa, Iowa City, 16 April 1970.
21. Tzvetan Todorov, "Les Catégories du récit littéraire," *Communications* 8 (1966): 132–38.
22. *Ibid.,* p. 136.
23. Jakobson, *Shifters,* p. 2.
24. V. N. Voloshinov, "Reported Speech," in Matejka and Pomorska, *Russian Poetics,* pp. 149–75.
25. Mikael Baxtin, "Discourse Typology in Prose," Matejka and Pomorska, *Russian Poetics,* pp. 176–98.
26. Lubomír Doležel, "The Typology of the Narrator: Point of View in Fiction," in *To Honor Roman Jakobson,* vol. I (The Hague: Mouton, 1967), pp. 541–52.
27. Norman Friedman, "Point of View in Fiction," in *The Novel: Modern Essays in Criticism,* ed. R. M. Davis (Englewood Cliffs, N.J.: Prentice-Hall, 1969), pp. 142–72.
28. Tzvetan Todorov, "Structural Analysis of Narrative," *Novel* 3 (1969): 70–72.
29. *Ibid.,* p. 71.
30. Roland Barthes, *Critique et vérité* (Paris: Editions du Seuil, 1966).
31. Roman Jakobson, "On the Boundary Between Studies of Folklore and Literature," in Matejka and Pomorska, *Russian Poetics,* pp. 91–93.
32. Roland Barthes, "Science Versus Literature," in *Structuralism: A Reader,* ed. Michael Lane (London: Jonathan Cape, 1970), pp. 410–17.
33. The paradigm of structuralist homages to Robbe-Grillet no doubt is Barthes's "Objective Literature: Alain Robbe-Grillet," in *Two Novels by Robbe-Grillet,* trans. Richard Howard (New York: Grove Press, 1965), pp. 11–26.
34. Italo Calvino, "Notes toward the Definition of the Narrative Form as a Combinative Process," *Twentieth Century Studies* 3 (1970): 93–102.
35. Roland Barthes, "The Structuralist Activity," in *Critical Essays,* tr. Richard Howard (Evanston, Ill.: Northwestern University Press, 1972), pp. 213–20.
36. Barthes, *S/Z,* pp. 3–5.
37. Stephen Heath on *Touch of Evil,* "Film and System: Terms of Analysis," *Screen* 16, no. 1 (Spring 1975).
38. Raymond Bellour, *Analyse du film* (Paris: Albatros, 1980).
39. Louis Marin's work is extensively reviewed in *Diacritics* 7, no. 2 (Summer 1977).
40. In cinema studies, see the journal *Camera Obscura* as well as Stephen Heath, "Sexual Difference and Representation," *Screen* 19, no. 3 (Autumn 1978): 51–112.
41. Eugenio Donato, "The Two Languages of Criticism," in *The Languages*

of Criticism and the Sciences of Man, ed. Richard Macksey and Eugenio Donato (Baltimore: Johns Hopkins Press, 1970), pp. 89–97.

42. Maurice Merleau-Ponty, "The Prose of the World," *TriQuarterly,* no. 20 (1971): 14–17.
43. William Hendricks, "Linguistic Models and the Study of Narration," *Semiotica* 5 (1972): 267.
44. See, respectively, Paul Ricoeur, "Structure, Word, Event," in *The Philosophy of Paul Ricoeur,* ed. Charles E. Reagan and D. Stewart (Boston: Beacon Press, 1978), pp. 109–19; Paul Ricoeur, *The Rule of Metaphor* (Toronto: University of Toronto Press, 1978); and Paul Ricoeur, *Interpretation Theory: Discourse and the Surplus of Meaning* (Fort Worth: Texas Christian University Press, 1976).
45. See Ricoeur, *Rule of Metaphor,* study 5.
46. Paul Ricoeur, in a letter to the author, has expressly praised Steiner's *After Babel* (London: Oxford University Press, 1975).

CHAPTER 6

1. For this idea I am indebted to a paper written by Dana Benelli in a class at the University of Iowa, autumn term 1979.
2. The "city symphony" is a genre of the 1920's which includes up to fifteen films all built on formal or abstract principles, yet dedicated to the presentation of a single city, be it Berlin, Paris, Nice, Moscow, or the like.
3. In the theory of interpretation this is generally attributed to Wilhelm Dilthey, although Martin Heidegger has made much of it in our century.
4. Frank McConnell, *Storytelling and Mythmaking* (New York: Oxford University Press, 1979).
5. André Bazin, *What Is Cinema?* (Berkeley: University of California Press, 1968), p. 142.
6. *Ibid.,* p. 107.
7. *Ibid.,* p. 67.
8. George Bluestone, *Novels into Film* (Berkeley: University of California Press, 1957), and Jean Mitry, "Remarks on the Problem of Cinematic Adaptation," *Bulletin of the Midwest Modern Language Association* 4, no. 1 (Spring 1971): 1–9.
9. Gombrich, *Art and Illusion,* p. 370.
10. Goodman, *Languages,* esp. pp. 143–48.
11. Keith Cohen, *Film and Literature: The Dynamics of Exchange* (New Haven: Yale University Press, 1979), p. 4. Cohen's citation from Metz comes from Metz, *Langage et cinéma,* pp. 20–21.
12. *Ibid.,* p. 92.

13. Bazin, *What Is Cinema?*, p. 76.
14. François Truffaut, "A Certain Tendency in French Cinema," in Nichols, *Movies*, pp. 224–36.
15. Emile Zola, "Naturalism and the Theater," in *The Experimental Novel and Other Essays*, tr. by Belle Sherman (New York: Haskell House, 1964).

CHAPTER 7

1. Wellek and Warren felt the need to close their classic *Theory of Literature* (New York: Harcourt Brace, 1948) with a chapter on "Literary History," though their commitment to the autonomy of the work of art is evident even here. Twenty years later, Geoffrey Hartmann referred to this essay in his "Towards Literary History" in his collection significantly titled *Beyond Formalism* (New Haven: Yale University Press, 1970).
2. Metz in "Cinematographic Language," and Eco in *Semiotics*, pp. 276–98, esp. 289, imply a context-sensitive concern for the production of signification. Note also that the *Cahiers du cinéma* essay on *Young Mr. Lincoln* opens with an extensive discussion of the economic, political, and artistic climate in which the film appeared.
3. Frye, *Anatomy of Criticism*, esp. the "Polemical Introduction."
4. Sylvia Harvey, *May 1968 and Film Culture* (London: British Film Institute, 1978).
5. Heath, *Questions of Cinema*, p. 16.
6. *Ibid.*, p. 62.
7. See, for example, Bill Nichols, "Documentary Theory and Practice," *Screen* 17, no. 4 (1976): 74–92, and Annette Kuhn, "The Camera I: Observations on Documentary," *Screen* 19, no. 2 (Summer 1978): 71–84. Trailers have been analyzed by Mary Beth Haralovich and Cathy Root Klaprat in *Enclitic* (Fall 1981, Spring 1982): 66–74. Robert Vianello is preparing a doctoral thesis on TV commercials (UCLA, forthcoming).
8. Harvey, *May 1968*, ch. 3, and Bill Nichols, *Ideology and the Image* (Bloomington: Indiana University Press, 1981), present good surveys of the function of ideology in the cinema. Terry Lovell's *Pictures of Reality* (London: British Film Institute, 1980) contains in addition a fine bibliography. The most substantial treatment of the topic in relation to cinema is surely Philip G. Rosen, "The Concept of Ideology and Contemporary Film Criticism" (unpublished Ph.D. dissertation, University of Iowa, 1978).
9. See especially Heath's "On Screen, in Frame," the opening essay of *Questions of Cinema*.
10. Tzvetan Todorov, *The Fantastic* (Ithaca, N.Y.: Cornell University Press, 1975).

11. An excellent summary of this movement of criticism is Sarah Lawall, *Critics of Consciousness* (Cambridge: Harvard University Press, 1968).

12. Thomas Schatz introduces his book *Hollywood Genres* (New York: Random House, 1981) with this dynamic view, taking his cue from other theorists of popular culture, especially John Cawelti in his *Adventure, Mystery, Romance* (Chicago: University of Chicago Press, 1976). Popular genre theories balancing invention and convention are supported by important studies in the other arts. See especially, Leonard Meyer, *Music, the Arts, and Ideas* (Chicago: University of Chicago Press, 1967), Gombrich, *Art and Illusion,* and James S. Ackerman, "A Theory of Style," *Journal of Aesthetics and Art Criticism* 20 (1962): 227.

13. Todorov, *The Fantastic,* pp. 82–86.

14. Seymour Chatman, *Story and Discourse* (Ithaca, N.Y.: Cornell University Press, 1978), sects. 4 and 5.

15. James Collins, "An Introduction to Aesthetic Ideology" (unpublished Ph.D. dissertation, University of Iowa, 1984).

16. Jean Narboni and Jean-Louis Comolli, "Cinema, Ideology, Criticism" in *Screen Reader* (London: British Film Institute, 1978), pp. 2–11, trans. from the October–November 1969 issue of *Cahiers du cinéma.*

17. Pamela Falkenberg has urged this point in "Textual Analysis, the Western, and the Critique of Corporate Capitalism" (unpublished Ph.D. dissertation, University of Iowa, 1983).

18. Barthes, *S/Z,* p. 4.

19. Narboni and Comolli in "Cinema" actually suggest an eight-tier categorization of films which I am here modifying.

20. George Lukács's reverence for Balzac and Tolstoy has always caused consternation among Marxists. See his *Studies in European Realism* (New York: Grosset & Dunlap, 1964), p. 9.

21. Laura Mulvey, "Visual Pleasure and the Narrative Cinema," *Screen* 16, no. 3 (Autumn 1975): 6–18, attacks all standard films. So also does Peter Gidal in "Theory and Definition of Structural/Materialist Film," his contribution to the anthology he edited, *Structural Film Anthology* (London: British Film Institute, 1976), pp. 1–21. Stephen Heath edges up to this position at the end of his essay "Narrative Space." in *Questions of Cinema,* pp. 19–75.

22. Peter Wollen, "Appendix 2," *Signs and Meanings in the Cinema* (Bloomington: Indiana University Press, 1969, 1st ed.), pp. 166 and 167.

23. Barthes, *S/Z,* pp. 4–6.

24. P. Adams Sitney, *The Visionary Cinema* (New York: Oxford University Press, 1974).

25. In addition to the work of Wollen, Mulvey, and Gidal already cited, Malcolm LeGrice has contributed to the self-consciousness of this movement

in his *Abstract Film and Beyond* (London: Studio Vista, 1977). David Rodowick focuses precisely on the British avant-garde and its political aspirations, "The Political Avant-Garde: Ideology and Epistemology in Post-1968 Film Theory" (unpublished Ph.D. dissertation, University of Iowa, 1983).

26. Heath, *Questions of Cinema,* ch. 7.
27. Gidal, *Structural Film Anthology,* pp. 1–4.
28. Stephen Heath, "The Question Oshima," originally published in *Wide Angle* 2, no. 1 (1977), now is ch. 6 of *Questions of Cinema.*
29. Julia Kristeva, *Desire in Language* (New York: Columbia University Press, 1980).
30. "Young Mr. Lincoln," *Cahiers du cinéma,* no. 223, (1970), sect. 1.
31. Barthes, *S/Z,* pp. 4–6.
32. Thierry Kuntzel, "Le Travail du film II," *Communications 23* (1976), trans. in *Camera Obscura* 5 (Spring 1980), pp. 7–71.

CHAPTER 8

1. Hugo Münsterberg, *Psychotherapy* (New York: Moffat, Yard, 1909), cited by Richard Griffith in the "Preface" to Münsterberg, *Film: A Psychological Study* (New York: Dover Publications, 1970), p. ix.
2. Charles F. Altman, "Psychoanalysis and Film," *Quarterly Review of Film Studies* 2, no. 3 (Summer 1977): 260–64.
3. Andrew, *Major Film Theories,* pp. 29, 109–14, and 147–49.
4. *Ibid.,* pp. 190–92.
5. Christian Metz, *Imaginary Signifier,* pp. 25–41.
6. Sigmund Freud, "Creative Writers and Daydreaming" (1908), *Standard Edition,* vol. 9, pp. 141–53, and *Leonardo da Vinci: A Study of Psychosexuality, Standard Edition,* vol. 11, pp. 59–138, Trans. James Strachey (London: Hogarth, 1955).
7. Freud, "Creative Writers," p. 143.
8. *Ibid.,* p. 153.
9. Sarah Kofman, *L'Enfance de l'art* (Paris: Payot, 1970), p. 20.
10. Freud's classic formulation of modern doubt is found in his "A Difficulty in the Path of Psychoanalysis" (1917), *Standard Edition.*
11. Norman Holland, *Five Readers Reading* (New Haven: Yale University Press, 1975). Holland's passing references to film response have been greatly expanded in his recent lectures at Harvard (1979), Iowa (1981), and elsewhere.
12. Norman Holland, "Unity Identity Text Self," in J. Tompkins, ed., *Reader Response Criticism* (Baltimore: Johns Hopkins University Press, 1980), pp. 122–27.

13. Don Frederickson, "Jung/Sign/Symbol/Film," *Quarterly Review of Film Studies* 4, no. 2 (Spring 1979): 167–92 and 5, no. 4 (Fall 1980): 459–79.

14. Todorov, "Fantastic in Fiction," p. 88.

15. I wish to thank Dennis Giles for discussions about the psychological basis of narrative. His Ph.D. dissertation is an important starting point for such ideas, "The Retrieve: A Theory of Narrative Structure in Film" (Northwestern University, 1977).

16. Raymond Bellour, "Le Blocage symbolique," *Communications* 23 (1975): 235–50.

17. Sigmund Freud, "Delusions and Dreams in Jensen's *Gradiva*," *Standard Edition*, vol. 9, pp. 7–93.

18. Paul Ricoeur, "Psychoanalysis and Art," lecture delivered in Washington, D. C. in 1979.

19. Bellour, "Le Blocage symbolique," p. 235.

20. Tzvetan Todorov, "La Rhétorique de Freud," in his *Théories du symbole* (Paris: Editions Seuil, 1977), pp. 285–322.

21. Paul Ricoeur, *Freud and Philosophy* (New Haven: Yale University Press, 1970), pp. 525–31.

22. Thierry Kuntzel, "The Film Work 2," *Camera Obscura* 5 (1980), trans. Nancy Huston from *Communications* 23 (1975): 136–90.

23. These titles represent the most ambitious close analyses invoking psychoanalysis in the 1970's. *M* is dealt with by Thierry Kuntzel, "le Travail du film," *Communications* 19 (1972): 25–39, trans. in *Enclitic* 2, no. 1 (Spring 1978): 39–61; *Touch of Evil* was analyzed by Stephen Heath in "Film and System," and *Young Mr. Lincoln* is analyzed by the editors of *Cahiers du cinéma*, no. 223 (September 1970), trans. in Nichols, *Movies*, pp. 493–528, in *Screen Reader I*, pp. 113–51, and in Gerald Mast and Marshall Cohen, *Film Theory and Criticism*, 2nd ed. (New York: Oxford University Press, 1979), pp. 778–831. The same editors analyzed *Morocco* in *Cahiers du cinéma*, no. 225 (November–December 1970).

24. Heath, *Questions of Cinema*, chs. 1 and 2.

25. Berger, *Ways of Seeing*, and Pierre Francastel, *Peinture et société* (Lyon: Audin, 1950), esp. the Preface and p. 1. See also Francastel's later *La Réalité figurée*.

26. Heath, "Sexual Difference," pp. 51–112.

27. Mulvey, "Visual Pleasure," pp. 6–18.

28. See, for example, David Rodowick, "The Difficulty of Difference," *Wide Angle* 5, no. 1 (1982): 1–14; Mary Ann Keane, "A Closer Look at Scopophilia," paper delivered at Society for Cinema Studies Conference, Pittsburgh 1983; and most important, Laura Mulvey, "Feminism, Film, and the Avant Garde," *Framework*, no. 10 (1979): 3–10.

29. Jean-Louis Baudry, "Ideological Effects of the Basic Cinematographic

Apparatus," *Film Quarterly* 28, no. 2 (Winter 1974–75): 39–47, trans. Alan Williams from *Cinéthique*, pp. 7–8.

30. Christian Metz, "The Fiction Film and Its Spectator," in *Imaginary Signifier*, pp. 99–148.
31. Jean-Louis Baudry, "Le Dispositif," *Communications* 23 (1975): 69, 70. This essay, translated in *Camera Obscura*, no. 1 (Fall 1976), substantially influenced Metz as can be seen in his *Imaginary Signifier*, p. 49.
32. Christian Metz, "The Fiction Film and Its Spectator," in *Imaginary Signifier*, pp. 99–148.
33. This term, coming from Bakhtin, has been directed explicitly against Metz's system by Doane, "The Dialogic Text," chs. 1 and 2. I am indebted to Mary Ann Doane for this and many other insights.
34. Ricoeur discusses the "indestructible" character of the instincts in *Freud and Philosophy*, p. 442. Freud's classic formulation appears in "On Dreams," *Standard Edition*, vol. 5, pp. 553, 577.
35. Sigmund Freud, "Analysis Terminable and Interminable," *Standard Edition*, vol. 23, pp. 209–54.
36. Ricoeur, *Freud and Philosophy*, pp. 483–93 and 514–23.
37. Ricoeur, "Psychoanalysis and Art."

CHAPTER 9

1. See Chapter 4, Sect. III, "Critique of Semiotics."
2. Jacques Lacan, "The Agency of the Letter in the Unconscious," *Ecrits: A Selection* (New York: W. W. Norton, 1977), ch. 5. For a thorough discussion of this issue see also *Speech and Language in Psychoanalysis* by Lacan with a commentary by Anthony Wilden (Baltimore: Johns Hopkins University Press, 1981).
3. Jean-François Lyotard, *Discours, figure* (Paris: Klincksieck, 1971).
4. Buñuel has been the subject of numerous excellent recent publications: Linda Williams, *Figures of Desire* (Urbana: University of Illinois Press, 1981); Paul Sandro "Assault and Disruption in the Cinema, Four Films by Louis Buñuel" (unpublished Ph.D. dissertation, Cornell University, 1974); and Marvin D'Lugo, "Glances of Desire in *Belle du Jour*," *Film Criticism* 2, nos. 2–3 (Winter/Spring 1978): 84–89. Other recent studies of dense filmmakers would include Paisley Livingston, *Ingmar Bergman and the Rituals of Art* (Ithaca: Cornell University Press, 1982), and Donald P. Costello, *Fellini's Road* (Notre Dame, Ind: University of Notre Dame Press, 1983).
5. Metz, "Metaphor and Metonymy," pp. 174–82. Metz deals with Roman Jakobson's seminal essay "Two Aspects of Language and Two Types of

Aphasia,'' in Roman Jakobson and Morris Halle, *Fundamentals of Language* (The Hague: Mouton, 1956).

6. Metz, "Metaphor and Metonymy," opens with a sophisticated analysis of the problem of "secondarization" and it is a topic that persists throughout this important and lengthy essay.

7. Edward B. Lowry, "Filmology: Establishing a Problematic for Film Study in France 1946–55" (unpublished Ph.D. dissertation, University of Texas, 1982). Lowry explicitly links filmology to semiotics through the early essays of Christian Metz.

8. Metz was clearly already aware of this in his 1964 essay "Cinema: Language or Language System," in *Film Language,* ch. 3. Stephen Heath has commented most fully and subtlely on this issue first in his "Cinema/Text/Cinetext," pp. 102–28, and more recently in "Language, Sight, and Sound," in *Questions of Cinema,* ch. 9. This latter essay indicates the complications that the psychoanalytic turn in theory have brought to the issue of "language and cinema."

9. Metz, "Metaphor and Metonymy," pp. 245–52, reverses the standard direction of thinking about figures. The more standard views are laid out and criticized in Ricoeur, *Rule of Metaphor,* studies 1 and 2. Also see Tzvetan Todorov, *Theories of the Symbol* (Ithaca: Cornell University Press, 1982).

10. Metz, "Metaphor and Metonymy," p. 275.

11. Ricoeur, *Rule of Metaphor,* studies 4–7.

12. *Ibid.,* pp. 132–33.

CHAPTER 10

1. The history of interpretation theory is the subject of many books. I am most indebted to Gerald L. Bruns, *Inventions* (New Haven: Yale University Press, 1982). The first two chapters of this book, "Secrecy and Understanding" and "The Originality of Texts in a Manuscript Culture," force the modern reader to confront the issue of the difference of interpretation in an earlier age.

2. See especially notes 14 and 16 in chapter 2 above.

3. See note 22 in chapter 2 above. Also see Mary Warnock, *Imagination* (Berkeley: University of California Press, 1976), pp. 184–95.

4. At the University of Kansas Conference on Hermeneutics in the Social Sciences and the Humanities (May 1981) Richard Rorty expounded at length on the connection between Continental post-structuralism (Foucault, Deleuze, et al.) and American post-pragmatism (James and Dewey). He has often referred to this connection. See, for example, Richard Rorty, "The Fate of Philosophy," *The New Republic,* October 18, 1982, p. 29.

5. Michael Polanyi and H. Prosch, *Meaning* (Chicago: University of Chicago Press, 1975).

6. William Butler Yeats, "The Circus Animals' Desertion," *Last Poems*.

7. Maurice Merleau-Ponty, *The Prose of the World* (Evanston: Northwestern University Press, 1973).

8. The terse history which follows here depends substantially upon Richard Palmer, *Hermeneutics* (Evanston: Northwestern University Press, 1969), which contains an excellent annotated bibliography, although the reader must be cautioned that the years since the publication of Palmer's book have produced additional voluminous writings on the topic.

9. This distinction between "meaning" (the logic of a text or of its parts) and "significance" (its thrust and impact for any reader in any context) is dealt with at length by P. D. Juhl in *Interpretation* (Princeton: Princeton University Press, 1980). Juhl is expressly indebted to E. D. Hirsch's *Validity in Interpretation* (New Haven: Yale University Press, 1967).

10. Erich Auerbach's *Mimesis* (Princeton: Princeton University Press, 1953) is surely the most exemplary philological undertaking of our era. Spitzer surveyed a comparably broad range of literatures in his essays published in such collections as *Essays on English and American Literature* (Princeton: Princeton University Press, 1962), *Classical and Christian Ideas of World Harmony* (Baltimore: John Hopkins University Press, 1963), and especially *Linguistics* and *Literary History: Essays in Stylistics* (New York: Russell and Russell, 1962).

11. Edward Said, *Beginnings* (Baltimore: Johns Hopkins University Press, 1975), p. 9.

12. See Juhl, *Interpretation,* pp. 27*ff.,* and Hirsch, *Validity in Interpretation,* pp. 8, 62, 140–44*ff.*

13. Ricoeur has charted his intellectual history in an appendix to *Rule of Metaphor,* pp. 315–22.

14. Reagan and Stewart, *Philosophy of Paul Ricoeur,* contains essays which represent each of these phases. A bibliography which can guide the interested reader well beyond this sample is found in Charles Reagan, *Studies in the Philosophy of Paul Ricoeur* (Athens, Ohio: Ohio University Press, 1978).

15. Ricoeur, *Interpretation Theory,* pp. 71–89.

16. For a comprehensive view and discussion of Barthes's career and major phases, see Steven Ungar, *Roland Barthes: The Professor of Desire* (Lincoln: University of Nebraska Press, 1984). I am indebted to Steven Ungar for more than his clear and evocative explication of Barthes.

17. Susan Sontag, *Against Interpretation* (New York: Farrar, Straus, & Giroux, 1966).

18. Barthes, "The Third Meaning," in *Image, Music, Text,* pp. 52–68.

19. See the final section of chapter 3, above, for a critique of Barthes's original conception of connotation.

20. Jacques Dubois, *A General Rhetoric* (Baltimore: Johns Hopkins University Press, 1982).

21. Ricoeur, "Structure, Word, Event" in his *The Conflict of Interpretations* (Evanston: Northwestern University Press, 1974), pp. 92–96.

22. Barthes, *A Lover's Discourse,* trans. Richard Howard (New York: Hill & Wang, 1978), pp. 5–9.

23. Barthes, *S/Z,* pp. 4–7.

24. Nelson Goodman, *Languages,* pp. 51–66.

25. Marie-Claire Ropars and P. Sorlin, *Octobre: écriture et idéologie,* 2 vols. (Paris: Albatros, 1976).

26. Jean-Louis Schefer, *L'Homme ordinaire du cinéma* (Paris: Gallimard, 1981).

Appendix: Classified Bibliography

The following bibliography is separated into topics according to the subjects covered in each chapter of the book. However, only items written since 1965 and only those specifically addressing the cinema are included. The reader is urged to consult the notes for each chapter since these contain references to essential texts from philosophy, literary theory, psychoanalysis, and so on that undergird this purely film-oriented bibliography.

Books and anthologies indispensable to modern theory as a whole are listed in the very first category even though they are relevant to many other topics. Hence the reader ought first to consult this initial category before referring to any of the more specialized topics.

Finally, it should be mentioned concerning the scope of this bibliography, that an effort was made to include all important items relating to these topics written in English, together with a few indispensable French ones. I have been far more selective with regard to those books and essays that are primarily film analyses since the number of close textual analyses of films is astronomical. I chose those that seem to me to represent a particularly transparent application of a theoretical stance or those that, in the analysis itself, question certain assumptions crucial to recent theory. Most of these analyses are grouped in the final category of the bibliography but some are so closely linked to a particular topic that they have been lodged under the rubric of that topic.

CHAPTER 1: THE STATE OF FILM THEORY

General Anthologies and Overviews

Screen Reader 1. London: Society for Education in Film and Television, 1977.

Screen Reader II. London: British Film Institute, 1982.

Altman, Rick, ed. *Cinema/Sound. Yale French Studies,* no. 60 (Spring 1980).

Andrew, Dudley. *The Major Film Theories: An Introduction.* New York: Oxford University Press, 1976.

Andrew, Dudley. "The Neglected Tradition of Phenomenology in Film Theory." *Wide Angle* 2, no. 2 (1978): 44–49.

Aumont, Jacques et al. *Esthétique du film.* Paris: Nathan, 1983.

Cadbury, William and Leland Poague. *Film Criticism: A Counter Theory.* Ames: Iowa State University Press, 1983.

Daney, Serge. *La Rampe: Cahiers Critique 1970–1982.* Paris: Gallimard, 1983.

Eberwein, Robert T. *A Viewer's Guide to Film Theory and Criticism.* Metachen, N.J.: Scarecrow Press, 1979.

Heath, Stephen. *Questions of Cinema.* Bloomington: Indiana University Press, 1981.

Henderson, Brian. *A Critique of Film Theory.* New York: Dutton, 1980.

Lawton, Ben et al., eds. *Film: Historical-Theoretical Speculations: The 1977 Film Studies Annual, Part Two.* Pleasantville, N.Y.: Redgrave Publishing, 1977.

Mast, Gerald and Marshall Cohen, eds. *Film Theory and Criticism: Introductory Readings.* New York: Oxford University Press, 1979.

Nichols, Bill. "Critical Approaches to Film Then and Now." *Cinéaste* 5, no. 2 (1972): 8–14.

Nichols, Bill, ed. *Movies and Methods: An Anthology.* Berkeley: University of California Press, 1976.

Perkins, Victor F. *Film as Film: Understanding and Judging Movies.* New York: Penguin Books, 1972.

Tudor, Andrew. *Theories of Film.* New York: Viking Press, 1974.

Miscellaneous Approaches to Film Theory and Aesthetics

Carroll, John M. "A Program for Cinema Theory." *Journal of Aesthetics and Art Criticism* 35 (1977): 337–52.

Carroll, John M. *Toward a Structural Psychology of Cinema.* New York: Mouton, 1980.

Carroll, Noel. "Avant-Garde Film and Film Theory." *Millennium,* nos. 4–5 (1979): 135–43.

Carroll, Noel. "Film History and Film Theory: An Outline for an Institutional Theory of Film." *Film Reader,* no. 4 (1979): 81–96.

Khatchadourian, Haig. "Film as Art." *Journal of Aesthetics and Art Criticism* 33 (1975): 271–84.

Khatchadourian, Haig. "Remarks on the 'Cinematic/Uncinematic' Distinction in Film." *Quarterly Review of Film Studies* 3, no. 2 (1978): 193–98.

Mast, Gerald. *Film/Cinema/Movies: A Theory of Experience.* New York: Harper & Row, 1977.

Recent Views of Traditional Theory

Aumont, Jacques. *Montage Eisenstein.* Paris: Albatros, 1979.

Henderson, Brian. "Bazin Defended Against His Devotees." *Film Quarterly* 23, no. 4 (1970): 26–37.

Hudlin, Edward. "Film Language: Pudovkin, Eisenstein and Russian Formalism." *Journal of Aesthetic Education* 13, no. 2 (1979): 47–56.

Levaco, Ronald. "Eikhenbaum, Inner Speech and Film Stylistics." *Screen* 15, no. 4 (1974–75): 47–58.

Lewis, Brian. "Jean Mitry on Film Language." *Sub-stance,* no. 9 (1974): 5–14.

Metz, Christian. "Current Problems of Film Theory: Jean Mitry's *L'Esthétique et psychologie du cinéma.*" *Screen* 14, nos. 1–2 (1973): 40–87.

Pleynet, Marcel. "The *Left* Front of Art: Eisenstein and the Old 'Young' Hegelians." *Screen* 13, no. 1 (1972): 101–19.

Polan, Dana B. "Eisenstein as Theorist." *Cinema Journal* 17, no. 1 (1977): 14–29.

Wicclair, Mark. "Film Theory and Hugo Münsterberg's *The Film; A Psychological Study.*" *Journal of Aesthetic Education* 12, no. 3 (1978): 33–50.

Williams, Alan. "The Camera Eye and the Film: Notes on Vertov's Formalism." *Wide Angle* 3, no. 3 (1980): 12–17.

Wollen, Peter. "On Ontology and Materialism in Film." *Screen* 17, no. 1 (1976): 7–23.

Wollen, Peter. *Signs and Meanings in the Cinema.* Bloomington: Indiana University Press, 1969.

CHAPTER 2: PERCEPTION

Anderson, Barbara. "Eye Movement and Cinematic Perception." *Journal of University Film Association* 32, nos. 1–2 (1980): 23–26.

Barthes, Roland. *Camera Lucida: Reflections on Photography.* New York: Hill & Wang, 1980. Translated by Richard Howard from Barthes. *La Chambre claire.* Paris: Gallimard, 1980.

Belton, John. "The Bionic Eye: Zoom Esthetics." *Cinéaste* 11, no. 1 (1980/81): 20–27.

Biro, Yvette. *Profane Mythology: The Savage Mind of the Cinema.* Bloomington: Indiana University Press, 1982.

Chion, Jean. *Le Champ sonore.* Paris: Gallimard, 1983.

Cornwell, Regina. "Paul Sharits: Illusion and Object." *Artforum* 10, no. 1 (1971). Reprinted in Nichols. *Movies and Methods.*

Francastel, Pierre. "Seeing-Decoding." *Afterimage,* no. 5 (Spring 1974): 4–21.

Hester, Marcus B. "Are Paintings and Photographs Inherently Interpretative?" *Journal of Aesthetics and Art Criticism,* 31 (1972): 235–48.

Jenkins, Bruce. "Structures of Perceptual Engagement in Film: Toward a Technology of Embodiment." *Film Reader,* no. 2 (1977): 141–45.

Metz, Christian. "Aural Objects." *Yale French Studies,* no. 60 (1980): 24–32.

Michelson, Annette. "Camera Lucida/Camera Obscura." *Artforum* 11, no. 5 (January 1973): 30–37.

Salniker, S. "Visual Responses in Perceptual Cinema." *Journal of University Film Association* 32, nos. 1/2 (1980): 33–40.

Small, Edward S. "Introduction: Cinevideo and Mental Images." *Journal of University Film Association* 32, nos. 1/2 (1980): 3–9.

Wees, William C. "The Cinematic Image as a Visualization of Sight." *Wide Angle* 4, no. 3 (1981): 28–37.

CHAPTER 3: REPRESENTATION

Representation and the Cinema

Benjamin, Walter. "The Work of Art in the Age of Mechanical Reproduction." In Mast and Cohen. *Film Theory and Criticism.* From Benjamin, Walter. *Illuminations.* New York: Schocken Books, 1969.

Bonitzer, Pascal. *Le Champ aveugle.* Paris: Gallimard, 1983.

Bonitzer, Pascal. "Experience on the Inside." *Sub-stance,* no. 9 (1974): 115–20.

Bonitzer, Pascal. *Le Regard et la voix: essais sur le cinéma.* Paris: Union Generale d'éditions, 1976.

Bonitzer, Pascal. "The Two Looks." *On Film,* no. 7 (1977/78): 20–26.

Braudy, Leo. *The World in a Frame: What We See in Films.* Garden City, N.Y.: Anchor Doubleday, 1976.

Burch, Noel. *Theory of Film Practice.* Translated by Helen R. Lane. Introduction by Annette Michelson. New York: Praeger, 1973.

Cavell, Stanley. *The World Viewed: Reflections on the Ontology of Film.* Cambridge: Harvard University Press, 1979.

Danto, Arthur C. "Moving Pictures." *Quarterly Review of Film Studies* 4, no. 1 (1979): 1–21.

De Cordova, Richard. "From Lumière to Pathé: The Break-Up of Perspectival Space." *Cine-Tracts* 4, nos. 2–3 (1981): 55–63.

De Lauretis, Teresa. "Imaging." *Cine-Tracts* 3, no. 2 (1980): 3–12.

Earle, William. "Phenomenology and the Surrealism of Movies." *Journal of Aesthetics and Art Criticism* 38 (1980): 255–60.

Heath, Stephen. "Screen Images, Film Memory." *Cine-Tracts* 1, no. 1 (1977): 27–36.

Kolker, R. P. et al. "A Phenomenology of Cinematic Time and Space." *British Journal of Aesthetics* 13 (1973): 388–96.

Laffay, Albert. *Logique du cinéma: création et spectacle.* Paris: Masson, 1964.

Sesonske, Alexander. "Time and Tense in Cinema." *Journal of Aesthetics and Art Criticism* 38 (1980): 419–26.

Vernet, Marc. "Structuration of Space." *On Film*, no. 7 (1977/78): 12–18.

Technological Aspects of Representation

Altman, Rick. "Moving Lips: Cinema as Ventriloquism." *Yale French Studies*, no. 60 (1980): 67–79.

Bordwell, David. "Camera Movement and Cinematic Space." *Cine-Tracts* 1, no. 2 (1977): 19–25.

Bordwell, David. "Camera Movement, The Coming of Sound, and the Classical Hollywood Style." *Film: Historical-Theoretical Speculations.* Pleasantville, N.Y.: Redgrave Press, 1979.

Burnett, Ron. "Film/Technology/Ideology." *Cine-Tracts* 1, no. 1 (1977): 6–14.

Comolli, Jean-Louis. "Technique and Ideology: Camera, Perspective, Depth of Field." *Film Reader*, no. 2 (1977): 128–40. Translated and reprinted from *Cahiers du cinéma*, no. 229 (1971).

Doane, Mary Ann. "The Voice in the Cinema: The Articulation of Body and Space." *Yale French Studies*, no. 60 (1980): 33–50.

Harpole, Charles H. "Ideological and Technological Determinism in Deep Space Cinema Images." *Film Quarterly* 33, no. 3 (1980): 11–22.

Henderson, Brian. "Toward a Non-Bourgeois Camera Style." *Film Quarterly* 24, no. 2 (Winter 1970–71): 2–14. Reprinted in Nichols. *Movies and Methods.*

Ogle, Patrick. "Technological and Aesthetic Influences upon the Development of Deep Focus Cinematography." *Screen* 13, no. 1 (1972): 45–72.

Pasolini, Pier Paolo. "Observations on the Long Take." *October*, no. 13 (1980): 3–6.

Salt, Barry. "Film Style and Technology in the Forties." *Film Quarterly* 31, no. 1 (1977): 46–56.

Spellerberg, James. "Technology and Ideology in the Cinema." *Quarterly Review of Film Studies* 2, no. 2 (1977): 288–301.

The Problem of Realism

Barthes, Roland. "The Realistic Effect." *Film Reader,* no. 3 (1978): 131–35.

Burgoyne, Robert. "The Imaginary and the Neo-Real." *Enclitic* 3, no. 1 (1979): 16–34.

Lewis, Brian. "A Phenomenological Model of Representational Film Experience." *Wide Angle* 4, no. 4 (1976): 50–54.

Rees, Al. "Conditions of Illusionism." *Screen* 18, no. 3 (1977): 41–54.

Willemen, Paul. "On Realism and the Cinema." *Screen* 13, no. 1 (1972): 37–44.

Williams, Christopher, ed. *Realism and the Cinema: A Reader.* London: Routledge & Kegan Paul, 1980.

CHAPTER 4: SIGNIFICATION

Semiotics and the Cinema

Baseheart, Mary C. "Christian Metz's Theory of Connotation." *Film Criticism* 4, no. 2 (1979): 21–37.

Bellour, Raymond. "To Analyze, to Segment." *Quarterly Review of Film Studies* 1, no. 3 (1976): 331–53.

Bergstrom, Janet. "Alternation, Segmentation, Hypnosis: Interview with Raymond Bellour." *Camera Obscura,* Nos. 3/4 (1979): 70–103.

Bettetini, Gianfranco. *The Language and Technique of Film.* Translated by David Osmond-Smith. The Hague: Mouton, 1973.

Burch, Noel. "Propositions." *Afterimage,* no. 5 (Spring 1974): 40–67.

Cegarra, Michel. "Cinema and Semiology." *Screen* 14, nos. 1–2 (1973): 129–87.

Cinéthique. "Langage et Cinéma." *Screen* 14, nos. 1/2 (1973): 189–213.

Collet, Jean. *Lectures du film; éléments pour une semiologie du cinéma.* Paris: Albatros, 1975.

De Lauretis, Teresa. "Semiotics, Theory and Social Practice: A Critical History of Italian Semiotics." *Cine-Tracts* 2, no. 1 (1978): 1–14.

Dika, Vera. "Wide Angle Saxon: An Examination of the Film Viewer as Reader." *Film Reader,* no. 3 (1978): 222–38.

Durgnat, Raymond. "The Death of Cinesemiology (With not even a Whimper)." *Cinéaste* 10, no. 2 (1980): 10–19 and 10, no. 4 (1980): 12–21.

Eco, Umberto. *A Theory of Semiotics.* Bloomington: Indiana University Press, 1976.

Eikhenbaum, Boris. "Problems of Film Stylistics." Translated by T. Aman. *Screen* 15, no. 3 (1974): 7–32.

Gaggi, Silvio. "Semiology, Marxism, and the Movies." *Journal of Aesthetics and Art Criticism* 36 (1978): 461–70.

Guzzetti, Alfred. "Christian Metz and the Semiotics of Cinema." *Journal of Modern Literature* 3 (1973): 292–93.

Hanhardt, John G. "Linguistics, Structuralism, and Semiology: Approaches to the Cinema." *Film Comment* 9, no. 3 (1973): 52–59.

Harman, Gilbert. "Semiotics and the Cinema: Metz and Wollen." *Quarterly Review of Film Studies* 2, no. 1 (1977): 15–24. Reprinted in Mast and Cohen. *Film Theory and Criticism.*

Harrild, A. "A Context for Semiology." *Screen* 15, no. 4 (1974/75): 10–21.

Heath, Stephen. "Metz's Semiology: A Short Glossary." *Screen* 14, nos. 1–2 (1973): 214–26.

Heath, Stephen. "The Work of Christian Metz." *Screen* 14, no. 3 (1973): 5–28.

Kindem, Gorham A. "Peirce's Semiotic Phenomenalism and Film." *Quarterly Review of Film Studies* 4, no. 1 (1979): 61–69.

Lawson, Sylvia. "The Peirce/Wollen Code Signs: Functions and Values." *Australian Journal of Screen Theory,* no. 3 (1977): 47–65.

Lotman, Juri. *Semiotics of Cinema.* Translated and Foreword by Mark E. Suino. Ann Arbor: University of Michigan Press, 1976.

Lovell, Terry. "Cultural Studies." *Screen* 14, no. 3 (1973): 115–22.

McTaggart, Andrew. "Signs and Meanings in the Cinema," *Screen* 10, no. 6 (1969): 67–75.

Metz, Christian. "Connotation Reconsidered." *Discourse,* no. 2 (1980): 18–31. Translated from *Essais sur la signification au cinéma, II.* Paris: Klincksieck. 1971.

Metz, Christian. *Essais Semiotiques.* Paris: Klincksieck, 1977.

Metz, Christian. *Film Language: A Semiotics of the Cinema.* Translated by Michael Taylor. New York: Oxford University Press, 1974.

Metz, Christian. "L'Incandescence et le Code." *Cahiers du cinéma* (March 1977): 5–22.

Metz, Christian. *Language and Cinema.* Translated by D. J. Umiker-Sebeok. The Hague: Mouton, 1974.

Metz, Christian. "Methodological Propositions for the Analysis of Film." *Screen* 14, nos. 1–2 (1973): 89–101.

Noguez, Dominique, ed. *Cinéma: Théorie, Lectures.* Paris: Klincksieck, 1973.

Nowell-Smith, Geoffrey. "Moving On From Metz." *JumpCut,* nos. 12/13 (1977): 39–41.

Rohdie, Sam. "Metz and Film Semiotics: Opening the Field." *JumpCut,* no. 6 (1975): 22–24.

Salvaggio, Jerry L. "Neglected Areas of Semiotic Criticism." *Quarterly Review of Film Studies* 4, no. 1 (1979): 53–60.

Sandro, Paul. "Christian Metz's *Essais,* vols. I and II, and *Language and Cinema.*" *Diacritics* 4, no. 3 (1974): 42–50.

Screen Reader 2: Cinema and Semiotics. London: British Film Institute, 1982.

Van Wert, W. F. et al. "Julia Kristeva/Cinematographic Semiotic Practice." *Sub-stance,* no. 9 (1974): 97–114.

Walsh, Martin. "Noel Burch's Film Theory." *JumpCut,* no. 10/11 (1977): 61–62.

Wollen, Peter. *Readings and Writings: Semiotic Counter Strategies.* London: Verso, 1982.

Wollen, Peter. *Signs and Meanings in the Cinema.* Bloomington: Indiana University Press, 1969.

Worth, Sol. "The Development of a Semiotic of Film." *Semiotica* 3 (1976): 282–321.

Particular Codes in the Cinema

Bellour, Raymond. "The Obvious and the Code." *Screen* 15, no. 4 (1974/75): 7–17.

Benequist, Lawrence. "The Semiotic Mode: Anchor and Relay as Sign Function in *Red River.*" *Cine-Tracts* 3, no. 2 (1980): 72–82.

Branigan, Edward. "The Articulation of Color in a Filmic System." *Wide Angle* 1, no. 3 (1975): 20–31.

Dayan, Daniel. "The Tutor-Code of Classical Cinema." *Film Quarterly* 28, no. 1 (1974): 22–31.

Eco, Umberto. "Towards a Semiotic Inquiry into the Television Message." *Working Papers in Cultural Studies,* no. 3 (1972): 103–22.

Kindem, Gorham. "Towards a Semiotic of Color in Popular Narrative Films: Color Signification in John Ford's *The Searchers.*" *Film Reader,* no. 2 (1977): 78–84.

Metz, Christian. "Ponctuations et démarcations dans le film de diégèse." *Cahiers du cinéma,* no. 234–35 (1972): 63–78. Reprinted in *Essais sur la signification au cinéma II.*

Miller, Jean-Alain. "Suture (Elements of the Logic of the Signifier)." *Screen* 18, no. 4 (1977/78): 24–35.

Oudart, Jean-Pierre. "Cinema and Suture." *Screen* 18, no. 4 (1977/78): 35–47.

Pasquier, Sylvain du. "Buster Keaton's Gags." *Journal of Modern Literature* 3 (1973): 269–91.

Rothman, William. "Against 'The System of Suture' (Remarks Occasioned by Daniel Dayan's Article, 'The Tutor-Code of Classical Cinema')." *Film Quarterly* 29, no. 1 (1975): 45–50.

Williams, Alan. "Is Sound Recording Like a Language?" *Yale French Studies*, no. 60 (1980): 51–66.

CHAPTER 5: NARRATIVE STRUCTURE

Cinematic Structure and Narrative

Barthes, Roland. "An Introduction to the Structural Analysis of Narrative." In *Image, Music, Text*. Translated by Stephen Heath. New York: Hill & Wang, 1980. Translated from *Communications* 4 (1964).

Bellour, Raymond. "Cine-Repetitions." *Screen* 20, no. 2 (1979): 65–72.

Brewster, Ben. "Structuralism in Film Criticism." *Screen* 12, no. 1 (1971): 49–58.

Cook, David A. "Some Structural Approaches to Cinema: A Survey of Models." *Cinema Journal* 14, no. 3 (1975): 41–54.

Crawford, Larry. "Verbal Categories and Filmic Narrative." *Enclitic* 1, no. 2 (1977): 89–110.

Crick, Peter. "Towards an Aesthetic of Film Narrative." *British Journal of Aesthetics* 17, no. 2 (1977): 185–88.

Eckert, Charles N. "The English Cine-Structuralists." *Film Comment* 9, no. 3 (1973): 46–51.

Fell, John L. "Darling This Is Bigger Than Both of Us." *Cinema Journal* 12, no. 2 (1973): 56–64.

Fell, John L. "Structuring Charts and Patterns in Film." *Quarterly Review of Film Studies* 3, no. 3 (1978): 311–88.

Gardies, Réné. "Structural Analysis of a Textual System: Presentation of a Method." *Screen* 15, no. 1 (1974): 11–31.

Goldmann, Annie. "Genetic Structuralism and Film. Problems of Methodology." *Australian Journal of Screen Theory* 1, no. 1 (1976): 51–68.

Hedges, Ines. "Substitutionary Narration in the Cinema?" *Sub-stance*, no. 9 (1974): 45–51.

Luhr, William and Peter Lehman. *Authorship and Narrative in the Cinema: Issues in Contemporary Aesthetics*. New York: Putnam, 1977.

Mayne, Judith. "*S/Z* and Film Criticism." *JumpCut*, nos. 12–13 (1976): 41–45.

Nowell-Smith, Geoffrey. "Cinema and Structuralism." *Twentieth Century Studies,* no. 3 (1970): 131–39.

Nowell-Smith, Geoffrey. "I Was a Star-struck Structuralist." *Screen* 14, no. 3 (1973): 92–99.

Pasolini, Pier Paolo. "The Scenario as a Structure Designed to Become Another Structure." *Wide Angle* 2, no. 1 (1978): 40–47.

Sandro, Paul. "The Management of Destiny in Narrative Form." *Cine-Tracts* 4, no. 1 (1981): 50–56.

Scholes, Robert. "Narration and Narrativity in Film." *Quarterly Review of Film Studies* 1, no. 3 (1976): 283–96. Reprinted in Mast and Cohen. *Film Theory and Criticism.*

Sub-stance 9 (1974). Entire issue is devoted to film semiotics and structuralism.

Williams, Alan. "The Circle of Desire: Representation in *La Ronde.*" *Film Quarterly* 27, no. 1 (1973): 35*ff.*

Williams, Alan. "Deceit, Desire, and Film Narrative." *Cine-Tracts* 4, no. 1 (1981): 38–49.

Williams, Alan. "Narrative Patterns in *Only Angels Have Wings.*" *Quarterly Review of Film Studies* 1, no. 4 (1976): 357–72.

Williams, Alan. "Structures of Narrativity in Lang's *Metropolis.*" *Film Quarterly* 27, no. 4 (1974): 17–24.

Wollen, Peter. "Introduction to *Citizen Kane.*" *Film Reader,* no. 1 (1975): 9–15.

CHAPTER 6: ADAPTATION

Literature and Film: Comparative Aesthetics

Arnold, Robert, Nicholas Humy, and Ana Lopez. "Rereading Adaptation: *A Farewell to Arms.*" *Iris* 1, no. 1 (1983): 101–14.

Conger, Syndy and Janice Welsch, eds. *Narrative Strategies: Original Essays in Film and Prose Fiction.* Macomb, Ill.: Western Illinois University, 1980.

Eidsvik, Charles. *Cineliteracy: Film Among the Arts.* New York: Random House, 1978.

Guzzetti, Alfred. "The Role of Theory in Films and Novels." *New Literary History* 3, no. 3 (1972): 547–55.

Hulseberg, R. A. "Novels and Films: A Limited Inquiry." *Literature Film Quarterly* 6, no. 1 (1978): 57–65.

Johnson, William C., Jr. "Literature, Film, and the Evolution of Consciousness." *Journal of Aesthetics and Art Criticism* 38 (1979): 29–38.

Kittredge, William. *Stories into Film.* New York: Harper & Row, 1979.

McConnell, Frank D. *Storytelling and Mythmaking*. New York: Oxford University Press, 1979.

McConnell, Frank D. *The Spoken Seen: Film and the Romantic Imagination.* Baltimore: Johns Hopkins University Press, 1975.

Mayer, Peter C. "Film Ontology and the Structure of the Novel." *Film Literature Quarterly* 8, no. 3 (1980): 204–12.

Morrissette, Bruce. "Post-Modern Generative Fiction: Novel and Film." *Critical Inquiry* 2, no. 2 (1975): 253–62.

Morse, Margaret. "Paradoxes of Realism: The Rise of Film in the Train of the Novel." *Cine-Tracts* 4, no. 1 (1981): 27–37.

Poague, Leland A. "Literature vs. Cinema: The Politics of Aesthetic Definition." *Journal of Aesthetic Education* 10, no. 1 (1976): 75–91.

Shattuck, Roger. "Fact in Film and Literature." *Partisan Review* 44 (1977): 539–50.

Silverstein, Norman. "Film and Language, Film and Literature." *Journal of Modern Literature* 2 (1971): 154–60.

Von Abele, Rudolph. "Film as Interpretation: A Case Study of *Ulysses*." *Journal of Aesthetics and Art Criticism* 31 (1973): 487–500.

CHAPTER 7: VALUATION (OF GENRES AND AUTEURS)

Genre, Auteur, Industry

Altman, Charles F. "The American Film Musical: Paradigmatic Structure and Mediatory Function." *Wide Angle* 2, no. 2 (1978): 10–17.

Altman, Charles F. "Towards a Theory of Genre Film." *Film: Historical-Theoretical Speculations*. Pleasantville, N.Y.: Redgrave Press, 1979.

Altman, Rick, ed. *Genre: The Musical*. London: Routledge & Kegan Paul, 1981.

Andrae, Thomas. "Theory: The Culture Industry Reconsidered: Adorno on Film and Mass Culture." *JumpCut*, no. 20 (1979): 34–37.

Baxter, Peter. "On the History and Ideology of Film Lighting." *Screen* 16, no. 3 (1975): 83–106.

Bellour, Raymond, ed. *Le Cinéma américain*, Paris: Flammarion, 1980.

Bordwell, David. "The Art Cinema as a Mode of Film Practice." *Film Criticism* 4, no. 1 (1979): 56–64.

Buscombe, Edward. "Ideas of Authorship." *Screen* 14, no. 3 (1973): 75–85.

Caughie, John, ed. *Theories of Authorship: A Reader*. London: Routledge & Kegan Paul, 1981.

Dadoun, Roger. "Fetishism in the Horror Film." *Enclitic* 1, no. 2 (1977): 39–63.

Dyer, Richard. "Entertainment and Utopia." *Movie,* no. 24 (1977): 2–13.

Feuer, Jane. *The Hollywood Musical.* Bloomington: Indiana University Press, 1982.

Grant, Barry K., ed. *Film Genre: Theory and Criticism.* Metuchen, N.J.: Scarecrow Press, 1977.

Heath, Stephen. "The Idea of Authorship." *Screen* 14, no. 3 (1973): 86–91.

Heath, Stephen. "*Jaws:* Ideology and Film Theory." *Framework,* no. 4 (1976): 25–27. Reprinted in *Film Reader,* no. 2 (1977): 166–68.

Kaminsky, Stuart M. *American Film Genres: Approaches to a Critical Theory of Popular Film.* Dayton: Pflann, 1974.

Kane, Pascal. "*Sylvia Scarlett:* Hollywood Cinema Reread." *Sub-stance* 9 (1974): 35–43.

Kazis, Richard. "Benjamin and the Age of Mechanical Reproduction." *Jump-Cut,* no. 15 (1977): 23–25.

Kitses, Jim. *Horizons West.* Bloomington: Indiana University Press, 1970.

MacCabe, Colin. "Theory and Film: Principles of Realism and Pleasure." *Screen* 17, no. 3 (1976): 7–27.

Mellencamp, Patricia. "Spectacle and Spectator: Looking Through the American Musical Comedy." *Cine-Tracts* 1, no. 2 (1977): 27–35.

Schatz, Thomas G. *Hollywood Genres: Formulas, Filmmaking, and the Studio System.* New York: Random House, 1981.

Vernet, Marc. "Genre." *Film Reader,* no. 3 (1978): 13–17.

Waldman, Diane. "Critical Theory and Film: Adorno and 'The Culture Industry' Reconsidered." *New German Critique,* no. 2 (1977): 39–60.

Wright, Will. *Sixguns and Society: A Structural Study of the Western.* Berkeley: University of California Press, 1975.

Alternative and Political Film Practice

Gidal, Peter. "The Anti-Narrative." *Screen* 20, no. 2 (1979): 73–93.

Gidal, Peter. "Theory and Definition of Structural/Materialist Film." *Studio International* 190, no. 978 (November-December 1975): 42–45.

Godard, Jean-Luc. *Introduction à une véritable histoire du cinéma.* Paris: Albatros, 1980.

Heath, Stephen. "The Anti-Narrative (1978): Afterword." *Screen* 20, no. 2 (1979): 93–99.

Heath, Stephen. "Lessons From Brecht." *Screen* 15, no. 2 (1974): 103–28.

MacCabe, Colin. "The Discursive and the Ideological in Film: Notes on the Conditions of Political Intervention." *Screen* 19, no. 4 (1978–1979): 29–43.

Mulvey, Laura. "Feminism, Film, and the Avant Garde." *Framework,* no. 10 (1979): 3–10.

Polan, Dana B. "Brecht and the Politics of Self-Reflexive Cinema." *Jump-Cut,* no. 17 (1978): 29–32.

Rodowick, David. "The Political Avant-Garde: Modernism and Epistemology in Post-1968 Film Theory." Ph.D. dissertation, University of Iowa, 1983.

Walsh, Martin. "The Frontiers of Language: Brecht and Straub/Huillet: *History Lessons." Afterimage,* no. 7 (1978): 12–31.

Walsh, Martin. *Brechtian Aspects of Radical Cinema.* London: British Film Institute, 1981.

Ideology and Recent Film Theory

Aristarco, Guido. "Marx, le cinéma et la critique du film." *Etudes cinématographiques* 88–92 (1972): 1–219.

Britton, Andrew. "The Ideology of *Screen:* Althusser, Lacan, Barthes." *Movie* 26 (Winter 78/79): 2–28.

Comolli, Jean-Louis and Jean Narboni. "Cinema/Ideology/Criticism." *Screen* 13, no. 1 (1972): Reprinted in *Screen Reader I,* 2–12.

Coward, Rosalind and John Ellis. *Language and Materialism.* London: Routledge & Kegan Paul, 1977.

Dworkin, Martin S. "Criticism and Ideology: A Note on Ideology." *Journal of Aesthetic Education* 11, no. 4 (1977): 93–101.

Harvey, Sylvia. *May 1968 and Film Culture.* London: British Film Institute, 1978.

Kristeva, Julia. "The Subject in Signifying Practice." *Semiotext(e)* 1, no. 3 (1975): 19–34.

Kuhn, Annette. "Ideology, Structure and Knowledge." *Screen Education,* no. 28 (1978): 34–41.

Kuntzel, Thierry. "The Treatment of Ideology in the Textual Analysis of Film." *Screen* 14, no. 3 (1973): 44–54.

Lebel, Jean-Patrick. *Cinéma et Idéologie.* Paris: Editions Sociales, 1972.

Lovell, Terry. *Pictures of Reality: Aesthetics, Politics, and Pleasure.* London: British Film Institute, 1978.

Neale, Steven. "Propaganda." *Screen* 18, no. 3 (1977): 9–40.

Nichols, Bill. *Ideology and the Image in the Cinema and Other Media.* Bloomington: Indiana University Press, 1981.

Rosen, Philip. *"Screen* and the Marxist Project in Film Criticism." *Quarterly Review of Film Studies* 2, no. 3 (1977): 273–87.

Wood, Robin. "Ideology, Genre, Auteur." *Film Comment* 13 (Jan/Feb 1977): 46–51.

Wood, Robin. "Realism and Revolution." *Film Comment* 13 (May/June 1977): 17–23.

Zimmer, Christian. "All Films Are Political." *Sub-stance,* no. 9 (1973): 123–36. Translated from *Les Temps modernes* by Lee Leggett.

CHAPTER 8: IDENTIFICATION

Psychoanalysis and the Cinema

Altman, Charles F. "Psychoanalysis and Cinema: The Imaginary Discourse." *Quarterly Review of Film Studies* 2, no. 3 (1977): 257–72.

Augst, Bertrand. "The Apparatus: An Introduction." *Camera Obscura,* no. 1 (1976): 97–101.

Augst, Bertrand. "The Defilement Into the Look." *Camera Obscura,* no. 2 (1977): 92–103.

Augst, Bertrand. "The Order of [Cinematographic] Discourse." *Discourse* 1 (Fall 1979): 38–57.

Baxter, Peter. "On the Naked Thighs of Miss Dietrich." *Wide Angle* 2, no. 2 (1978): 18–25.

Bellour, Raymond. "Le Blocage symbolique" *Communications* 23 (1975): 235–350.

Bellour, Raymond. "Psychosis, Neurosis, Perversion." *Camera Obscura,* nos. 3–4 (1979): 104–34.

Brewster, Ben and Stephen Heath. "Critical Dialogue: Psychoanalysis and Film: An Exchange." *JumpCut,* no. 9 (1975): 27–28.

Brewster, Ben. "Notes on the Text of *Young Mr. Lincoln* by the Editors of *Cahiers du cinéma.*" *Screen* 14, no. 3 (1973): 29–43.

Buscombe, Edward et al. "Statement: Psychoanalysis and Film." *Screen* 16, no. 4 (1975/76): 119–30.

Curry, Robert. "Films and Dreams." *Journal of Aesthetics and Art Criticism* 33 (1974): 83–89.

Doane, Mary Ann. "Misrecognition and Identity." *Cine-Tracts* 3, no. 3 (1980): 25–32.

Fredericksen, Don. "Jung/Sign/Symbol/Film." *Quarterly Review of Film Studies* 4, no. 2 (1979): 167–92, and 5, no. 4 (1980): 459–79.

Houston, Beverley and Marsha Kinder. *Self and Cinema: A Transformalist Perspective.* Pleasantville, N.Y.: Redgrave Publishing Company, 1980.

Hunter, Ian. "Fetishism in Film 'Theory' and 'Practice.' " *Australian Journal of Screen Theory,* nos. 5–6 (1979): 48–66.

Johnson, Catherine. "Narrative, Spectacle and the Sexes in Ophuls' *Le Plaisir.*" *Film Criticism* 4, no. 3 (1980): 17–24.

Kuntzel, Thierry. "The Film-Work." *Enclitic* 2, no. 1 (1978): 39–62.

Kuntzel, Thierry. "The Film-Work 2." *Camera Obscura,* no. 5 (1980): 6–69.

Leaming, Barbara. "Towards a Psychoanalytic Reading of a Contemporary American Film." *Cine-Tracts* 1, no. 3 (1978): 15–29.

Rose, Jacqueline. "Paranoia and the Film System." *Screen* 17, no. 4 (1977): 85–104.

The Spectator Before the Screen

Baudry, Jean-Louis. "The Apparatus." *Camera Obscura,* no. 2 (1976): 104–27.

Baudry, Jean-Louis. *L'Effet Cinema.* Paris: Albatros, 1978.

Baudry, Jean-Louis. "Ideological Effects of the Basic Cinematographic Apparatus." Translated by Alan Williams. *Film Quarterly* 28, no. 2 (1974/75): 39–47.

Bonitzer, Pascal. "Here: The Notion of the Shot and the Subject of Cinema." *Film Reader,* no. 4 (1979): 108–19. Translated from *Cahiers du cinéma* (Jan/Feb 1977).

Doane, Mary Ann. "The Dialogic Text: Filmic Irony and the Spectator." Ph.D. dissertation, University of Iowa, 1979.

Elsaesser, Thomas. "Primary Identification and the Historical Subject: Fassbinder and Germany." *Cine-Tracts* 3, no. 3 (1980): 43–52.

Giles, Dennis. "Hard Times: The Lack and the Other." *Film Reader,* no. 2 (1977): 85–89.

Giles, Dennis. "Pornographic Space: The Other Place." *Film: Historical-Theoretical Speculations.* Pleasantville, N.Y.: Redgrave Press, 1979.

Heath, Stephen. "Anata Mo (Oshima and Lacan)." *Screen* 17, no. 4 (1977): 49–66.

Heath, Stephen. "The Turn of the Subject." *Cine-Tracts* 2, no. 2 (1979): 32–48.

Humphries, Reynold. "*Peeping Tom:* Voyeurism, the Camera, and the Spectator." *Film Reader,* no. 4 (1980): 193–200.

Kristeva, Julia. "Ellipsis on Dread and the Specular Seduction." *Wide Angle* 3, no. 3 (1980): 42–47.

MacCabe, Colin. "Presentation of the Imaginary Signifier." *Screen* 16, No. 2 (1975): 7–13.

Metz, Christian. *The Imaginary Signifier.* Translated by Alfred Guzzetti et al. Bloomington: Indiana University Press, 1981.

Michaels, Lloyd. "The Imaginary Signifier in Bergman's *Persona.*" *Film Criticism* 2, nos. 2–3 (1978): 72–7.

Penley, Constance. "*What Maisie Knew:* Childhood as Point of View." *Camera Obscura,* no. 2 (1977): 133–38.

Silverman, Kaja. "Masochism and Subjectivity." *Framework,* no. 12 (1980): 2–9.

Stern, Lesley. "Point of View: The Blind Spot." *Film Reader,* no. 4 (1979): 214–36.

Willemen, Paul. "Notes On Subjectivity: On Reading Edward Branigan's 'Subjectivity Under Siege.' " *Screen* 18, no. 1 (1978): 41–69.

Sexual Difference in Film

Flitterman, Sandy. "Women, Desire, and the Look: Feminism and the Enunciative Apparatus in Cinema." *Cine-Tracts* 2, no. 1 (1978): 63–68.

Gledhill, Christine. "Recent Developments in Feminist Criticism." *Quarterly Review of Film Studies* 3, no. 4 (1978): 457–93.

Heath, Stephen. "Difference." *Screen* 19, no. 3 (1978): 50–112.

Johnston, Claire. "The Subject of Feminist Film Theory/Practice." *Screen* 21, no. 2 (1980): 27–34.

Kaplan, E. Ann., ed. *Women in Film Noir.* London: British Film Institute, 1978.

Kuhn, Annette. *Women's Pictures: Feminism and Cinema.* London: Routledge & Kegan Paul, 1982.

Lesage, Julia. "Feminist Film Criticism: Theory and Practice." *Women and Film* 1, nos. 5–6 (1974): 12–19.

Mulvey, Laura. "Visual Pleasure in the Narrative Cinema." *Screen* 16, no. 3 (1975): 6–18.

CHAPTER 9: FIGURATION

Figurative Meaning in the Cinema

Bresson, Robert. *Notes on Cinematography.* Translated by Jonathan Griffin. New York: Urizen, 1975.

Cahiers du cinéma editors. "John Ford's *Young Mr. Lincoln.*" *Cahiers du cinéma,* no. 223 (1970): 29–47. Translated in *Screen* 13, no. 2 (1972); and in Nichols. *Movies and Methods.*

Hanhardt, John G. "Boris Upensky's 'A Poetics of Composition.' " *Film Reader,* no. 4 (1979): 189–92.

Linderman, Deborah. "Uncoded Images in the Heterogeneous Text." *Wide Angle* 3, no. 3 (1980): 34–41.

Lyotard, Jean-François. "Added Attraction: Acinema." *Wide Angle* 2, no. 3 (1978): 52–59.

Metz, Christian. "Metaphor and Metonymy in Film: the Imaginary Referent." In Metz. *The Imaginary Signifier.* Bloomington: Indiana University Press, 1981.

Metz, Christian. *"Trucage* and the Film." *Critical Inquiry* 3 (1977): 657–75.

Nelson, Thomas Allen. "Film Styles and Film Meanings." *Film Criticism* 3, no. 3 (1979): 2–17.

Ropars, Marie-Claire. "The Function of Metaphor in Eisenstein's *October."* *Film Criticism* 2, no. 2 (1978): 109–27.

Ropars, Marie-Claire. "The Overture of *October." Enclitic* 2, no. 2 (1978): 50–72; and 3 no. 1 (1979): 35–47.

Thompson, Kristin. *"Playtime:* Comedy on the Edges of Perception." *Wide Angle* 3, no. 2 (1979): 18–25.

Williams, Linda. *"Hiroshima* and *Marienbad:* Metaphor and Metonymy." *Screen* 17, no. 1 (1976): 34–39.

Filmic Narration

Bellour, Raymond. "Hitchcock: The Enunciator." *Camera Obscura,* no. 2 (1977): 66–91.

Bergstrom, Janet. "Enunciation and Sexual Difference (Part I)." *Camera Obscura,* nos. 3–4 (1979): 32–69.

Browne, Nick. "The Spectator-In-The-Text: The Rhetoric of *Stagecoach." Film Quarterly* 29, no. 2 (1976): 26–38.

Jaffe, Ira S. "Film as the Narration of Space: *Citizen Kane." Literature Film Quarterly* 7, No. 2 (1979): 99–111.

Kavanagh, Thomas M. "The Middle Voice of Film Narration." *Diacritics* 9, no. 3 (1979): 54–61.

Kawin, Bruce F. *Mindscreen: Bergman, Godard and First-Person Film.* Princeton, N.J.: Princeton University Press, 1978.

McGlynn, Peter. "Point of View and the Craft of Cinema: Notes on Some Devices." *Journal of Aesthetics and Art Criticism* 32 (1973): 187–95.

Thompson, Kristin. *Eisenstein's* Ivan the Terrible: A *Neoformalist Analysis.* Princeton: Princeton University Press, 1981.

CHAPTER 10: INTERPRETATION

Film Criticism and Interpretation: Issues and Methods

Agel, Henri. *Poétique du Cinéma: Manifeste essentialiste.* Paris: Presses Universitaires, 1966.

Andrew, Dudley. "Film Analysis or Film Therapy." *Quarterly Review of Film Studies* 2, no. 1 (1977): 33–41.

Bordwell, David. "Criticism, Theory, and The Particular." *Film Criticism* 4, no. 1 (1979): 1–8.

Cohen, Robert. "Mizoguchi and Modernism: Structure, Culture, Point of View." *Sight and Sound* 47, no. 2 (1978): 110–18.

Kinder, Marsha and Beverley Houston. *Close-Up: A Critical Perspective on Film.* New York: Harcourt Brace Jovanovich, 1972.

Koch, Christian. "Cinema, Discourse, and the Event." *Journal of University Film Association* 32, nos. 1–2 (1980): 45–47.

Marty, Alain. "L'analyse du film." *Image et son,* no. 266 (1972): 3–28.

Schefer, Jean-Louis. *L'Homme ordinaire du cinéma.* Paris: Gallimard, 1981.

Schrader, Paul. *Transcendental Style in Film: Ozu, Bresson, Dreyer.* Berkeley: University of California Press, 1972.

Wood, Robin. *Personal Views: Explorations in Film.* London: G. Fraser, 1976.

Close Analysis of Films: Its Theory and Practice

"Papers From the *Enclitic* International Conference on the Textual Analysis of Film, May 15–17, 1981." *Enclitic* 5–6, nos. 2/1 (1981/82): entire issue.

Andrew, Dudley. "The Gravity of *Sunrise.*" *Quarterly Review of Film Studies* 2, no. 3 (1977): 356–87.

Bellour, Raymond. *L'Analyse du film.* Paris: Albatros, 1979.

Bellour, Raymond. "The Unattainable Text." *Screen* 16, no. 3 (1975): 19–27.

Bordwell, David. *The Films of Carl-Theodor Dreyer.* Berkeley: University of California Press, 1981.

Browne, Nick. "Narrative Point of View: The Rhetoric of *Au Hasard Balthazar.*" *Film Quarterly* 31, no. 1 (Fall 1977): 19–33.

D'Lugo, Marvin. "Glances of Desire in *Belle de Jour.*" *Film Criticism* 2, nos. 2–3 (1978): 84–89.

Drummond, Peter. "Textual Space in *Un Chien Andalou.*" *Screen* 18, no. 3 (1977): 55–119.

Fischer, Lucy. "The Lady Vanishes: Women, Magic and the Movies." *Film Quarterly* 33, no. 1 (Fall 1979): 30–40.

Heath, Stephen. "Film and System, Terms of Analysis, Part I and Part II on *Touch of Evil.*" *Screen* 16, nos. 1 and 2 (1975): 7–77 and 91–113.

Klinger, Barbara. "Renoir's *Le Crime de Monsieur Lange:* Visual Environments." *Wide Angle* 3, no. 2 (1979): 54–61.

Lehman, Peter. "An Absence Which Becomes a Legendary Presence: John Ford's Structured Use of Off-Screen Space." *Wide Angle* 2, no. 4 (1978): 36–42.

Nichols, Bill. "*The Birds:* At the Window." *Film Reader,* no. 4 (1980): 120–44.

Nolleti, Art. "A Fissure in the Spider Web: A Reading of Rossen's *Lilith.*" *Film Criticism* 2, nos. 2/3 (1978): 90–103.

Nowell-Smith, Geoffrey. "Six Authors In Pursuit of *The Searchers.*" *Screen* 17, no. 1 (1976): 26–33.

Petric, Vlada. "For a Close Cinematic Analysis." *Quarterly Review of Film Studies* 1, no. 4 (1976): 453–73.

Ropars, Marie-Claire et al. Muriel: *Histoire d'une recherche.* Paris: Editions Galilee, 1974.

Ropars, Marie-Claire and Pierre Sorlin. Octobre: *Ecriture et idéologie.* 2 vols. Paris: Albatros, 1976.

Rothman, William. *Hitchcock: The Murderous Gaze.* Cambridge: Harvard University Press, 1982.

Seidman, Steven. *"The Innocents:* Point of View as an Aspect of the Cinefantastic." *Film Reader,* no. 4 (1980): 201–13.

Index

CALL STEPHANIE
FINISH TAPE FOR WORK.
CABLE T.V. ?